Lecture Notes in Economics and Mathematical Systems

For information about Vols. 1–156, please contact your bookseller or Springer-Verlag

Vol. 157: Optimization and Operations Research. Proceedings 1977. Edited by R. Henn, B. Korte, and W. Oettli. VI, 270 pages. 1978.

Vol. 158: L. J. Cherene, Set Valued Dynamical Systems and Economic Flow. VIII, 83 pages. 1978.

Vol. 159: Some Aspects of the Foundations of General Equilibrium Theory: The Posthumous Papers of Peter J. Kalman. Edited by J. Green. VI, 167 pages. 1978.

Vol. 160: Integer Programming and Related Areas. A Classified Bibliography. Edited by D. Hausmann. XIV, 314 pages. 1978.

Vol. 161: M. J. Beckmann, Rank in Organizations. VIII, 164 pages. 1978.

Vol. 162: Recent Developments in Variable Structure Systems, Economics and Biology. Proceedings 1977. Edited by R. R. Mohler and A. Ruberti. VI, 326 pages. 1978.

Vol. 163: G. Fandel, Optimale Entscheidungen in Organisationen. VI, 143 Seiten. 1979.

Vol. 164: C. L. Hwang and A. S. M. Masud, Multiple Objective Decision Making – Methods and Applications. A State-of-the-Art Survey. XII, 351 pages. 1979.

Vol. 165: A. Maravall, Identification in Dynamic Shock-Error Models. VIII, 158 pages. 1979.

Vol. 166: R. Cuninghame-Green, Minimax Algebra. XI, 258 pages. 1979.

Vol. 167: M. Faber, Introduction to Modern Austrian Capital Theory. X, 196 pages. 1979.

Vol. 168: Convex Analysis and Mathematical Economics. Proceedings 1978. Edited by J. Kriens. V, 136 pages. 1979.

Vol. 169: A. Rapoport et al., Coalition Formation by Sophisticated Players. VII, 170 pages. 1979.

Vol. 170: A. E. Roth, Axiomatic Models of Bargaining. V, 121 pages. 1979.

Vol. 171: G. F. Newell, Approximate Behavior of Tandem Queues. XI, 410 pages. 1979.

Vol. 172: K. Neumann and U. Steinhardt, GERT Networks and the Time-Oriented Evaluation of Projects. 268 pages. 1979.

Vol. 173: S. Erlander, Optimal Spatial Interaction and the Gravity Model. VII, 107 pages. 1980.

Vol. 174: Extremal Methods and Systems Analysis. Edited by A. V. Fiacco and K. O. Kortanek. XI, 545 pages. 1980.

Vol. 175: S. K. Srinivasan and R. Subramanian, Probabilistic Analysis of Redundant Systems. VII, 356 pages. 1980.

Vol. 176: R. Färe, Laws of Diminishing Returns. VIII, 97 pages. 1980.

Vol. 177: Multiple Criteria Decision Making-Theory and Application. Proceedings, 1979. Edited by G. Fandel and T. Gal. XVI, 570 pages. 1980.

Vol. 178: M. N. Bhattacharyya, Comparison of Box-Jenkins and Bonn Monetary Model Prediction Performance. VII, 146 pages. 1980.

Vol. 179: Recent Results in Stochastic Programming. Proceedings, 1979. Edited by P. Kall and A. Prékopa. IX, 237 pages. 1980.

Vol. 180: J. F. Brotchie, J. W. Dickey and R. Sharpe, TOPAZ – General Planning Technique and its Applications at the Regional, Urban, and Facility Planning Levels. VII, 356 pages. 1980.

Vol. 181: H. D. Sherali and C. M. Shetty, Optimization with Disjunctive Constraints. VIII, 156 pages. 1980.

Vol. 182: J. Wolters, Stochastic Dynamic Properties of Linear Econometric Models. VIII, 154 pages. 1980.

Vol. 183: K. Schittkowski, Nonlinear Programming Codes. VIII, 242 pages. 1980.

Vol. 184: R. E. Burkard and U. Derigs, Assignment and Matchir Problems: Solution Methods with FORTRAN-Programs. VIII, 14 pages. 1980.

Vol. 185: C. C. von Weizsäcker, Barriers to Entry. VI, 220 pages. 198

Vol. 186: Ch.-L. Hwang and K. Yoon, Multiple Attribute Decisic Making – Methods and Applications. A State-of-the-Art-Survey. X 259 pages. 1981.

Vol. 187: W. Hock, K. Schittkowski, Test Examples for Nonlinea Programming Codes. V. 178 pages. 1981.

Vol. 188: D. Bös, Economic Theory of Public Enterprise. VII, 142 page 1981.

Vol. 189: A. P. Lüthi, Messung wirtschaftlicher Ungleichheit. IX, 28 pages. 1981.

Vol. 190: J. N. Morse, Organizations: Multiple Agents with Multipl Criteria. Proceedings, 1980. VI, 509 pages. 1981.

Vol. 191: H. R. Sneessens, Theory and Estimation of Macroeconomi Rationing Models. VII, 138 pages. 1981.

Vol. 192: H. J. Bierens: Robust Methods and Asymptotic Theory i Nonlinear Econometrics. IX, 198 pages. 1981.

Vol. 193: J. K. Sengupta, Optimal Decisions under Uncertainty. VI 156 pages. 1981.

Vol. 194: R. W. Shephard, Cost and Production Functions. XI, 10 pages. 1981.

Vol. 195: H. W. Ursprung, Die elementare Katastrophentheorie. Ein Darstellung aus der Sicht der Ökonomie. VII, 332 pages. 1982.

Vol. 196: M. Nermuth, Information Structures in Economics. VIII, 23 pages. 1982.

Vol. 197: Integer Programming and Related Areas. A Classifie Bibliography. 1978 – 1981. Edited by R. von Randow. XIV, 33 pages. 1982.

Vol. 198: P. Zweifel, Ein ökonomisches Modell des Arztverhaltens XIX, 392 Seiten. 1982.

Vol. 199: Evaluating Mathematical Programming Techniques. Proceedings, 1981. Edited by J.M. Mulvey. XI, 379 pages. 1982.

Vol. 200: The Resource Sector in an Open Economy. Edited by H. Siebert. IX, 161 pages. 1984.

Vol. 201: P. M. C. de Boer, Price Effects in Input-Output-Relations A Theoretical and Empirical Study for the Netherlands 1949–1967 X, 140 pages. 1982.

Vol. 202: U. Witt, J. Perske, SMS – A Program Package fo Simulation and Gaming of Stochastic Market Processes and Learning Behavior. VII, 266 pages. 1982.

Vol. 203: Compilation of Input-Output Tables. Proceedings, 1981. Edited by J. V. Skolka. VII, 307 pages. 1982.

Vol. 204: K. C. Mosler, Entscheidungsregeln bei Risiko: Multivariate stochastische Dominanz. VII, 172 Seiten. 1982.

Vol. 205: R. Ramanathan, Introduction to the Theory of Economic Growth. IX, 347 pages. 1982.

Vol. 206: M. H. Karwan, V. Lotfi, J. Telgen, and S. Zionts, Redundancy in Mathematical Programming. VII, 286 pages. 1983.

Vol. 207: Y. Fujimori, Modern Analysis of Value Theory. X, 165 pages. 1982.

Vol. 208: Econometric Decision Models. Proceedings, 1981. Edited by J. Gruber. VI, 364 pages. 1983.

Vol. 209: Essays and Surveys on Multiple Criteria Decision Making. Proceedings, 1982. Edited by P. Hansen. VII, 441 pages. 1983.

Vol. 210: Technology, Organization and Economic Structure. Edited by R. Sato and M. J. Beckmann. VIII, 195 pages. 1983.

Lecture Notes in Economics and Mathematical Systems

Managing Editors: M. Beckmann and W. Krelle

305

Geert-Jan C. Th. van Schijndel

Dynamic Firm and Investor Behaviour under Progressive Personal Taxation

Springer-Verlag
Berlin Heidelberg New York London Paris Tokyo

Managing Editors

Prof. Dr. M. Beckmann
Brown University
Providence, RI 02912, USA

Prof. Dr. W. Krelle
Institut für Gesellschafts- und Wirtschaftswissenschaften
der Universität Bonn
Adenauerallee 24–42, D-5300 Bonn, FRG

Author

Dr. Geert-Jan C. Th. van Schijndel
Juristenlaan 5
NL-5037 GJ Tilburg, The Netherlands

ISBN-13: 978-3-540-19230-5 e-ISBN-13: 978-3-642-46637-3
DOI: 10.1007/978-3-642-46637-3

Library of Congress Cataloging-in-Publication Data. Schijndel, Geert-Jan C. Th. van (Geert-Jan Cornelis Theresia), 1956- Dynamic firm and investor behaviour under progressive personal taxation / Geert-Jan C. Th. van Schijndel. p. cm.–(Lecture notes in economics and mathematical systems; 305) Bibliography: p. ISBN 0-387-19230-1 (U.S.)
1. Corporations–Finance. 2. Investments. 3. Taxation, Progressive. 4. Income tax. I. Title. II. Series.
HG4011.S3385 1988 336.24'2–dc 19 8812237

aan mijn ouders

aan Wendy

ACKNOWLEDGEMENTS

Apart from the already mentioned financial support of the Common Research Pool of Tilburg University and Eindhoven University of Technology, many people have contributed to the completion of this thesis.

First of all I like to mention my promotors. I owe in particular Prof.Dr. Piet Verheyen very much for initiating, stimulating and supervising the project. I admire the way and his ability to manage complex scientific problems and struggles. Besides the perfect introduction into the subject on this project that I got by reading the drafts of his thesis, I am very grateful to Prof.Dr. Paul van Loon for his critical but still stimulating remarks. Dr. Jan de Jong, finally, showed that many econometric research may benefit from the cooperation between the Tilburg and Eindhoven Universities. He was not only able to quard me for serious mathematical mistakes, but he also questioned the necessity and purpose of the many assumptions I have to made in order to solve the economic problem under consideration.

Although many former colleagues of the department of econometrics have contributed to the project, I like to mention in particular my final-year-room-mate, Drs. Peter Kort, for his comments and corrections on a earlier draft of this thesis.

I have got the opportunity to visit many international conferences and to meet interesting people. Especially I like to mention Dr. Steffen Jørgensen and prof.Dr. Gustav Feichtinger.

Last but not least I like to thank Mrs. Lenie Spoor, who accurately typed the present text. The illustrations are drawn on a Philips personal computer by using Diagrammaster.

Geert-Jan van Schijndel

Tilburg, January 1988.

CONTENTS

CHAPTER ONE

SCOPE AND OUTLINE OF THE BOOK

1.1. Principal aim of the book

This book aims to include the effects of a progressive personal tax into the deterministic dynamic theory of the firm. To that end we investigate the impact of a progressive personal tax on the optimal dividend, financing and investment policy of a shareholder controlled value maximizing firm. More specific, the principal aim is the justification of the thesis that during each stage of their evolution firms will be controlled by investors in different tax brackets. To that end we develop a dynamic equilibrium valuation and portfolio theory under certainty, that considers

- the market value of an arbitrary firm such that no excess demand for or supply of shares exists
- the portfolio selection of differently taxed investors
- the succession of differently taxed investors, who possess the shares of any value maximizing firm, in the course of time
- the optimal resulting policy string and corresponding evolution of a firm in the course of time.

The above description of the problem field finds its origins in the theory of corporate finance and the theory of the dynamics of the firm.

1.2. Theory of corporate finance

The impact of both corporate and personal taxation on the optimal policy of the firm and the behaviour of investors is still a central issue in recent contributions in finance theory. One of the principal motives to study this subject is the so-called 'non neutrality' of most of the tax regimes with regard to the policy of firms and the choices by investors: corporate and personal decisions are affected by taxation. Moreover the inclusion of a progressive personal tax, that is, a personal tax rate which rises with the income or initial wealth of the investor, brings on the notion that personal taxes will induce tax clienteles: due to its policy a firm will attract investors in specific tax brackets. The announcement of a particular policy by the firm's management thus induces individuals in specific tax brackets to invest in the firm. On the other hand taxation provides an incentive for decision makers to prefer one method or possibility over another. This situation occurs if the investor or shareholder is capable to control the firm, so that the policy of the firm corresponds with the investor's preferences. Although we consider in this book also the notion of tax induced clienteles, we emphasize on the latter mentioned implication of personal taxation.

With regard to the topic of this book the above choice brings on two issues to point out.

Firstly, we mostly assume that the shareholder of a particular firm is both owner and controller of that firm, that is, we assume non separability of ownership and management. In this way we thus exclude corporations which are controlled by its management that afterwards may be called to account at the shareholders'-meeting. In such a situation the shareholders have delegated the decision making process to the management of the firm. However, the shares of such large firms are owned by so many unknown investors that it will be quite impossible to achieve a common policy by consulting the owners. Moreover, it is beyond doubt that the number of (relative) small private firms, owned and controlled by e.g. families and partners, is of such proportion, that we still consider the majority of firms in the total business market.

Secondly, we focus throughout the book at three important features of the firm: the financing, the dividend and the investment policy. This selection is not supposed to imply that all other decision problems are of minor importance. Since we restrict ourselves, however, to finance theory, this selection covers well the corresponding research field. Besides, this selection links up with the dynamic financial models, the second origin of our problem field.

1.3. Dynamics of the firm

Time is of utmost importance with regard to the economic decision making process. All kind of decisions should be seen in the context of time. Moreover, the real world is a process of dynamic change. It is thus no surprise that the inclusion of time in a variety of management science problems has attracted the attention of many economists. The introduction of dynamic optimization techniques, such as the Maximum Principle and Dynamic Programming, has opened the possibility to analyse the intertemporal structure of many economic problems under consideration. In particular 'Optimal Control Theory' has proved to be a very efficient tool to study the dynamics of economic processes. It can fruitfully be applied to several problems in management science. An important application is the research field coined 'the dynamics of the firm'. These studies mostly consider the optimal dynamic behaviour of a value maximizing firm by determining simultaneously the optimal financing, dividend and investment policies. This selection of controls may be extended by including others, such as the choice of production techniques and the location of capital and labour.

The general result of these studies is that the optimal evolution pattern of a firm can be described by a succession of different policies concerning the above mentioned controls. So, the firm will not immediately pursue an equilibrium steady state policy, but it will continuously adjust its policy to the circumstances.

These dynamic models, also named dynamic growth models, are already extended in several ways. Although many authors are aware of the effects of personal taxation their studies in a dynamic setting are lacking this subject, however. Research into this subject has been conducted by some authors. As a result of their specific assumptions, however, a number of interesting topics are still left out of consideration.

1.4. Relevance and motivation of the book

The aim of this book, the inclusion of personal taxation into the dynamic theory of the firm, is quite obvious. We may clarify this purpose both from a theoretical as well as from an empirical point of view.

In order to point out the theoretical motive, we recall some conclusions of the theory on corporate finance and the theory on the dynamics of the firm, that are indicated in the previous sections and will be considered in depth in the chapters two and three:

- a mutual dependence can be observed between some financial policies of the firm and the level of the personal tax rate of the firm's shareholders. This conclusion holds in particular with respect to the financing, dividend and, as it will turn out, the investment policy.
- the evolution of a firm can be described by a succession of different policies concerning e.g. finance, dividend and investment.

The confrontation of these features in one problem setting is thus by no means surprising, since the two statements amplify each other. Moreover, this book fills up a gap in both the theories; that is, we extend the theory on corporate finance in this respect by including another dimension: dynamics, and we extend the dynamic theory of the firm by including personal taxation.

Empirically, we are now able to get a better description of that what we observe in the real world. Since we include some very important features, we may get a better insight in the decisions both corporations and investors make in the course of time.

Of course, we still neglect some other characteristics of the real world in our problem formulation. One of them is the uncertainty we daily face. From a pure theoretical point of view uncertainty can be included in a dynamic problem by applying stochastic optimization techniques, such as stochastic optimal control. However, due to the mathematical difficulties, that then will be encountered, less striking, less clear and less interpretable results will be obtained.

1.5. Subproblems

In order to fulfill our principal aim, we will carry out the analysis stepwise by considering the next subproblems:

- In which way are the three main decisions in finance theory, viz. the financing, the dividend and the investment policy, affected by personal taxation?
- What will be the equilibrium values of firms in a market with progressive personal taxation within a static setting?
- What is the impact of personal taxation on the optimal evolution of a single value maximizing firm?
- Is it possible that the state of the firm is such that other shareholders will take over the control of the present shareholders in order to pursue the policy they advocate? That is, we consider the case of one single value maximizing firm and more differently taxed investors.
- What is the dynamic equilibrium situation in case of more firms and more investors?

The above enumeration indicates the contents of the remaining chapters of this book which we elucidate in the next subsection.

1.6. Outline of the book

The contents of this book can be divided into three parts. In the chapters two and three we survey for convenience of the reader some relevant elements of the theory on corporate finance and the dynamic theory of the firm. Readers familiar with these theories will not find anything new in them, but others will get the information necessary to understand the origin and topic of this book. The first mentioned readers may regard these chapters to be unnecessarily long; the last mentioned readers may appreciate its length from a pedagogical point of view. Thereafter, in chapter four, we discuss, extend and improve some topics in finance theory. Finally, we focus on the principal aim of the book: in the chapters five, six and seven we investigate stepwise the impact of personal taxation within the dynamic theory of the firm.

In more detail the contents of the chapters are as follows:

In chapter two we focus on the relevance of time with regard to the economic decision process. We stress the general interest of economists to include time into a variety of management science problems by presenting some examples, which are taken from the literature and which illustrate in addition the progress in dynamic optimization theory. It turns out that in particular 'Optimal Control Theory' has provided a useful framework for the analysis of intertemporal economic decision processes. We apply this optimization theory, when we focus in this chapter on the so-called 'dynamics of the firm', the field of research that forms the topic of the book. We consider in particular a basic model that describes the optimal dynamic behaviour of a value maximizing firm. We determine simultaneously the optimal financing, dividend and investment policy in the course of time.

We describe the impact of taxation, both corporate and personal, on the optimal policy of the firm as well as on the behaviour of investors in chapter three. We elaborate on the concept of 'fiscal (non) neutrality' and illustrate this concept by means of some examples, in particular with respect to the value of a firm in relation to its leverage, that is, the debt to equity ratio. We start this analysis with the well known Modigliani & Miller leverage irrelevancy theorem, that is derived under absence of any taxation, and end up with Miller's irrelevancy theorem, which is based on an 'after tax' equilibrium theory with a progressive personal tax.

In chapter four we once again elaborate on the firm's equilibrium market value under taxation and its implication with respect to tax induced clienteles: due to its policy a firm will attract investors subject to particular tax rate levels. We use a model, based on the DeAngelo & Masulis model, in order to clarify once again Miller's irrelevancy theorem and to show the existence of tax induced 'dividend' and 'financial leverage' clienteles. In addition, we introduce 'investment clienteles' as a result of the corporate investment policy and extend the DeAngelo & Masulis framework by considering the implications of different tax regimes. A main part of this chapter is devoted to a comprehensive discussion of the Gordon criticism of Miller's result. We point out a corrected version of the equilibrium approach that Gordon uses, and we question the adjustment process he describes.

In chapter five we return to the dynamic theory of the firm. We formulate a basic model which describes the dynamic dividend, financing and investment problem of a value maximizing firm under personal taxation during a fixed planning period. We elaborate on the analytical solution, that we obtain by means of Optimal Control Theory and the iterative policy connecting procedure designed by Van Loon. We derive some decision rules with respect to the three mentioned policies and combine these in a way which enables us to indicate the optimal policy as a function of only the rate of return on equity. Furthermore, we present an analysis of the economic results, including a sensitivity analysis with regard to some financial and fiscal parameters. We compare the results of the problem under consideration with those of problems without personal taxation and discuss the striking differences.

Chapter six enlarges the analysis of the previous chapter by allowing investors to sell the shares of the firm under consideration at some unknown moment in time. In a way we consider an optimal control problem with a free end point at which a 'shareholder take-over' may occur. So, contrary to chapter five, at least two or more investors are now involved. We use several formulations and techniques to model and solve the problem, including a 'switching dynamics'-like approach and a cooperative differential game approach.

The purpose of chapter seven is an attempt to justify the principal thesis of the book that during each stage of their evolution firms will be controlled by investors in different tax brackets. To that end we consider in a dynamic setting the impact of personal taxation on the optimal policy string of many value maximizing firms and the equilibrium portfolio selection of differently taxed investors, both under the assumption of no separation of ownership and control. In this line a dynamic valuation and portfolio selection theory is derived, such as indicated in the first section.

Finally, we summarize the conclusion of this book in chapter eight.

In general, the chapters of this book are split up into sections, that may in turn be subdivided in subsections. All remaining chapters start with an introductory section and end up with the main conclusions. Technical derivations and proofs are placed in the appendices, whereas the chapters itselves emphasize on the economic presentation and interpretation of problem and solution respectively.

CHAPTER TWO

MODELS OF DYNAMIC FIRM BEHAVIOUR

2.1 Introduction

Time is of utmost importance with regard to the economic decision making process. Many, or perhaps all, decisions of enterprise behaviour are based on time dependent data, environmental circumstances and opportunities: decisions should be seen in the historical contexts. In addition, time brings along the necessity to plan ahead, not only because of the lagged response on present actions, but also because present decisions affect future events by making certain opportunities available, by precluding others and by altering the costs or revenues of still others. Present decisions are, therefore, always taken with a view towards the future. Quoting Kamien and Schwartz we may say:

> "If present decisions do not affect future opportunities, the planning problem is trivial. One need then only make the best decision for the present." [Kamien & Schwartz (1985), p. 3].

Observing the way business enterprises operate in the economy we discover clear differences among their behaviour. Some firms may keep on a stationary level and have no incentive to alter their steady state policy. Other firms, however, may have the opportunity to grow, that is, to enlarge their production capacity level and corresponding sales level, whereas still others are forced to pursue a contraction policy e.g. because of low efficiency or pessimistic future expectations. Accordingly, "the market is a process of dynamic change" and "it is no surpise that the position of enterprises change as well" [Appels (1986) p. 244 and p. 243 respectively]. We may stress this conclusion by a statement of Van Loon (1983) who quotes Hicks:

"In mechanics, statics is concerned with rest, dynamics with motion, but no economic system is ever at rest in anything like the mechanical sense." [Van Loon (1983), p. 4].

Studies in management science frequently consider comparative static or comparative dynamic analysis techniques. As implied by its name, a comparative static analysis is purely static and is concerned with the intratemporal effects of a change in a certain parameter or variable upon other variables such as prices and output. A comparative dynamic analysis is concerned with the comparison of different steady state equilibria of the system. "Because, however, it only yields steady state solutions, it does not give any information about the time path of the adjustment." [Friedlaender & Vandendorpe (1978), p. 9]. This is an important deficiency because the history and future course of any company differs from every other, that is every firm tells its own story. The use of dynamic models is, therefore, of utmost importance in order to describe the evolution of characteristic features or variables of the process in the course of the time.

The application of dynamic models with corresponding optimization techniques has assumed large proportions in management science since Pontryagin et al. (1962) published their pathbreaking work on the maximum principle. The formalism on which this principle is based, forms a basis for the field coined Optimal Control Theory. This theory in particular has provided an usefull framework for the analysis of intertemporal economic decision processes. Feichtinger argues that Optimal Control Theory is of importance in economics because "it is able to provide deeper insight into the dynamic interdependence between the model variables, i.e. into the intertemporal structure of the economic phenomenon under consideration." [Feichtinger (1985), p. v].

The above clarifies the general interest of economists during the last decade to apply Optimal Control Theory to a variety of management science problems. In line with this, we firstly present some examples showing in which manner time can be included in economic modelling (section 2.2). Thereafter, we focus on the so-called 'dynamics of the firm', the field of research that forms the topic of this book. We consider in particular the optimal dynamic behaviour of a value maximizing firm by determining simultaneously the optimal financing, investment and dividend policies over a finite horizon (section 2.3). The corresponding model and its solution are our starting-points for the further research of this book. Finally, we briefly survey the chapter and the most fruitful applications of continuous Optimal Control Theory in management science.

2.2. Dynamic and management modelling

In the two volumes of his book Tapiero (1977) comprehensively elaborates on the temporal dimensions relevant to operations management. One of his conclusions is: "The inclusion of time in the modeling and analysis of operational systems is by no means easy, but it is a factor that must be considered in the practice of operations management" [Tapiero (1977), p. 45]. This inclusion of time can be done in many ways. We give three examples which also illustrate the progress in dynamic optimization.

2.2.1. Exponential growth

The use of exponential growth is a well known procedure in economics to include time. All time dependent variables are assumed to change according a particular rate of growth, say g. The value of such a variable X is then fixed by:

$$X(T) = x_0(1+g)^T \qquad \text{discrete case} \tag{2.1}$$

$$X(T) = x_0 e^{gT} \qquad \text{continuous case} \tag{2.2}$$

where

T : time

x_0: initial value of X

A well known, nowadays classical, application of the exponential growth method is due to Gordon. In 1962 he published a model in order to fix the optimal division of the firm's net cash flow into retentions and dividend payments. The problem, that he hereby encounters, is that on the one hand a retention of profit reduces the amount of current dividend payments. On the other hand, however, the level of future dividend probably rises because of the increase of production capacity due to the current gross investment, financed through the retention under consideration.

Before presenting the model, we first define some variables and constants. In the present and next chapters we describe constants by small letters and variables by capitals:

CF(T): net cash flow at T
D(T) : dividend at T
K(T) : production capacity level at T
b : retention rate, $0 \leq b < 1$
i : time preference rate of shareholders
r' : net return on capital

Gordon considers a shareholder owned firm, that is, the firm is supposed to act as if it maximizes its value as conceived by its shareholders. The firm's value may then be defined as the present value of the dividend flow over an infinite horizon. The discount rate, we use, is represented by the time preference rate of the shareholders. Hence, the objective is to maximize

$$\int_{T=0}^{\infty} D(T).e^{-iT}dT \tag{2.3}$$

Dividend is assumed to equal the fraction (1-b) of the firm's cash flow implying that a fraction b is retained in order to finance new investment. The firm is all equity financed and issues of new shares are not allowed. Thus,

$$D(T) = (1-b).CF(T) \tag{2.4}$$

$$\dot{K}(T) := \frac{dK(T)}{dT} = b.CF(T) \tag{2.5}$$

A dot denotes the derivative of the variable with respect to the time. Gordon assumes constant returns to scale, so:

$$CF(T) = r'K(T) \tag{2.6}$$

The aim is to determine the retention rate b in such a way that the present value of the firm is maximized. To get this optimal solution, we reduce the model into one single expression. To that end, we firstly solve the differential equation (2.5), which is an easy task because of the constant-returns-to-scale-assumption (2.6). Thereafter, we substitute the expression, we found for K(T) in (2.6) and successively (2.6) in (2.4) and (2.4) on its turn in the objective functional (2.3). The result is the next maximization problem:

$$\underset{0<b<1}{\text{maximize}} \int_{T=0}^{\infty} (1-b)CF(0)e^{-i(1-b\frac{r'}{i})T} dT \tag{2.7}$$

The optimal retention rate b^* obviously depends on the value of the time preference rate in relation to the rate of return on capital. We distinguish three cases:

a) in case $r' < i$ the optimal retention rate equals zero: $b^* = 0$. Because the rate of return is less than the time preference rate, that is, the rate of return shareholders obtain elsewhere, cash flow is totally paid out as dividend.

b) the value of the firm is independent of the retention rate when $r' = i$. Shareholders take a neutral view with regard to the policy of the firm. With the exception of $b = 1$, all values of b over the range zero to one result in the same optimal value.

c) if $r' > i$ we only obtain results in case of finite horizons. The value of the firm is then maximized when the growth rate of capital equals the time preference rate. So, $b^* = i/r'$.

Due to the assumption of constant returns to scale we get a solution, which is constant in the course of time. The inclusion of time by means of exponential growth rates does not bring on a real dynamic solution in the sense that the current control affects the state and control space of future decisions. Expression (2.7) makes clear that the model can be reduced to a standard static optimization problem, which solution b^* satisfies the first order condition for optimality.

2.2.2. Multiperiod constraints

A second manner to include time in economic modeling is the introduction of time dependent restrictions or multiperiod constraints. We illustrate this way of modeling on the basis of the investment selection problem designed by Lorie & Savage (1955). This problem belongs to the so-called 'constrained capital budgeting problems' [see e.g. Copeland & Weston (1983), pp. 55-60].

Suppose a firm is comparing a finite number of investment projects with, for simplicity, equal duration. In addition to the known investment costs, each investment may periodically yield outlays. A meaningful multiperiod budget constraint is imposed on the firm, however. Let us further assume that cash flows can not be transferred between time periods, that external liabilities are not available, and that the cash budgets in the succeeding periods are known. The problem is then to find the set of investment projects which maximizes the net present value and satisfies the cash constraints. We may formulate the following model:

$$\underset{F_j}{\text{maximize}} \sum_{j=1}^{n} F_j NPV_j \tag{2.8}$$

$$\text{subject to} \sum_{j=1}^{n} F_j C_j(T) < \sum_{j=1}^{n} F_j R_j(T), \; T > 0 \tag{2.9}$$

where

$R_j(T)$: revenue project j in period T

F_j : acceptance indicator project j, $F_j = \{0,1\}$

$C_j(T)$: cash outlays project j in period T

NPV_j : net present value project j

n : number of projects

The inclusion of time by multiperiod constraints brings on the interesting result that a project with negative net present value may be accepted in the optimal solution if it supplies the funds needed during other time periods to undertake very profitable projects.

The optimal dynamic solution, however, is once again trivial, that is, in the decision making period the optimal values of F_j are determined and these values may not change in the course of time. If we assume that the planning period is restricted to a finite number of discrete time periods, say z, and that it is possible to undertake fractions of projects, then the problem may be formulated using linear programming. In fact, Weingarter (1963) solved the sample of Lorie & Savage by using linear programming. If projects are indivisible, then integer programming may be used.

So, the problem of multiperiod constraints, may be formulated as the maximization of an objective subject to at least z restrictions (other restrictions may exist), where z is the number of time periods under consideration.

2.2.3. Dynamic control

Following in the step of Verheyen (1976) we transform the model of Gordon in order to eliminate two major objections:

- the assumption of a constant retention rate
- the assumption of constant returns to scale.

We, therefore, remodel the expressions (2.4) through (2.6) into the following ones:

$$D(T) = (1-B(T)).CF(T) \tag{2.10}$$

$$\dot{K}(T) = B(T).CF(T) \tag{2.11}$$

$$CF(T) = S(K(T)) \tag{2.12}$$

where the retention rate B(T) may vary in the course of time and cash flow is a concave function of the production capacity K, S(K), at T, that is, we assume decreasing returns to scale.

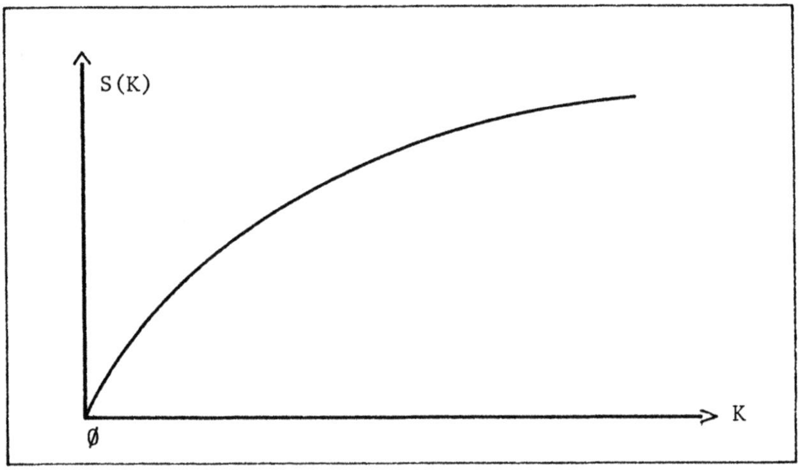

Figure 2.1: Cash flow as concave function of K: S(K).

The problem has now become truly dynamic because the current retention rate not only affects current dividend, but also future dividend decisions. In addition, the first order condition now depends on the production capacity level because of the decreasing returns to scale. Similar to the original Gordon model the optimal retention rate still depends on the value of the time preference rate in relation to the rate of return on capital, which is not a constant anymore. It is not surprising therefore, that the solution is a function $B^*(T)$, that gives the firm's optimal retention rate at each point in time over its planning period. This optimal solution, which can be found by means of several optimization techniques, is depicted in figure 2.2. To get such a solution we have to assume that $\frac{dS}{dK}(0) > i$.

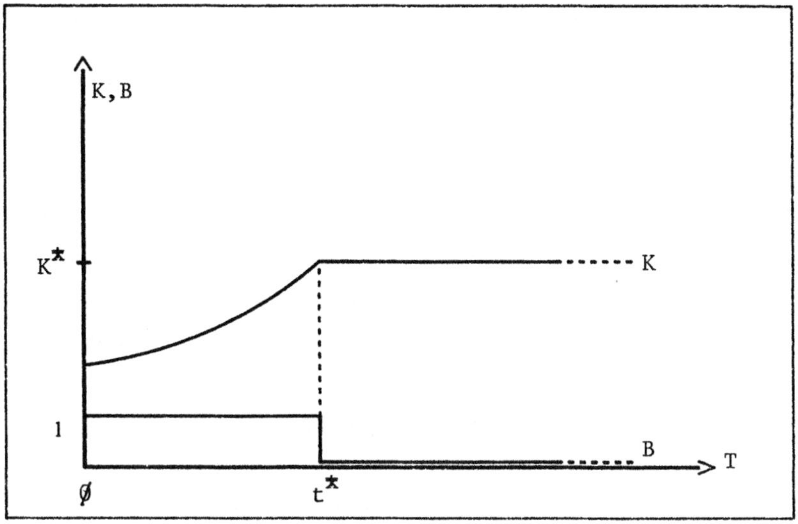

Figure 2.2: Optimal solution dynamic model of Gordon.

At first the firm retains its total cash flow in order to grow at maximum speed: $B^*(T) = 1$, $T < t^*$. This policy is the optimal one because net return on capital exceeds the time preference rate. However, net return on capital is not a constant, but a decreasing function of the production capacity level: $dS(K)/dK$. So, a retention policy not only produces an increase of production capacity level, but decreases the net return on capital, which is equivalent to marginal revenue, as well. As soon as the level K^* is reached, where

$$K(t^*) = K^* \Leftrightarrow \frac{dS}{dK}(K^*) = i \tag{2.13}$$

it is profitable to stop expansion and to pay out all earnings instead. If the firm would continue its expansion investment, marginal revenue would fall below the time preference rate. Similar to case a) of the original Gordon model a maximum pay out policy would be the result. So, from $T = t^*$ on the firm pays out its cash flow and keeps the production capacity on a constant level:

$$\left.\begin{array}{l} B^*(T) = 0 \\ K^*(T) = K^* \end{array}\right\} \quad \text{for } T > t^* \tag{2.14}$$

Finally, we notice that the time preference rate reflects the return shareholders may obtain elsewhere. Within this deterministic setting, and the absence of debt financing, the time preference rate is equivalent to the firm's cost of equity capital. The optimal policy, therefore, depends on the well known balance between marginal revenue and marginal costs: as long as revenue of an additional unit production capacity exceeds the capital costs of this unit, it is profitable to raise production capacity; as soon as an equality occurs, the optimal equilibrium level is reached. It is due to the decreasing net return function that this example clarifies the dynamics of the model: current policy affects the decision criterion of future policies.

For two purposes we may reformulate the dynamic variant of the Gordon model.

Firstly, the Gordon problem may be modeled in expressions that are common in the dynamic theory of the firm and in the formulations we use in the remainder of the book in particular. In addition, it will enable the reader to realize the correspondence between the dynamic Gordon model and the model that we will elaborate on in the following section and that will be the basis for the further analysis in the book. In fact, the dynamic Gordon model may be considered as a kind of precursor of the basic model of the next section.

Secondly, the formulation enables us to explain something about the jargon of 'Optimal Control Theory'. Although it is beyond our scope to deal in great detail with the field of dynamic optimization techniques, it will be convenient for the reader to have some knowledge of the common technical terms and language used in Optimal Control Theory. We suggest the reader who is in great detail interested in Optimal Control Theory, to read the available standard literature on this topic. A broad outline of dynamic modeling is given by the survey paper of Tapiero (1978), whereas more comprehensive and extensive, but still readable, considerations may be found in e.g. Sethi & Thompson (1981), Kamien & Schwartz (1985) or Feichtinger & Hartl (1986).

We reformulate the model by eliminating the retention rate $B(T)$ and introducing the dividend variable $D(T)$ as control variable instead. In particular, we rewrite expression (2.11) into:

$$\dot{K}(T) = B(T).CF(T)$$
$$= CF(T) - (1-B(T)).CF(T)$$
$$= S(K(T)) - D(T) \qquad (2.15)$$

We thus get the following optimal control problem:

$$\underset{D}{\text{maximize}} \int_{T=0}^{\infty} D(T)e^{-iT}dT \qquad (2.16)$$

subject to

$$\dot{K}(T) = S(K(T)) - D(T) \qquad (2.17)$$

$$K(0) = k_0 > 0 \qquad (2.18)$$

$$S(K(T)) - D(T) \geq 0 \qquad (2.19)$$

$$D(T) \geq 0 \qquad (2.20)$$

$$K(T) \geq 0 \qquad (2.21)$$

A description of the above problem in the jargon of Optimal Control Theory can now be given as follows [see e.g. Sethi & Thompson (1981), p. 2]:

The system to be controlled is the firm. The state of the system is represented by state variables. The above problem has only one state variable, viz. K(T). The value of K(T) is controlled by the decision or control variable D(T). Given the values of the state and control variable, the state equation (2.17) determines the instantaneous rate of change of the state variable. So, based on the initial value k_0, fixed by the initial condition (2.18), and the values of D(T) over the planning period, that is, the control history, we can integrate over time to get the state trajectory of the firm. The aim of the control is to maximize the value of the firm, that is, the objective functional (2.16). The decision maker has to reckon with the laws of motion as described in (2.17) and (2.18), with the state constraint (2.21), the control constraint (2.20) and the mixed constraint (2.19). Any plan, fulfilling these conditions is called a feasible solution; the optimal plan is named the optimal policy string and optimal state trajectory respectively.

2.3. A dynamic theory of the firm: investment, finance and dividend

In this section we investigate the optimal dynamic behaviour of a value maximizing firm by determining simultaneously the optimal financing, investment and dividend policy over a finite horizon. To do so, we elaborate on the formulation of an optimal control problem and its solution, which is determined by means of the so-called maximum principle. We will deal in great detail with the expressions of the model, which has much in common with both the model Lesourne (1973) has designed as well as with the underlying financial model of the activity analysis problem considered by Van Loon (1983). In addition, we survey formulations that have been considered by other authors. The model will form the basis for the research of next chapters.

2.3.1. The firm's objective

The specification of the firm's objective is of utmost importance, because it determines the direction of the firm's activities in a large measure. The objective considerably depends on the decision maker or party that has an interest in the firm.

We may distinguish three parties of goalsetters: managers, employees and shareholders. We elaborate on the latter party and glance at the two first mentioned ones because these are of nonimportance for our purpose.

Managers are generally supposed to pursue power, prestige and income. In case they are the dominant party within the firm, but supposed that they are not the owners, that is, ownership and control are separated, the objective of the firm will mostly be the maximization of growth in terms of discounted sales in combination with either a restriction on the minimal amount of dividend to be paid out, or a restriction on the minimal profit level per unit equity to be maintained [see e.g. Leland (1972)].

Labour may be the rulling party in so-called 'labour managed' firms. In this type of firms "Labour receives the residual revenue after the other input factors including capital, have received their predetermined renumeration". [Ekman (1978, p. 17]. In this situation, the firm maximizes income per employee.

In finance theory, however, shareholders mostly act as the dominant participating party in the firm's decisions. Accordingly, the firm is supposed to act as if it maximizes its value conceived by the shareholders. In the remainder of the book this will be named the assumption of no separation of ownership and control. The value of the firm is then defined as the present value of either the dividend or the cash flow, both over an infinite period of time [Krouse & Lee (1973), Sethi (1978)]. When a finite planning horizon is introduced, the firm's discount value at the end of the planning period has to reflect all future returns. This salvage value may be a function of the value of final equity or the discounted value of final equity itself [Ludwig (1978), Van Loon (1983)]. Depending on the problem under consideration we will use either the infinite horizon objective or the latter, more specific, finite horizon definition.

In this chapter we consider a shareholder owned value maximizing firm, which at some known planning time z may stop its activities. As we assume no separation of ownership and control, the objective functional is given by:

$$\int_{T=0}^{z} D(T)e^{-iT}dT + X(z)e^{-iz} \tag{2.22}$$

where

X(T): equity at T.

In general, the group of shareholders may change due to mutual buy and sell transactions among shareholders or due to issues of new shares. In these cases the objective is defined as: maximizing the value of the firm as conceived by the present shareholders. We will deal in detail with the former situation in chapters 6 and 7; the latter will be beyond our scope.

2.3.2. Input, and its transformation to output

A firm achieves its profit by transforming inputs into outputs. As any company may have its own unique combination of inputs and outputs, we need to specify the firm's production function. Although a firm may use a large variety of inputs, we restrict ourselves to only two: we assume that the firm produces output by means of labour and capital goods.

Most publications making this distinction between inputs postulate a perfect labour market, which implies a constant wage rate and perfect adaptability. Due to the resulting fixed optimal labour productivity, the amount of labour appears to adapt itself perfectly all the time [see e.g. Jorgenson (1963), (1967)]. Imperfections in labour markets may be due to a restriction on a firing policy or hiring and firing cost functions [Leban (1982), Feichtinger and Luptacik (1983)].

In the literature, the market of capital goods is mostly supposed to be perfect, so that the firm can buy its assets at fixed prices. Several authors, however, have studied the case of an imperfect market in the framework of so-called adjustment cost models: each firm does not immediately adapt its optimal size because of costs inherent to the adjustment proces. A survey of the theory on adjustment costs may be found in Söderström (1976), whereas Kort (1986, 1987) incorporates adjustment costs in a dynamic financing/investment model of the firm.

Using combinations of labour and capital the firm produces output. In the case of only one single production technique any output level corresponds with one combination of inputs. Although the assumption of a single production technique will mostly be satisfactory for the purpose of the topic under consideration, research has been done to the optimal choice of production techniques.

Many publications dealing with the allocation of labour and capital in the dynamic theory of the firm assume a continuous production function that mostly belongs to a specific class of Cobb-Douglas type function [see e.g. Lesourne & Leban (1978)]. Such a production function requires that the firm can choose at each moment in time between an infinite number of production possibilities.

In the opinion of Van Loon, a continuous production function is not a realistic concept, because "in reality the management of the firm always chooses between a limited number of production possibilities" [Van Loon (1983), p. 40]. He, therefore, introduces an activity analysis to describe the link between the inputs of labour and capital goods, and the output of the firm. In particular he considers two linear production activities, one that is capital intensive and one that is labour-intensive.

With regard to the output, the production quantity is as a matter of course positively correlated to the number of outputs. This dependence may be linear or nonlinear.

In the latter case production is mostly assumed to be an increasing, concave function of the inputs, which implies decreasing returns to scale. The output market may also be postulated as a perfect one, that is, the price does not change when the amount of output of the firm varies. In that case, the value of the output, that is the sales level, will be a concave function of the inputs too. If the labour market is also perfect, the optimal labour productivity will be fixed, which, accordingly, implies that both production and sales may be considered as concave functions of only capital. So, any value K of the amount of capital goods corresponds uniquely with a marginal productivity [see Van Loon (1983), p. 120].

In the former case output is proportional to input, the labour to capital rate is fixed and an imperfect output market is considered. Prices decrease when output quantity increases. Sales, however, are again a concave function of the amount of capital goods.

In this book we assume that the firm produces a single output by means of two inputs: labour and capital. The input markets are perfect and to facilitate the analysis, the value per unit of a capital good is fixed at one unit of money. We further assume absence of other imperfections, such as inflation and technical progress. We also equalize the technical deterioration rate and the depreciation rate, which implies that the value of the amount of capital goods in the firm equals the number of capital goods. The afore mentioned assumptions enable us to describe the impact of investments on the amount of capital goods by the nowadays generally used formulation of net investments. If we assume depreciation to be proportional to the amount of capital goods, we may write:

$$\dot{K}(T) = I(T) - aK(T) \tag{2.23}$$

where

I(T): gross investment, that is the number of assets bought or sold by the firm

a : depreciation rate

Assuming a fixed labour to capital rate, production will be proportional to the inputs:

$$Q(T) = qK(T) = \frac{q}{\ell} L(T) \tag{2.24}$$

where

L(T): labour

Q(T): production

ℓ : labour to capital rate

q : capital productivity

Let us assume, for simplicity, the capital productivity to equal one, $q = 1$. This implies that the amount of capital goods may be named the production capacity. For sake of readability we sometimes use both expressions for this phenomenon.

In this book we postulate an imperfect output market, which implies that the firm is operating under decreasing returns to scale. Due to the fixed labour to capital rate, sales less labour costs is a concave function of K. In addition, we introduce the phenomenon 'operating income', which stands for the revenue before interest payments and corporate taxation (see also subsection 2.3.3). In our terminology, operating income is equal to sales less labour costs and depreciation. Hence,

$$O(K) = S(K) - wL(K) - aK \qquad (2.25)$$

where

$O(K)$ = operating income

$S(K)$ = sales income

w = wage rate.

We should note that for the sake of readability we have dropped in (2.25) the obvious time argument T. Due to earlier assumptions, O(K) is a concave function of only the production capacity level K and its depiction is similar to that of S(K) in figure 2.1. We will use O(K) because of its convenience and simplicity.

2.3.3. Finance and government

Generally speaking the firm's assets are financed by either equity or debt. Because it is beyond our scope we do not elaborate on the existing variety of money capital. The reader may think of shares when speaking of equity, whereas loans and bonds are examples of debt money.

In the literature on dynamic modeling debt is treated in different ways with regard to its mathematical features. Leland (1972), who was the first to include aspects of production as well as of financing, assumes the total amount of debt to alter only due to inflow of new debt:

$$\dot{Y}(T) = B(T) \qquad (2.26)$$

where

$B(T)$ = inflow of debt

$Y(T)$ = total amount of debt

Ludwig (1978) amends Leland's state equation of debt by introducing a fixed redemption rate $b > 0$. Hence,

$$\dot{Y}(T) = B(T) - bY(T) \qquad (2.27)$$

Dealing with debt in this way, the firm is forced to keep a certain amount of debt all the time, due to the fixed redemption rate. That is, given a positive initial value the total amount of debt is always non-negative in the course of time. To Ludwig, this continuous presence of debt money in the firm is a realistic aspect of his approach. Van Loon (1983), however, wonders whether the origin of it, that is, the infinite pay off period, is such a realistic feature. He, therefore, treats the total amount of debt itself as a decision variable of the firm's management. As a consequence, debt may adjust instantaneously upwards and downwards. Moreover, it may be even negative, that is, the firm may also lend money.

This replacement of a state variable into a control variable is a far-reaching simplification of the model in view of the mathematical difficulties to encounter. In spite of this simplification, however, it turns out that the nature of the solution, that is the nature of the optimal policy of the management as a function of the time is not affected. The quantities may differ, the quality of the decision is the same, however.

Lenders of debt money may plead their interest either by making conditions on loans in such a way as to minimize risk or by claiming rewards proportional to their risk bearing.

The former formulation mostly assumes an imperfect capital market in such a way that the firm is subject to a certain kind of credit rationing. Credit rationing means that lenders are willing to invest funds into the firm only up to a certain limit. Such an upperbound, together with a fixed interest rate is an indication of the risk class to which the firm belongs. The upperbound may be considered as a condition on the financial structure of the firm, that must be fulfilled in order to stay in the relevant risk class. Ludwig (1978) surveys alternative ways to formulate these limits of borrowing as presented in the literature. One possible formulation is a definition in terms of flows, that is, the upperbound may be on new debt as a function of the cash flow [Lesourne (1973), p. 222] or of the investment expenditures [Ludwig (1978), p. 92]. Another formulation is one in terms of stock, e.g. an upperbound on the total amount of debt as a (linear) function of equity, implying a maximum leverage [Lesourne (1973), p. 206 or Van Loon (1983), p. 45].

In the latter formulation, the firm is allowed to invest in such a way that its risk profile changes. Authors dealing with this assumption formulate the demanded interest rate as a function of the leverage [Senchack (1975) and Tuovila (1983)].

Equity is the firm's most important liability as it is an necessity for viability. The amount of equity may increase through issues of new shares, enterprise subsidies by the government and through retentions.

Only few publications deal with the topic of issues of share. Mostly, those papers assume an imperfect capital market, that is, issuing new shares is subject to floatation costs [Senchack (1975)] or limitations [Tuovila (1983)]. For many purposes, however, it is not necessary to allow issues of new shares.

Enterprise subsidies are politically powerful and beloved governmental instruments to stimulate economic progress and innovation. The reader interested in this topic is referred to the comprehensive work of Appels (1986). Van Loon (1983) was the first to include enterprise subsidies in the dynamic theory of the firm. He argues that the firm can raise its equity also by acquiring investment grants. In his 1985 article Van Loon reviews the Dutch battlefield of finding the best way to stimulate trade, industry and employment by comparing the impact of alternative measures on the optimal trajectory of a firm. Although it is beyond doubt that investment grants affect the firm's policy, we will neglect it.

The last possibility to raise equity is through retentions. Instead of paying out dividend, the firm may decide to retain earnings, which may be used

- to pay back debt money, or, if the amount of debt is already negative, to lend money
- to get cash money or short term cash balance positions; short term cash policies, however, do not play an important part in investment policies when forecasts are certain
- to finance new investments.

Equity will fall when the firm pays out more dividend than it earns. With net earnings we mean the operating income after corporate taxation and tax deductible interest payments.

The firm under consideration, has only one asset: capital goods K. Because we postulate our basic model within a deterministic setting, we may neglect short term cash policies. The firm may attract the usual kinds of money capital: equity X(T) and debt Y(T). The balance sheet is therefore:

$$K(T) = X(T) + Y(T) \tag{2.28}$$

We furthermore assume that no transaction costs are incurred when borrowing or paying off debt money and corporate tax is proportional to profits and paid at once. Issues of new share are prohibited, interest payments are tax deductible and earnings after corporate tax are used to issue (nonnegative) dividend or to increase the level of equity through retentions. This leads to:

$$\dot{X}(T) = (1-\tau_c)[O(K) - rY(T)] - D(T) \tag{2.29}$$

where

r : interest rate

τ_c: corporate tax rate.

We limit debt, which is treated as a control variable, by introducing an upperbound in terms of a maximum debt to equity rate h:

$$Y(T) < hX(T), \quad h > 0 \tag{2.30}$$

Finally, we remark that the expressions we have designed up to now, may also be derived from the well known financial records of the firm: the balance sheet, the income statement and the cash account [see e.g. Van Loon (1983), pp. 43-44 and Van Schijndel (1986b)].

2.3.4. Additional assumptions

To complete the set of general assumptions for the basic model we discuss and add the next four.

1. $(1-\tau_c)\frac{dO}{dK}(0) > \max\{(1-\tau_c)r, i\}$ (2.31)

   The marginal revenue of the first product to be sold exceeds each of the financial costs implying that the firm will consider only those alternatives that are profitable from the start.

2. $i \neq (1-\tau_c)r$ (2.32)

   In this way we avoid degenerated solutions. Moreover, as Van Loon argues, only by coincidence the prices of equity and debt to be paid by the same firm, equal each other. As lenders of debt money and shareholders have different interests and intentions, the markets of debt and equity are separated [Van Loon (1983), p. 48]. When introducing personal taxation an additional justification of this assumption will be given (see section 5.2).

3. The firm owns certain known initial amounts of equity and debt, such that

$$Y(0) = hX(0) \qquad X(0) = x_0 > 0$$
$$X(0) + Y(0) = K(0) \qquad K(0) = k_0 > 0 \qquad (2.33)$$

4. All variables are nonnegative at all times. This assumption implies that the firm may not divest or lend money.

2.3.5. Summary of the basic model and general solution procedure

We are now ready to combine the analysis of the previous subsections into the basic model of the firm. The problem to be solved is formulated as an optimal control problem. The objective to maximize the present value of the firm is given by expression (2.22). The state equations governing the system are obtained from (2.23) and (2.29). Both the decision variables and the state variables are subject to constraints. The problem is to determine the time paths of the control variables D(T), I(T) and Y(T) so that the objective will be maximized. The dividend policy has a direct influence on the objective, whereas investment and debt enter indirectly via the state equations.

For convenience, we summarize the problem in its full length:

$$\underset{D,I,Y}{\text{maximize}} \int_{T=0}^{z} D(T)e^{-iT}dT + X(z)e^{-iz} \tag{2.22}$$

subject to the state equations

$$\dot{K} = I - aK \tag{2.23}$$

$$\dot{X} = (1-\tau_c)[O(K) - rY] - D \tag{2.29}$$

with the initial conditions

$$\begin{aligned} K(0) &= (1+h)x(0) \\ X(0) &= x_0 > 0 \end{aligned} \tag{2.33}$$

subject to the following constraints:

$$K = X + Y \tag{2.28}$$

$$Y < hX \tag{2.30}$$

$$D > 0,\ I > 0,\ Y > 0,\ K > 0,\ X > 0 \tag{2.34}$$

Furthermore, the additional assumptions (2.31) and (2.32) should hold.

This dynamic problem can be solved analytically by means of Optimal Control Theory [see e.g. Sethi & Thompson (1981), Kamien & Schwartz (1985) or Feichtinger & Hartl (1986)]. It is for convenience of the reader that in appendix A1 the necessary, and in our case also sufficient, conditions for an optimal solution are derived from a principle that strongly resembles on the standard maximum principle of Pontryagin c.s. (1962). This principle consists of a set of first order conditions with respect to the control variables, Euler Lagrange equations, complementary slackness conditions, transversality conditions and some additional conditions concerning continuity properties. We make use of these conditions by applying the 'iterative policy connecting'-procedure designed by Van Loon (1983, pp. 115-117). This procedure is a very fruitful and convenient method in order to determine from the set of necessary conditions a solution for the optimal policy of the firm over the whole planning period.

2.3.6. Optimal policy strings

In the description of the optimal policy strings we will, for simplicity only, disregard contraction policies by considering only those cases for which the initial value of K is sufficiently low.

Applying Van Loon's iterative solution procedure we may discern five different feasible optimal time paths, each characterized by different policies concerning leverage, investment and dividend. Although we have derived these policies analytically in appendix A1, it suffices for the moment to summarize the findings in the next table, in which the con-

policy	Y	D	I	$\dot{X}$	$\dot{Y}$	$\dot{K}$	K	feasible
1	hX	0	max	+	+	+	$< K^*_{YX}$	always
2	(0,hX)	0	aK	+	-	0	$= K^*_{YX}$	always
3	0	0	max	+	0	+	$> K^*_{YX}$	always
4	0	+	aK	0	0	0	$= K^*_X$	$i < (1-\tau_c)r$
5	hX	+	aK	0	0	0	$= K^*_Y$	$i > (1-\tau_c)r$

Table 2.1.: Features of feasible policies.

stant production capacities K^*_{YX}, K^*_X and K^*_Y satisfy:

$$K = K^*_{YX} \Leftrightarrow (1-\tau_c)dO/dK = (1-\tau_c)r \qquad (2.35)$$

$$K = K^*_X \Leftrightarrow (1-\tau_c)dO/dK = i \qquad (2.36)$$

$$K = K^*_Y \Leftrightarrow (1-\tau_c)dO/dK = \frac{1}{1+h} i + \frac{h}{1+h} (1-\tau_c)r \qquad (2.37)$$

With regard to the production capacity K we may distinguish three kinds of policies: growth policies, stationary policies and contraction policies. For the moment we elaborate only on the first two mentioned policies, for reason that contraction policies occur only then as an optimal policy, when the initial production capacity exceeds the desired optimal level. We assume, however, a sufficiently low initial production capacity level so that the latter situation will not ocuur. For that reason we neglect these policies in table 2.1.

Within the stationary policies we distinguish two stationary equilibrium policies and one consolidation policy. Dependent on the inequality in $(1-\tau_c)r \gtrless i$, that is the relative values of the cost of capital, two optimal equilibrium levels of the production capacity exist: K^*_X and K^*_Y respectively. If the total amount of capital goods equals such a value, the firm has no incentive to alter the size of the firm, because at those levels the marginal return to equity equals the shareholders time preference rate i. Because the latter expresses the rate of return that shareholders may obtain elsewhere, marginal return to equity equals marginal cost to equity. Accordingly, the optimal policy is to keep to the equilibrium level during the remaining planning period by investing such a level as necessary to replace absoleted capital goods. So, we postulate the next dividend/investment decision rule:

> The optimal policy is, in general, to pay out dividend and to invest only at replacement level as long as the marginal return to equity equals the time preference rate.

Van Loon (1983, p. 64) shows that in the dynamic model we consider the usual expression of marginal return to equity holds:

$$R_X = R + (R-C_Y)\,\frac{Y}{X}$$

or (2.38)

$$R_X = (1-\tau_c)\,d0/dK + (1-\tau_c)(d0/dK - r)\,\frac{Y}{X}$$

where

C_Y: (marginal) cost of debt

R_X: marginal return to equity

R : marginal return to total capital.

After substitution of marginal revenue and leverage of the stationary equilibrium levels K_X^* and K_Y^*, expression (2.38) points out that the corresponding policies 4 and 5 satisfy the abovementioned dividend/investment decision rule.

The firm's prime endeavour is to reach the desired stationary dividend level as quick as possible. For this purpose it may be profitable to stop at some time the expansion drift of the firm in order to rearrange its financial structure, characterized by the relative amounts of debt and equity. The former is restricted by the latter. So, the financial structure has two extreme cases: the case that the assets are financed by means of the maximum allowed amount of debt and the case that the firm is financed by equity only. Which of both is the optimal one depends on the marginal return to equity. Expression (2.38) clarifies the contribution of leverage to marginal return to equity. From this expression we can conclude that a decrease of the leverage factor Y/X results in a higher return to equity as soon as $(1-\tau_c)d0/dK < (1-\tau_c)r$. Using (2.35) we now postulate the financial decision rule:

> The firm will try to realize such a financial structure as to maximize at any state marginal return to equity. It chooses for a maximum debt financing policy as long as debt has a positive impact on the marginal return to equity. That is, it prefers a self-financing policy when $K > K_{YX}^*$ and a maximum debt financing policy when $K < K_{YX}^*$.

During the consolidation phase the firm uses all its revenue to replace debt by equity (policy 2). Such a redemption may stimulate future expansion due to the lower cost of capital.

Two policies are left to discuss: policy 1 and 3 respectively. Both policies have excellent possibilities for growth. Subject to these policies the firm will retain all earnings. If debt financing has still a positive contribution to marginal return to equity, the firm also attracts as much debt as possible (policy 1). Both retentions and debt are used to finance expansion investments in order to realize a maximum increase of the amount of capital goods.

We are ready to combine the different policies into optimal policy strings, which describe the evolution of the firm in the course of time. Dependent on the inequality in $(1-\tau_c)r \gtrless i$ we get two different master trajectories.

The first one occurs if $i < (1-\tau_c)r$ and is represented by figure 2.3. The desired optimal stationary production capacity level is equal to K^*_X. Although debt financing is more expensive than self financing the firm's initial optimal policy is to borrow the maximum amount that is possible given the size of equity. In case that the initial amount of debt is below the maximum allowed level, an instantaneously adjustment upwards turns out to be optimal. As borrowing increases profit and thus raises the rate of growth of equity, it is profitable to borrow as long as the resulting marginal cost is less than marginal revenue. Accordingly, the firm grows at maximum speed in order to realize a maximum increase of the income stream and amount of cheap equity (policy 1). Corresponding expression (2.38) and the financial decision rule this policy is the optimal one as long as $(1-\tau_c)dO/dK > (1-\tau_c)r$, or, equivalently, $K(T) < K^*_{YX}$.

As soon as the amount of capital goods K(T) reaches the level K^*_{YX}, where

$$K = K^*_{YX} \Leftrightarrow (1-\tau_c)dO/dK = (1-\tau_c)r \qquad (2.39)$$

it is profitable to use retentions to pay back debt money, for

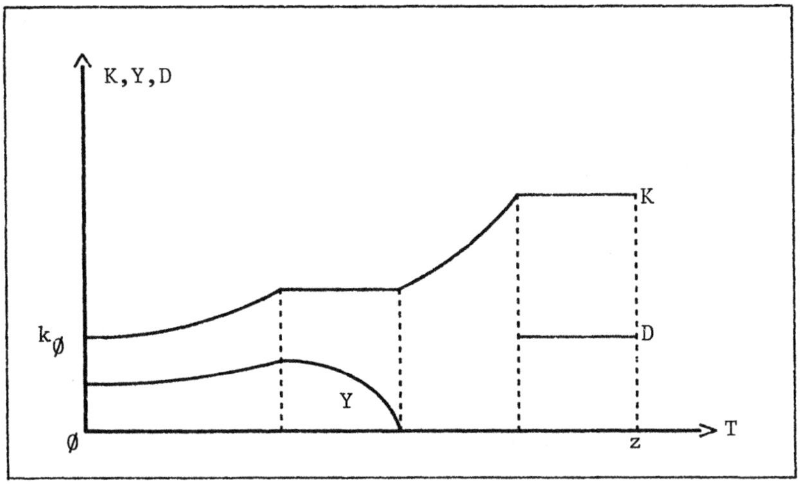

Figure 2.3: Optimal master trajectory if $(1-\tau_c)r > i$.

- issuing earnings is valued by the shareholders according their time preference rate $i < (1-\tau_c)r$
- continuing expansion investments yields a net return, $(1-\tau_c)dO/dK$, less than $(1-\tau_c)r$, due to the decreasing returns to scale
- paying back debt money saves $(1-\tau_c)r$ rent payments per unit.

So, the firm stops its expansion in order to use all its revenue to replace debt by equity (policy 2).

After this period of consolidation it still makes sense to expand the amount of capital goods, because it is financed now at lower costs by equity only. As no dividend is issued, the firm starts increasing as fast as possible again (policy 3).

In this way the state of maximum dividend pay out in a self-financing regime K_X^*, where

$$K = K_X^* \Leftrightarrow (1-\tau_c)dO/dK = i \qquad (2.40)$$

is reached as quick as possible. At this state it is useless to continue expansion investments because additional net cost will exceed net revenue (policy 4). Investment falls down to the replacement level and remaining earnings are issued to the shareholders.

The second optimal master evolution pattern or policy string occurs if debt is cheap compared to equity (see figure 2.4).

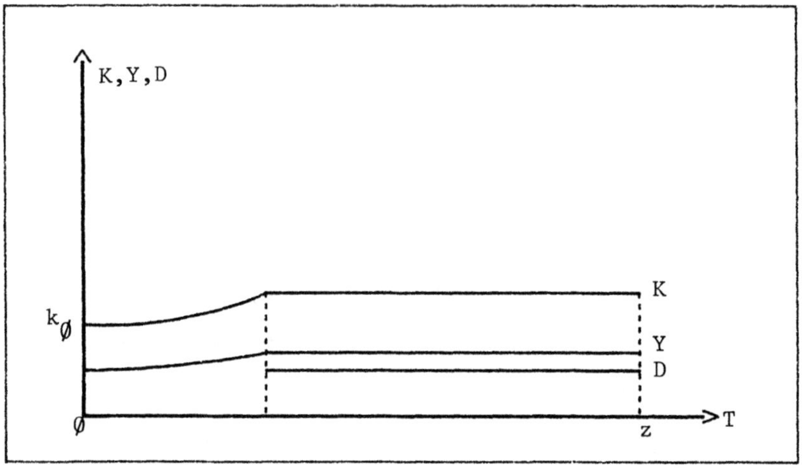

Figure 2.4: Optimal master trajectory if $(1-\tau_c)r < i$.

The start of this policy string is the same as the start of the previous one: due to the cheapness of debt money it is optimal to borrow the maximum amount that is possible and invest both retained earnings and debt in capital goods in order to realize a maximum growth of the income stream (policy 1).

It is worth investing at the maximum level till $K = K_Y^*$, because at levels lower that K_Y^* the marginal income after taxation exceeds marginal financing costs in case of maximum debt financing. As soon as the amount of capital goods equals K_Y^*, this accelerated growth is cut off abruptly because marginal net revenue equals the weighted sum of net costs of debt and equity:

$$(1-\tau_c)\frac{dO}{dK} = \frac{1}{1+h}\, i + \frac{h}{1+h}\,(1-\tau_c)r \qquad (2.41)$$

This expression implies an equality of marginal return to equity and the time preference rate i (see expression (2.38)). According to the dividend/investment decision rule it is optimal to keep to the equilibrium level K_Y^* during the remaining planning period by investing such a level as necessary to replace absoleted capital goods. Remaining earnings are again paid out to the shareholders.

2.3.7. Summary and conclusions

In the previous sections we elaborated on the optimal dynamic behaviour of a value maximizing firm by determining optimal policies and combine these in time to an optimal policy string. We emphasize the conclusion that the optimal evolution pattern consists of a string of subsequent policies concerning dividend, finance and investment. So, the firm will not immediately pursue an equilibrium steady state policy, but will continuously adjust its policy to the circumstances, that is the state of the firm, in order to reach its equilibrium level as quick as possible.

We did not pay attention to a further analysis. One may e.g. study the influence of environmental changes on features of the optimal policy string. This would be a sensitivity analysis concerning parameters that are interesting for economic analysis. For two reasons, however, we do not consider this kind of analysis at this moment. Firstly, it is beyond our scope to deal in great detail with the results of analyses which have been already carried out by other authors in the past [see e.g. Van Loon (1983)]. We only use the model presented here as a starting point for further research and as an introduction into the dynamics of the firm. Secondly, we will present some of the sensitivity results in one of the next chapters when we consider an extension of this basic problem.

The research postulated in this chapter may be extended in several ways. Most of the possible extensions are already mentioned in previous subsections: activity analysis, labour managed firms, adjustment costs, investment grants, issues of new shares, etc. The aim of our research is to extend the dynamic theory of the firm by introducing personal taxation, a topic which continues to be a central issue in recent contributions in finance theory.

Finally, we refer the reader interested in the application of dynamic optimization into the analysis of the dynamics of the firm to two survey papers. The first one is due to Stepan & Swoboda (1982). In their paper they survey the application of Optimal Control Theory to dynamic financing models by comparing a number of existing theories and models. The paper of Lesourne & Leban (1982) gives an overview of the general state-of-art by considering three types of problems: one firm facing a certain environment (deterministic control), a firm facing a stochastic environment with a risk of bankruptcy (stochastic control) and firms facing duopolistic competition (differential games).

2.4. Dynamic modeling: survey and conclusions

In the past two decades control theory has proved to be a very useful tool to study the dynamics of economic processes. The interest for this line of research is probably due to increasing insatisfaction raised by static analysis and by its unability to take into account changing environments.

The collections of papers of e.g. Bensoussan, Kleindorfer and Tapiero (1978) and Feichtinger (1982a, 1985) contain many examples in which the theory of the firm is extended by using Optimal Control Theory to solve real dynamic models analytically. Deterministic control theory has also fruitfully been applied to several problems in management science, such as advertising, production and inventory, maintenance and replacement, natural resources, transportation and cash balance. A survey of applications of Optimal Control Theory to management science has been written by Feichtinger (1982b), whereas also Sethi and Thompson (1981) pay attention to many economic applications.

In the last ten years papers began to appear on essential stochastic environments. "In most real situations the introduction of the time component leads simultaneously to the introduction of uncertainties" [Bensoussan et al. (1974), p. 30]. Uncertainty arises from external sources, from limited knowledge about the internal operation of the system and about the effects of decisions on the process and also from a partial observability of the state of the firm. An overview of stochastic Optimal Control Theory and its applications to operational research is given by Neck (1984). Stochastic control theory can be regarded as the most general approach for single decisionmaker problems. Even Tapiero (1977), a fervent advocate of optimal control theory, however, points out a severe limitation of it: stochastic control is mathematically difficult, which causes a larger than usual communication gap between theorists and potential appliers; analytical solutions are available only for very simple problems. Ten years after this statement the number of fruitful applications, which are solved analytically, is still poor.

Finally, some remarks on the theory of differential games, which has provided a convenient tool for an extension of the dynamic models to some classes of competitive situations. The most simple case is evidently the class of duopolistic competition. A survey paper by Feichtinger & Jørgensen (1983) reviews a number of differential games applications to management science, such as investment, consumption, employment, bargaining, production, inventory and maintenance. A survey of differential games models only in the field of advertising is due to Jørgensen (1982).

CHAPTER THREE

TAXATION AND SOME IMPLICATIONS

3.1. Introduction

The impact of both corporate and personal taxation on the optimal policy of the firm and the behaviour of investors continues to be a central issue in recent contributions in both finance theory and the theory of public policy. In these studies both firms and investors are operating in a particular environment that is characterized by several types of fiscal regime that apply to them. It appears, however, that most of the fiscal regimes are not 'neutral' with regard to the optimal policy of firms and investors' choices. For this reason fiscal policy is a major and flexible tool of governmental policy.

We restrict ourselves to finance theory, that is, we consider only the impact of a certain fiscal system on the optimal policy of both investors and firms. We do not care for which reasons a particular fiscal regime is postulated by the government. We focus on the interaction between the different taxes involved, both corporate profit tax and different personal taxes, particularly because of the importance regarding the effects of these taxes found in the finance literature.

Although of considerable importance, we neglect several other taxes, such as unit input/output tax, value added tax and lump sum tax. We also pay no attention to the impact of taxes on capital depreciation and investment allowances. These topics, which are discussed by e.g. Moerland (1978b), are, however, beyond our scope.

The outline of this chapter is as follows. Firstly, we illustrate the impact of taxation by means of some examples applied to management science. Afterwards, we define and explain, in section 3.3, the concept of 'fiscal (non) neutrality', a concept of utmost importance in fiscal theory. Section 3.4 contains a description of four different tax systems, that may be relevant to our study. This provides a basis for the analysis of the effect of taxation on corporate financial policy given in the remaining part of this chapter. We elaborate on the impact of leverage on the value of a firm, that is operating under different tax regimes, by considering the evolution and progress of the valuation theory. The value of a firm in relation to its leverage will appear to be an excellent example to illustrate the impact of taxation on corporate policy. In addition, it is a useful illustration in view of the topic of this book. We start the analysis with the well known leverage irrelevancy theorem of Modigliani & Miller (1958), derived under absence of any taxation, and end up with Miller's irrelevancy theorem, which is based on an 'after tax' equilibrium theory with a progressive personal tax [Miller (1977)].

Finally, we note that this chapter has been included for the reader's convenience; that is, readers familiar with the theory of finance will be acquainted with the contents of this chapter.

3.2. Some examples

In this section we illustrate some problems that occur as soon as taxation is involved in the decision making process. In our text, we borrow heavily from the literature, in particular from Verheyen (1981). Some of the examples are outside the scope of this book. Nevertheless, we use them in order to make the reader familiar with the impact of taxation on corporate policy.

The first example is related to merger and acquisition policy, which can be viewed as both an investment problem and a financial structure problem. The impact of a merger on the cash flow, the share value, the bond value and the total value of the firm depends on the nature of the economic system under consideration. As taxation is a part of the system, it will possibly influence the merger decision.

We illustrate this by considering two firms, one or both of which have outstanding risky debt before the merger. Haley & Schall (1979) now argue that as long as the income streams of the premerger firms are such that one firm can become insolvent (and goes bankrupt) while the other firm has a possitive equity position, a merger will produce a corporate coinsurance effect. If the firms are separate, the creditors of the bankrupt firm will sustain a loss. However, if the firms are merged, the cash flows of the solvent firm are available to service the debt requirement of the other firm. The merged firms, thus, provide each other with a form of corporate coinsurance, which reduces the bankruptcy risk to the creditors of the merged firm. In this situation lenders of debt money may well be willing to supply debt up to a higher level at the same rate.

As the cost of debt is tax deductible, synergistic effects may occur from the merger, and since the coinsurance is in effect provided by the equity shareholder, stock prices may fall. The final result of a merger thus depends on the balance between synergistic effects, such as tax reduction, and the coinsurance loss.

A second example is taken from the theory on maintenance and replacement. The problem of determining the lifetime of an asset simultaneously with its exploitation during that lifetime is an important problem in practice. An important result of the classic single machine replacement theory is that a replacement of an old machine by a new one is only optimal when the marginal costs of maintaining the old machine exceed the marginal costs of starting a new one. That is, the difference between the maintenance costs, productivity and capital costs of both the machines is in favour of the new asset. The management, however, may try to postpone the replacement by applying preventive maintenance, which will slow down the rate of decline of the resale value.

Schworm (1979) surveys the machine replacement problem subject to corporate taxation. Obviously, the cost of owning and operating capital depends on production decisions that can be influenced by tax policy. Schworm shows that changes in the tax rate, depreciation allowances and investment tax credits have an indeterminate qualititative effect on capital utilization and maintenance. As a consequence, accelerated depreciation or an investment tax credit can either increase or decrease the demand for new assets. Schworm thus concludes that "predicting the effect of tax policy on capital use and capital purchases requires detailed knowledge of the influence of capital use on operating costs and capital deterioration" [Schworm (1979), p. 192].

Our final example concerns the net return on riskless corporate and governmental securities. The existence of taxes represents one of the more important ways in which actual security markets differ from the ideal markets assumed in finance theory.

Due to the changing market interest rates over time, the market value or price of a security may be above or below its parity. Under the theoretical assumption of perfect security markets, the equilibrium price of two different securities will be such that their returns, that is the sum of the discounted interest yields (coupon) and the capital gain or loss due to drawings over the market price, equal each other. Furthermore, all investors attach homogeneous returns.

The introduction of a progressive personal tax, however, provides heterogeneous returns because of the different tax treatment of interest yields and capital gains or losses. As a consequence, the value of bonds varies along investors subject to different personal tax rates. On its turn, this results in 'tax induced clienteles', that is, a security is rationally held by investors in only particular tax brackets. Schaeffer (1982) illustrates the former point by considering the prices of two hypothetical one-period bonds and the cash flows received by a tax-exempt investor and a tax payer. If the prices are such that the tax-exempt investor faces the same return on both bonds, then from his point of view, neither bond dominates the other. However, the tax payer obtains a higher return from the bond with the lower coupon interest rate, due to the difference between the personal tax rates on interest and capital gain. So, for him there is an important difference.

3.3. Fiscal (non) neutrality

The effects of taxation on corporate behaviour are often described by means of the concept of 'fiscal (non) neutrality'. Neutrality of a fiscal system does not necessarily imply that taxation has no impact on corporate values: tax payments e.g. reduce net profit of the firm. A tax system is neutral, however, if decisions are not affected by taxation that is, it provides no incentive for the decision maker to prefer one alternative over another.

In the theory of the firm corporate decisions are mostly based on marginal values of the relevant variables. So, "a fiscal regime is defined as neutral in the context of an individual firm if its introduction or modification does not affect the marginal costs of the inputs" [Moerland (1978a), p. 43].

We may illustrate fiscal non-neutrality by considering the well known 'tax-correction proposition' of Modigliani & Miller (1963). When the government subsidizes interest payments to providers of debt capital by allowing the corporation to deduct interest payments as an expense, the market value of a corporation can increase when the corporation takes on more and more risk free debt. With the tax deductibility of interest - contrary to the cost of equity - debt is clearly prefered to equity. In the framework of Modigliani and Miller corporate profit tax thus is non-neutral with respect to the cost of capital.

Finally, we refine the definition of fiscal (non) neutrality by quoting Moerland: "The degree of fiscal (non) neutrality is expressed by the semi-elasticity of the marginal cost of an input with respect to some relevant characteristic of a fiscal regime. ...The degree of fiscal non-neutrality - for a particular firm - may differ between inputs. Also, taxation may be neutral with respect to the marginal costs of some inputs while it is non-neutral with respect to the marginal costs of others.... If the degrees of (non) neutrality are identical for all inputs, we call the fiscal regime homogeneously (non) neutral". If there is at least one degree that differs from the others, the fiscal system is called non-homogeneously non-neutral. "By definition, a neutral regime is homogeneous. Non-homogeneity can only apply to non-neutral systems" [Moerland (1978b), pp. 17-18].

3.4. Different types of profit and income tax regimes

"One major weakness in much popular discussion on taxation is the failure to consider the interaction between different taxes involved" [King (1977), p. 6]. The effect of a tax may depend quite critically on the constellation of other taxes with which it is employed. We will, therefore, take a look at the tax system as a whole. To do so, we review four different tax systems, that may be relevant to our study: the classical system, the two-rate system, the imputation system and the integrated system.

As stated before, we pay no attention to several kinds of special corporate taxes, investment allowances and capital depreciation possibilities. We elaborate on the interaction between the different tax rates that are relevant to the purpose of our research, such as corporate profit tax and personal taxes on dividend, interest and capital gain. This is done in order to make the reader familiar with the topic of taxation.

Before discussing the four basic tax systems, we remark that capital gain is mostly treated separate from other personal taxes. As a consequence, it is no part of the fiscal regimes we next consider. When evaluating the fiscal (non) neutrality, however, capital gain tax need to be included.

3.4.1. Classical system

The classical system consists of the known concept of separate taxation of the company and its shareholders, with the tax liability of the company to corporation tax being independent of personal taxes. Under this system of taxation, total corporate profits (distributed or retained) are taxed by a flat rate of corporate profit tax, which we shall denote by τ_c, while only distributed profits are additionaly taxed by a personal income tax. No attempt is made to allow shareholders credit for tax paid by the company. This system thus effects double taxation of dividends. The total tax liability excluding the tax payments on interest, capital gain, wages and other personal income, TTL, is therefore given by

$$TTL = \tau_c E + \tau_p D \tag{3.1}$$

or, using the expression of our basic model of chapter 2:

$$TTL = \tau_c [O(K) - rY] + \tau_p D \tag{3.2}$$

where

E : total corporate profit

τ_p: personal tax rate on private income

As a consequence, the tax rate on dividend, τ_d, equals the private income tax rate: $\tau_d = \tau_p$.

The classical system is used in a number of countries, notably the United States and the Netherlands. In most of these countries, however, a small amount of dividend is tax exempt from income tax. The classical system was also tried and subsequently abandonned in France, West Germany and the United Kingdom.

3.4.2. Two rate system

One of the major objections to the classical system is that it involves a double taxation of dividends. The two-rate system (also named split-rate or dual-rate system) aims to alleviate at least some of the double taxation of dividends by taxing distributed profits at a lower rate than undistributed profits. Hence,

$$TTL = \tau_c[O(K) - rY - D] + \tau_{cd}D + \tau_p D$$

$$= \tau_c[O(K) - rY] + [\tau_p - (\tau_c - \tau_{cd})]D \qquad (3.3)$$

where

τ_{cd}: corporate tax rate on distributed profits, $\tau_{cd} < \tau_c$.

As $\tau_c - \tau_{cd} > 0$, the two-rate system relieves the double taxation of dividend by alleviations in the corporate tax sphere.

Variants of the two-rate system have been tried in e.g. West Germany and the United Kingdom.

3.4.3. Imputation system

As with the two-rate system, the imputation system attempts to give shareholders credit for tax paid by the company. Unlike the two-rate system, however, there is only a single rate of corporate profit tax. So, total profits (distributed or retained) are taxed by the corporate profit tax, while profits distributed are taxed, once again, by a modified personal income tax. Part of the corporate tax liability on distributed profits is imputed to the shareholders and regarded as a pre-payment, which the shareholders receive in the form of a tax credit. Some fraction of the corporation tax paid on dividends is allowed to be subtracted from the personal income tax. Hence,

$$TTL = \tau_c[O(K) - rY] + (\tau_p - \tau_s)D \qquad (3.4)$$

where

τ_s: rate of imputation.

The imputation system relieves the double taxation of dividends by alleviations in the personal tax sphere.

The imputation system and its variants are employed in e.g. Belgium, France and the United Kingdom.

3.4.4. Integrated system

Neither the two-rate nor the imputation system succeeds in eliminating the tax discrimination between dividends and retentions completely. Only the integrated system completely integrates the corporate tax system with the personal tax system. Profits are imputed to shareholders in proportion to their shareholdings, and this imputed income is subject to personal income tax. Under such a system we have

$$TTL = \tau_p[O(K) - rY] \qquad (3.5)$$

Although a fully integrated system was recommended for Canada and was seriously considered by West Germany, neither country has adopted the system, however.

3.4.5. Neutrality of the tax regimes

The choice of tax system is a topic of almost constant debate in political circles, as evidenced by the number of changes of the system that have occured. As stated before, fiscal policy is a major tool of governmental policy. The choice of a fiscal system mostly is a political issue, which may be illustrated by the variety of corporate tax systems in the EEC-countries. In this context it is not surprising, that there has been much discussion about tax harmonization in the EEC.

The degree to which a tax system is neutral with respect to financing policy is one of the more important considerations in choosing the system. As this book is not concerned with the policy problem of the choice of tax system, we will not evaluate the tax systems with respect to their fiscal (non) neutrality characteristic. This, as a matter of fact, has already been done by several authors, such as King (1977), Moerland (1978b), Stapleton & Burke (1977) and Atkinson & Stiglitz (1980). To illustrate the results of the studies, we quote King: "Only the classical and integrated system, therefore, are capable of achieving neutrality with respect to the choice of financial policy for any value of the income tax rate. The imputation and two-rate system could be neutral only if there were a single rate of personal income tax". [King (1977), p. 110]. For the classical system e.g. to be neutral, capital gains must be taxed as income and no deductibility provision may be extended to interest payments.

3.5. Leverage and the value of a firm

Given the firm's investment policy, the management must determine the means of financing. In this section we consider the question how financing decisions affect the value of the firm to its shareholders, which is a very important issue in finance theory. It turns out that the impact of leverage on the market value of the firm considerably depends on the fiscal regime under consideration. We focus on this well-known theory because its result is relevant to our research with regard to the dynamic theory of the firm.

We examine the above mentioned problem by considering two almost identical firms, that is, except of the financial structure, both firms are in the same risk class and are anticipated to have the same total cash earnings or operating income. One of both firms is levered, that is, it finances its investment by both equity and debt, whereas the other firm is unlevered, that is, its capital structure is composed entirely of common stock. In addition we assume that except for their taxation the firms face perfect markets. We thus assume:

- firms are in the same risk class
- capital markets are frictionless
- individuals can borrow and lend at the risk free rate
- there are no costs to bankruptcy
- firms issue only two types of claims: risk-free debt and equity
- all cash flow streams are perpetuities.

We will study three different cases:

- no taxes, personal nor corporate
- corporate taxes, no personal taxation
- taxes on corporate and personal incomes.

Finally, we define following variables, which we will use in the next subsections.

firm	U	L
amount of debt	nil	Y
operating income	O(K)	O(K)
market value equity	S_U	S_L
market value debt	-	B_L
total market value	V_U	V_L

3.5.1. Irrelevancy theorem of Modigliani & Miller

We start our analysis in an imaginary world without taxes of any kind. We consider an investor who holds (a fraction of) the shares of the unlevered firm U. The market value of both firm and shares is $V_U = S_U$. His return on this investment is O(K). Thus,

return firm U	O(K)
market value shares U	S_U

Firm L, on the contrary, has to pay interest on debt. If the total amount of debt financing is equal to Y, shareholder's earnings equal O(K) - rY. The market value of these shares is S_L.

The investor may, however, obtain exactly the same return as in the first case by buying (the same proportions of) both the common stock and bonds of the levered firm, that is, he could invest B_L in the debt of the levered firm and S_L in the shares of the levered firm. Since rY is the payment to the firm's debt-holders, investor's total earnings are O(K). In this way, the firm's leverage is cancelled out by a 'homemade' or personal leverage. Hence,

earnings shares L	O(K) - rY
earnings bonds L	rY
total return	O(K)
value shares L	S_L
value bonds L	B_L
total value investment	$S_L + B_L$

Under the assumption of perfect capital markets, equilibrium requires that equal earnings imply equal market values. Thus

$$S_U = S_L + B_L \qquad (3.5)$$

and

$$V_L = S_L + B_L \qquad (3.6)$$

We now easily derive that

$$V_U = S_U = S_L + B_L = (V_L - B_L) + B_L = V_L \tag{3.7}$$

We conclude that in equilibrium the total market value of the two firms must equal each other. This conclusion is consistent with the well known leverage irrelevancy theorem of Modigliani & Miller: "The average cost of capital to any firm is completely independent of its capital structure". [Modigliani & Miller (1958), p. 268], or: given their production and investment decisions, the market values of firms, operating in perfect capital markets, are unaffected by differences in their capital structure.

3.5.2. Corporate tax correction theorem

In this subsection we give attention to corporate tax laws by which a firm can deduct interest payments on its debt in computing its income tax purposes, but other payments, that is, dividends to security holders are not tax deductible. In their 1963 tax-correction paper Modigliani & Miller argue that the inclusion of such a tax law results in a higher market value of a levered firm than of an identical unlevered firm.

The analysis, we carry out to clarify this statement, is analoguous to that of the previous subsection. We assume again the existence of two firms identical in all aspects except their capital structure. The shareholders posttax earnings of the unlevered firm are now $(1-\tau_c)O(K)$, whereas the market value is assumed to be S_U. Thus,

earnings shares U	$(1-\tau_c)O(K)$
market value shares U	S_U

The aftertax earnings available to the investor holding the shares of an identical levered firm are $(1-\tau_c)[O(K) - rY]$. Those shares have a proposed market value of S_L. Accordingly, an investment in the shares of the levered firm will yield exactly the same return as an investment in the shares of the unlevered firm by adding only such an amount of debt that yields a return of $(1-\tau_c)rY$. Because the bonds of the levered firm yield rY, we see that the aftertax earnings available to the security holders of the levered firm, that is, both the share- and bondholders, are greater than those available to the security holders of the unlevered firm by the quantity $\tau_c rY$. It is as if the government pays a subsidy of $\tau_c rY$ to the levered firm for having debt in its capital structure. Since we assume that a risk free security with a return of rY has a market value of B_L, the investor's total investment is $S_L + (1-\tau_c)B_L$. Summarizing the above, we get

earnings shares L	$(1-\tau_c)[0(K) - rY]$
earnings bonds L	$(1-\tau_c)rY$
total earnings L	$(1-\tau_c)0(K)$
value shares L	S_L
value bonds L	$(1-\tau_c)B_L$
total value investment	$S_L + (1-\tau_c)B_L$

Equal earnings again require equal market values. Hence,

$$S_U = S_L + (1-\tau_c)B_L \tag{3.8}$$

Using expression (3.6) we get

$$V_U = S_U = (V_L - B_L) + (1-\tau_c)B_L = V_L - \tau_c B_L \tag{3.9}$$

or, equivalently:

$$V_L = V_U + \tau_c B_L \tag{3.10}$$

The value of the levered firm is equal to the value of the unlevered firm plus the tax shield provided by debt. "This is perhaps the single most important result in the theory of corporation finance obtained in the last 25 years. It says that in the absence of any market imperfections including corporate taxes (i.e. if $\tau_c = 0$), the value of the firm is completely independent of the type of financing used for its projects. However, when the government subsidizes interest payments to providers of debt capital by allowing the corporation to deduct interest payments on debt as an expense, the market value of the corporation can increase as it takes on more and more (risk free) debt. Ideally (given the assumptions of the model) the firm should take on 100% debt." [Copeland & Weston (1983), pp. 387-389].

We notice that the market values of the shares ceteris paribus decline when leverage increases. By investing the difference $S_U - S_L$ in risk free bonds total return increases, however.

Of course, when the market values of the two firms are in the equilibrium given by equation (3.10), there are no advantages or disadvantages to the investor who purchases shares of the unlevered rather than the equivalent unlevered position involving the bonds and the shares of the levered firm. However, the shareholders of any firm are better off, whenever the firm increases its leverage.

3.5.3. Leverage related costs

Following the publication of the Modigliani & Miller (1963) tax correction paper, many writers have sought to reconcile the M&M maximum leverage prediction with observed capital structure. Such a 'corner solution' is, of course, an unsatisfactory result, because actual firms do not, and in fact cannot, achieve anywhere near that degree of leverage. Clearly, the analysis of the previous subsection did not capture all the relevant factors influencing the financing decision.

Many writers have attempted to explain the low levels of leverage by resort to 'leverage related costs'. They are convinced that a capital structure equilibrium for corporations requires at least some market imperfections, such as leverage related costs, which increase with the debt-to-equity ratio in order to avoid a corner solution of 100% debt. These leverage related costs need to be very large and include bankruptcy costs [Brennan & Schwartz (1977), Kim (1978)], contracting and monitoring costs [Jensen & Meckling (1976)], information and signaling costs [Vermaelen (1981)] and incomplete markets [Modigliani (1982)]. In addition De Angelo & Masulis argue that the presence of corporate tax shield substitutes for debt, such as accounting depreciation, depletion allowances and investment tax credits implies "a market equilibrium in which each firm has a unique interior optimum leverage decision (with or without leverage related costs)" [De Angelo & Masulis (1980a), p. 3].

The inclusion of these increasing leverage related costs results in the U-shaped curve, which is depicted in figure 3.1.

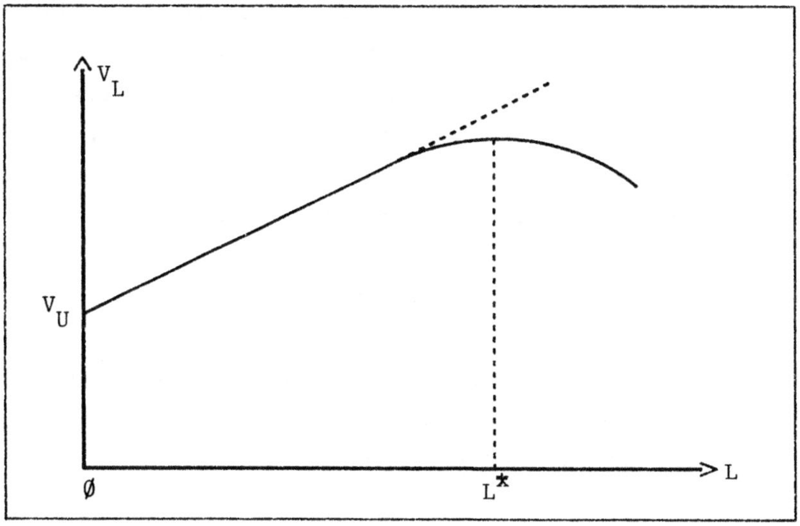

Figure 3.1: market value of a levered firm subject to corporate taxation and leverage related costs.

The striking feature of this analysis is the existence of an optimal debt-to-equity ratio. Up to the point L^* of figure 3.1. the value of the firm rises as debt is introduced into the capital structure; however, beyond this point, increasing the use of leverage lowers the value of the firm, because the leverage related costs become dominant. So, the balancing of the leverage related costs against the tax gains of debt finance gives rise to an optimal capital structure, just as the traditional view has always maintained, though for somewhat different reasons.

3.5.4. Personal taxes

In addition to the leverage related costs also market imperfections on the other side of the trade-off may be used to explain the variety of debt-to-equity ratios and thus to avoid the unrealistic corner solution of 100% debt. Moreover, the great emphasis on the then known leverage related costs seems to Miller to have been misplaced: "For big business, at least (...), the supposed trade-off between tax gains and bankruptcy costs looks suspiciously like the recipe for the fabled horse-and-rabbit stew - one horse and one rabbit" [Miller (1977), p. 264]. In addition, Miller cannot understand, why observed capital structure have shown so little change over time? Miller is convinced, that personal taxes could offset corporate taxes, such that in equilibrium even the value of any individual firm would be independent of its leverage.

This far reaching conclusion will be discussed in one of the next subsections. For the moment being we focus on the impact of uniform personal taxes on the value of the firm in relation to its leverage. We will use the same framework as in the previous subsections.

Let τ_e be the personal tax rate on equity income. So, τ_e equals τ_d when the firm distributes all profit; it equals the personal tax rate on capital gain τ_g when the company adopts a zero dividend policy and it will, finally, take on an intermediate value when a policy of dividend distribution is combined with capital gains as well.

An individual who owns the shares of the unlevered firm will have a post tax income equal to $(1-\tau_e)(1-\tau_c)O(K)$, while the market value is supposed to be S_U. This individual can obtain an identical income stream by purchasing the shares of the levered firm and an amount of bonds that yields a net return of $(1-\tau_e)(1-\tau_c)rY$. Since, interest income is taxed according to the personal tax rate τ_r, the investor thus has to buy an amount of corporate debt equal $(1-\tau_e)(1-\tau_c)rY/(1-\tau_r)$, however. We still assume that a risk free security with a pre-tax return of rY has a market value of B_L. Hence,

earnings shares L	$(1-\tau_e)(1-\tau_c)[O(K) - rY]$
earnings bonds L	$(1-\tau_r)r(1-\tau_e)(1-\tau_c)Y/(1-\tau_r)$
total earnings L	$(1-\tau_e)(1-\tau_c)O(K)$
value shares L	S_L
value bonds L	$B_L(1-\tau_e)(1-\tau_c)/(1-\tau_r)$
total value investment	$S_L + B_L(1-\tau_e)(1-\tau_c)/(1-\tau_r)$

In accordance to previous analyses and again using expression (3.6) we now get:

$$V_U = S_U = S_L + B_L(1-\tau_e)(1-\tau_c)/(1-\tau_r)$$

$$= (V_L - B_L) + B_L(1-\tau_e)(1-\tau_c)/(1-\tau_r) \tag{3.11}$$

or

$$V_L = V_U + [1 - \frac{(1-\tau_e)(1-\tau_c)}{(1-\tau_r)}]B_L \tag{3.12}$$

Note that expression (3.12) confirms both the Modigliani & Miller irrelevancy theorem and their 1963 tax correction paper: in a world without any taxation the market value of a firm is independent of its financial leverage, while the introduction of corporate taxation benefits debt financing. However, due to the introduction of a tax rate on income from shares, which is less than the tax on interest yields, this gain from leverage will be reduced. In fact, for a wide range of values for τ_c, τ_e and τ_r, the gain from leverage vanishes or even turns negative. An illustration of this result is given in figure 3.2.

Finally, we note that under a maximum dividend policy and the classical tax system, implying $\tau_e = \tau_d = \tau_r$, the impact of personal taxes is abolished, that is, we get the Modigliani-Miller maximum debt prediction.

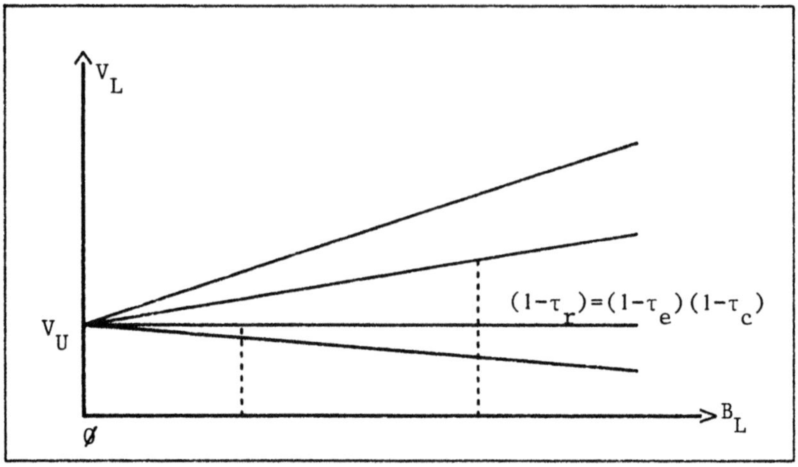

Figure 3.2: market value of a firm under uniform personal taxation.

3.6. Leverage and market equilibrium

In the previous section we have found an expression to indicate the value of a firm as a function of its leverage and the personal tax rate of its shareholder. The problem now is to find an equilibrium market value of the firm in the case that the shareholders are partitioned into tax groups. In this line, the final result of the previous section may be used to analyse the impact of leverage on the equilibrium market value of a firm in case share and debt income are taxed at different rates, but with each rate the same for all investors. In fact, this variation in the firm's value with its leverage is described by Arditti, Levy & Sarnat (1977). The results are similar to those depicted in figure 3.2.

In this section we focus on the equilibrium valuation problem under a progressive personal income tax, that is, we consider different income tax rates varying along investors. As a consequence, investors may have different opinions with regard to the value of the firm's securities. Given these different taxes and valuations, we now explore how adjustment in the demand for, and supply of, these differently taxed securities affect the resulting set of equilibrium values of debt and equity. To do so, we distinguish two major models of equilibrium, that are the most widely accepted in the literature on financial theory at this time.

The first one is labeled the 'Before Tax Theory' and is associated with Modigliani & Miller (1963), as well as with Miller & Scholes (1978). The second one, with which we will be concerned with in the next chapter, is called the 'After Tax Theory' and is most frequently associated with Miller (1977).

3.6.1. Before Tax Theory

The 'Before Tax Theory' essentially concludes that all personal income taxes to investors can be effectively laundered. The corporate profit tax is thus the only tax imperfection. Consequently, the resulting situation can be appropriately described by means of the tax correction model of Modigliani & Miller (1963) in combination with at least some other market imperfection, such as leverage related costs. In this way a corner solution of 100% debt is avoided, so that the model can be used to explain the variety of debt-to-equity ratios.

The tax laundery may, for example, be illustrated by the Miller & Scholes' "Dividend and taxes" (1978) argument. They claim that many fiscal systems establishes so many easy ways to save and invest at before tax rates of return, so that the effective personal tax rate applicable on a dollar of dividends is essentially zero. This result would hold for any shareholder in any and all tax brackets under the assumption of an approximately zero tax rate on capital gain.

The procedure required to avoid paying personal taxes on dividends is to borrow on personal account ensuring that the interest expense on his personal debt, which is tax deductible, equals the net dividend received, so that they cancel out. The proceeds of the loan can then be invested at a before tax rate of return. In this way the dividend income tax is eliminated, whereas the individual's personal capital structure is not affected and tax rules not violated.

Finally, we remark that the same method can be applied, in principle, on a dollar of interest received from bonds.

3.6.2. After Tax Theory

In "Debt and taxes" Miller (1977) argues that personal taxes could offset corporate taxes such that in equilibrium the value of any individual firm would be independent of its leverage. In addition to the usual assumptions, we have mentioned before, this 'After Tax Theory' is explored under the following suppositions.

Firstly, Miller assumes that the effective personal tax rate on equity income, τ_e, is zero. Miller sets this rate equal to zero in order to facilitate his equilibrium analysis. This assumption may be fairly realistic, since a firm, which should minimize the combined tax exposures to itself and its investors, should adopt a zero dividend policy, that is, the stockholders pay the capital gain tax rather that the personal tax. In many countries the former is equal or close to zero. However, similar qualitative results may be obtained in case of a positive, but relative small and constant, personal tax rate τ_e [see e.g. Hamada & Scholes (1985)].

Secondly, in some countries such as the United States, individuals may invest in risk free, tax exempt municipal bonds to earn a tax free yield r_0. For that reason, the rate of interest on taxable bonds must include compensation for the personal tax burden that these bonds impose on the investor. An individual with a marginal tax rate on income from bonds equal to τ_{rp} will only hold bonds if they pay $r_0/(1-\tau_{rp})$, that is, their return must be 'grossed up'. Furthermore, the existence of a progressive personal tax structure means that this compensation must increase when larger quantities of bonds are issued. The demand for bonds is thus given by the upward sloping curve labeled $r_d(Y)$, that is depicted in figure 3.3. The flat stretch of the curve represents the demand for fully taxable bonds by fully tax exempt investors.

On the supply side firms are willing to issue only bonds relative to equity as long as the before tax cost of debt is below the 'grossed up' after tax cost of equity, which under the presented assumptions equals $r_0/(1-\tau_c)$. The factor 'gross up' reflects the fact that corporate debt is tax deductible. Therefore, the supply curve is drawn at the horizontal level $r_0/(1-\tau_c)$.

Equilibrium in the corporate bond market, then, is established, where supply is equal to demand, that is, where the before-tax cost of corporate debt is equal to the rate which would be paid by tax-exempt organizations 'grossed up' by the corporate tax rate. So, "there will be an equilibrium level of aggregate corporate debt, Y^*, and hence an equilibrium debt-equity ratio for the corporate sector as a whole. But there would be no optimum debt ratio for any individual firm" [Miller (1977), p. 269]. To see that this is true, let us recall that the personal tax

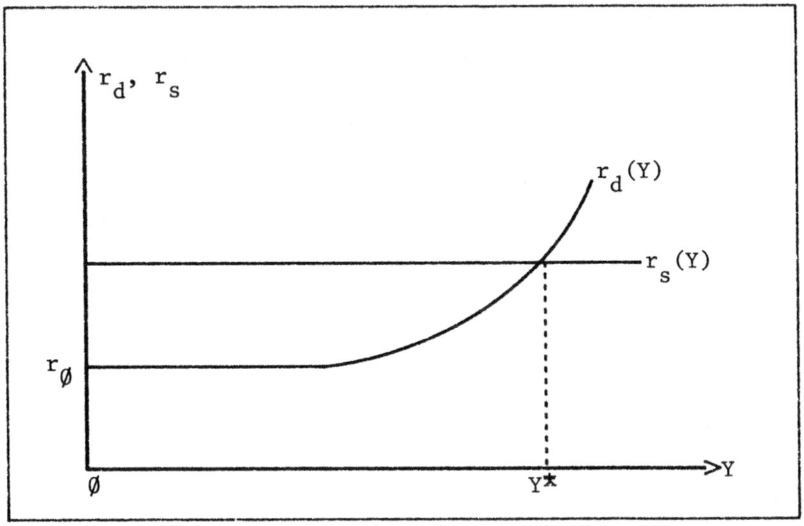

Figure 3.3: aggregate supply and demand for corporate bonds.

rate on equity income is assumed to be zero and rewrite the value of a levered firm:

$$V_L = V_U + [1 - (1-\tau_c)/(1-\tau_{rp})]B_L \tag{3.13}$$

The equilibrium prices (or costs) of debt and equity are such that

$$r_s = r_0/(1-\tau_c) = r_d = r_0/(1-\tau_{rm}) \tag{3.14}$$

where τ_{rm} is the personal tax rate of the marginal investor and r_s the label of the supply curve. Consequently,

$$(1-\tau_c) = (1-\tau_{rm}) \tag{3.15}$$

which on its turn implies that V_L equals V_U. If the supply rate of return differs from then the gain from leverage will be positive or negative and all corporations will either try to have a capital structure containing 100% debt or issue no debt at all.

Anticipating the next chapter, we indicate an important implication of Miller's argument, which says that "companies following a no-leverage or low leverage strategy (...) would find a market along investors in the high tax brackets; those opting for a high leverage strategy (...) would find the natural clientele for their securities at the other end of the scale. But one clientele is as good as the other". [Miller (1977), p. 269]. This phenomenon, which was first noticed by Farrar & Selwyn (1967), is often called the 'financial leverage clientele' effect. In the next chapter we will pay more attention to it, when discussing some important subsequent contributions, which study and extend the Miller hypothesis.

3.7. Conclusion

In this section an introduction has been given to the impact of taxation on corporate policy. We restricted ourselves to the leverage decision of a firm, which appeared to be an illustrative example. In the next chapter, however, we enlarge the analysis by additionally considering the dividend and investment policy of the firm as well as the investors's choices with respect to their desired kind of income. To do so, we elaborate on some contributions that study, extend and dispute the 'After Tax' equilibrium theory of Miller.

We close this chapter with a remark with regard to the distinction between the two equilibrium theories, presented in section 3.6 and which to some extend are competitive. This distinction does not seem very feasible with what most people consider our current real world. In Hamada & Scholes (1985) a comprehensive discussion and comparison of both theories is given. They conclude that theoretically "the answer to our question, why two separate tax theories, rests on who is the marginal investor". [p. 201]. In addition, "some (empirical) evidence supports the before tax and some the after tax equilibrium model". [p. 217].

Therefore, we finally mention the attempt of Harris (1980) to combine both theories by including leverage related costs within the Miller framework. He derives an adjusted value function of a levered firm:

$$V_L = V_U + [1 - \frac{(1-\tau_e)(1-\tau_c)}{(1-\tau_{rp})}]B_L - C(L) \tag{3.16}$$

where C(L) denoted the impact of leverage L related costs on the value of the levered firm. Harris states that the evidence presented in his book provides support for an affirmative answer to the question whether the inclusion of personal income taxes in the model at corporate capital structure will a dequately explain observed patterns of behaviour. His conclusions are: "marginal investors incorporate personal taxes in their valuation and investment decisions. Financial managers may pursue widely divergent capital structure policies all of which may be optimal. Optimality results from the dominance of personal effects, which offset the differences in non-tax related expected cash outflows to third parties" such as bankruptcy, monitoring and other agency costs. [Harris (1981), p. 175].

CHAPTER FOUR

FINANCIAL MARKET EQUILIBRIUM UNDER TAXATION AND TAX INDUCED CLIENTELES EFFECTS

4.1 Introduction

In this chapter we enlarge the analysis given in the previous one. In addition to the leverage irrelevancy theorem we discuss the impact of taxation on the corporate dividend and investment policy as well as on the investors' choices as a function of their disposable personal income. To do so, we once again elaborate on the firm's equilibrium market value onder taxation and its implications with respect to tax induced clienteles.

The notion that personal taxes will induce tax clienteles was first suggested by Farrar & Selwyn (1967). Although their analysis was not based on an equilibrium valuation framework, and thus their conclusion about financial leverage clienteles in particular was largely conjectural, more recent contributions, such as that of Brennan (1970), Stapleton (1972) and Stiglitz (1973), did not reject them. Moreover, in the previous chapter we have seen that Miller (1977) uses the idea of financial leverage clienteles to argue that personal taxation could offset corporate taxes such that in equilibrium the value of any individual firm would be independent of its leverage.

Miller's approach stimulated several contributions studying, extending and disputing his hypothesis that companies following a low leverage strategy will find a market along investors in high tax brackets, while the stock of highly levered firms will be held by investors with low personal tax rates.

At first, many subsequent papers by Kim, Lewellen & McConnell (1979), DeAngelo & Masulis (1980b), Auerbach & King (1983), and others, accepted and clarified the thruth of Miller's conclusion. In 1982, however, the discussion was again opened through Gordon, who "could not understand how Miller reached this conclusion". [Gordon (1982), p. 483]. The correctness of Gordon's result, that the equilibrium value of a firm is a convex function of its leverage, is to our opinion on its turn doubtful.

We first present a model, based on DeAngelo & Masulis (1980a), to clarify once again Miller's irrelevancy theorem (section 4.2). In section 4.3 a dividend irrelevancy theorem and the existence of dividend clienteles is discussed, that is, depending on its dividend policy, a firm will attract investors subject to specific tax brackets. In addition, the framework of DeAngelo and Masulis is extended by specifying the relations between the personal tax rates, that is, by considering some tax regimes. Section 4.4 presents Gordon's criticism of Miller's results, followed by a comprehensive discussion in which we will show that the equilibrium concept, that Gordon uses, is not correct. In section 4.6 we point out a corrected equilibrium approach, which will turn out to be a valuable tool for the dynamic analysis of chapter 7 in particular. Finally, we introduce 'tax induced investment clienteles' as a result of the corporate investment policy. Contrary to the 'financial leverage' and 'dividend'-clientele-effects this phenomenon is not yet based on an equilibrium framework. The inclusion of this topic, however, completes our analysis with respect to the impact of personal taxation on three important issues that we consider throughout this book: the financing, dividend and investment policy.

4.2. Dividend and leverage irrelevancy theorem under personal taxation

The model, we describe below, is a simplified version of the framework that DeAngelo & Masulis (1980b) explored in order to show that in equilibrium the market value of any firm is independent of its financing and dividend policy. Contrary to DeAngelo and Masulis, we eliminate differences in risk by assuming that all rates of return are certainty equivalents. Since DeAngelo and Masulis assume complete markets in which firms can issue a complete set of so-called Arrow-Debreu securities in both debt and equity, there is no formal distinction between the analysis of certainty and uncertainty. The result of DeAngelo and Masulis thus is a natural extension of the result that holds under certainty [see e.g. Auerbach (1979)].

We employ a decision model in which value maximizing firms sell equity and debt claims in order to finance investments at a given level. These securities yield constant returns which are taxable to its holders according to the corresponding personal tax rates, which differ across investors. We assume all debt payments tax deductible to the firm and all firm net income taxable at the corporate tax rate τ_c, which is cross-sectionally constant. Both debt and equity markets are assumed complete, perfectly competitive and frictionless, so that no single investor or firm is significant enough to alter security prices. In addition, both markets are effectively segmented against personal arbitrage.

Given the level of investment, the problem of the firm is to determine its financial structure and its dividend policy. It will adopt the financing-dividend decision which provides the greatest total net present market value. Hence, the firm maximizes

$$V_L = S_L + B_L \tag{4.1}$$

where

S_L: market value of shares or equity claims

B_L: market value of bonds or debt claims

The equity claims may be separated into dividend and capital gain components respectively. Thus,

$$S_L = S_D + S_G \tag{4.2}$$

where

S_D: market value dividend claims

S_G: market value capital gain claims

Let P_D, P_G and P_Y be the current market prices per dollar of dividend, capital gain and debt income respectively. We may now write the objective as to maximize

$$V_L = (P_D \cdot D + P_G \cdot G) + P_Y \cdot rY$$

$$= P_D \cdot D + P_G[(1-\tau_c)(0(K)-rY) - D] + P_Y \cdot rY \qquad (4.3)$$

where

G: capital gain through retained earnings.

The optimal dividend and financing policies depend on the sign of the first order derivatives with respect to the control variables D and Y respectively. Hence,

$$\frac{\partial V_L}{\partial D} = P_D - P_G \qquad (4.4)$$

$$\frac{\partial V_L}{\partial Y} = r[P_Y - (1-\tau_c)P_G] \qquad (4.5)$$

Since all firms face the same market prices and by assumption the same corporate tax rate, the analysis applies to each and every firm. For example, the aggregate supply of equity claims (both dividend as capital gain) will be zero if $P_D = P_G$ and $P_Y - (1-\tau_c)P_G > 0$.

On the demand side we assume the existence of many investors with personal tax rates, that are continuously distributed over the range of feasible values. For simplicity, DeAngelo and Masulis (1980a,b) assume in particular that investors are differently taxed so that at least one investor is in each of the following mutually exclusive and exhaustive personal tax brackets:

bracket 1:

$$(1-\tau_{ri}) > (1-\tau_{di})(1-\tau_c)$$

bracket 2:

$$(1-\tau_{ri}) = (1-\tau_{di})(1-\tau_c)$$

bracket 3:

$$(1-\tau_{ri}) < (1-\tau_{di})(1-\tau_c)$$

The debt-equity demand of an individual depends on his personal preferences represented by an utility function subject to a budget constraint. In order to facilitate the analysis we may transform the objective of any investor into the maximization of the net return on investment. Hence,

$$\max_{\alpha_{ji}}\{\alpha_{1i}\cdot\frac{(1-\tau_{di})}{P_D} + \alpha_{2i}\cdot\frac{(1-\tau_{gi})}{P_G} + \alpha_{3i}\cdot\frac{(1-\tau_{ri})}{P_Y}\} \tag{4.6}$$

$$\text{subject to } \sum_j \alpha_{ji} = 1 \tag{4.7}$$

$$\alpha_{ji} > 0 \tag{4.8}$$

where

τ_{gi}: personal tax rate on capital gain subject to investor i

We now argue that positive quantities of both debt and equity can be supplied in the aggregate simultaneously only if there is no after tax premium. Hence,

$$P_Y^* = P_D^*(1-\tau_c) = P_G^*(1-\tau_c) \tag{4.9}$$

To clarify this result, let us assume a premium such that

$$P_Y > P_D(1-\tau_c) = P_G(1-\tau_c) \tag{4.10}$$

Using (4.5) we obtain that market prices at such levels will stimulate firms to supply only debt claims in order to increase the value of the firm. However, investors i for whom

$$(1-\tau_{di})(1-\tau_c) > (1-\tau_{ri}) \tag{4.11}$$

prefer equity to debt claims if P_D, P_G and P_Y are at levels satisfying (4.10), that is, investors i will pay a price for any equity claim that exceeds any P_Y satisfying (4.10). To see that this is true, let us recal the objective functional (4.6) which says that any investor i will prefer the firm to make available equity securities if

$$\max\left\{\frac{(1-\tau_{di})}{P_D}, \frac{(1-\tau_{gi})}{PG}\right\} > \frac{(1-\tau_{ri})}{P_Y} \tag{4.12}$$

If we assume, only for simplicity, that $\tau_{di} = \tau_{gi}$, market prices at levels satisfying (4.10) imply for any investor i that

$$\underbrace{\frac{(1-\tau_{di})}{P_D} > \frac{(1-\tau_{ri})}{(1-\tau_c)P_D}}_{(4.11)} \underbrace{> \frac{(1-\tau_{ri})}{P_Y}}_{(4.10)} \tag{4.13}$$

which in turn implies that investors i prefer equity claims rather than debt claims. But, with $P_Y-(1-\tau_c)P_D > 0$, expression (4.5) points out that no firm will issue any equity. This means that any P_Y, P_D and P_G satisfying (4.10) in a market with no equity available cannot be in equilibrium. Moreover, investors i will offer up to prices that make them indifferent between debt and equity; that is, they are willing to pay more for equity claims than their going price P_D (or P_G). This will drive up the equity claim prices as an result.

On the other hand, a similar reasoning can be made when $P_Y-(1-\tau_c)P_D < 0$ by recalling the existence of investors j with $(1-\tau_{dj})(1-\tau_c) < (1-\tau_{rj})$. These investors will prefer debt claims although no firm is willing to supply such claims.

Notice, that similar results may be obtained when $\tau_{di} \neq \tau_{gi}$ or when other premiums are assumed. So, no premium can exist at equilibrium if there are i- and j-type investors in the market. The interaction of supply and demand will cause an equilibrium with prices P_Y^*, P_D^* and P_G^* satisfying (4.9), at which firms will issue both debt and equity claims. Moreover, such an equilibrium confirms the Miller hypothesis that the value of a firm is independent of its leverage rate. This result can easily be obtained by substituting the equilibrium prices in the first order condition (4.5). In addition, the firm's value may be independent of its dividend policy too.

So, under the assumption that investors are continuously distributed over the range of possible tax rates, at equilibrium the choice among debt, dividends and capital gain is a matter of indifference to any given firm.

4.3. Dividend and financial leverage clienteles

Proceeding on the assumptions and results of the previous section we now derive the phenomenon of tax induced clienteles; that is, depending on its policy, a firm will attract investors subject to specific tax brackets. In this section we focus on dividend and financial leverage clienteles in particular. Moreover, we consider the latter phenomenon under both the classical and the imputation tax system. Finally, the tax induced net return clienteles as a result of the firm's investment policy will be discussed in section 4.7.

Recalling the results of the previous section, we know that at equilibrium the value of any firm will be independent of its dividend policy, that is, the choice of equity claim to be supplied is a matter of indifference to the firm.

On the demand side, however, the revenues of these claims are differently taxed. According to the objective functional (4.6) the choice of investors depends on which ever (in)equality holds in:

$$\frac{(1-\tau_{di})}{P_D^*} \gtreqless \frac{(1-\tau_{gi})}{P_G^*} \qquad (4.14)$$

which, due to equality of P_D^* and P_G^*, is equivalent to

$$\tau_{di} \lesseqgtr \tau_{gi} \qquad (4.15)$$

So, capital gain claims are prefered by investors subject to tax rates on capital gain less than their tax rate on dividend. As the latter tax rate mostly exceeds the former, only fully tax exempt investors are willing to hold dividend claims, however. The result of dividend clienteles thus is on one hand obvious and on the other hand trivial.

To obtain the result of financial leverage clienteles, we firstly define P_E^* as the equilibrium market value of one dollar equity claim. P_E^* may take on the polar values P_D^* and P_G^* respectively, or interior values due to a combination of both equity claims.

In the previous section we have seen that equilibrium prices are such that firms are willing to issue simultaneously both equity and debt claims, that is $P_E^*(1-\tau_c) = P_Y^*$. Consequently, investors' preferences depend on whichever (in)equality holds in

$$\frac{(1-\tau_{ei})}{P_E^*} \gtreqless \frac{(1-\tau_{ri})}{P_Y^*} \tag{4.16}$$

or, equivalently,

$$(1-\tau_{ei})(1-\tau_c) \gtreqless (1-\tau_{ri}) \tag{4.17}$$

This condition corresponds to the results of the third chapter. In addition, it confirms the statement of Miller (1977) that low-income investors prefer corporate debt and high-income investors personal debt. This notion of financial leverage clienteles may be easily obtained by setting τ_e equal to zero. However, the existence of the phenomena strongly depends on the kind of equity claim as well as on the tax system under consideration.

To clarify the above mentioned statement we first consider the case in which the firm is supplying dividend claims only, and thereafter the case in which the firm is supplying capital gain claims as well. Accordingly, we rewrite (4.17) into

$$(1-\tau_{di})(1-\tau_c) \gtreqless (1-\tau_{ri}) \tag{4.18}$$

Under the classical tax system ($\tau_{di} = \tau_{ri}$) this condition implies that no single investor, neither subject to personal taxation nor tax exempt, will demand a positive quantity of equity claims. The introduction of a dividend personal tax shelter [see DeAngelo & Masulis (1980b)] or a reform of the tax system into an imputation tax system may establish such a positive demand. In the latter case ($\tau_{di} = \tau_{ri} - \tau_s$) expression (4.18) turns into

$$\frac{\tau_s}{\tau_c}(1-\tau_c) \gtreqless (1-\tau_{ri}) \tag{4.19}$$

So, in case $\tau_s = \tau_c$, that is, the total fraction of the corporate tax paid on distributed profit is allowed to be subtracted from the personal income tax, investor i's choice depends on the balance between the corporate tax rate and the personal tax rate on debt income. This result is in particular similar to Miller's result when assuming $\tau_{di} = 0$.

Secondly, we consider the case in which the firm is supplying both dividend and capital gain claims. In addition we introduce the following relation between the personal tax rates on debt and dividend income respectively:

$$\tau_{di} = \tau_{ri} - \tau_s = \tau_{ri} - s.\tau_c \tag{4.20}$$

where

s: imputation factor.

Using the investor's objective (4.6) and the equilibrium condition (4.9) we obtain following conditions:

Investor i prefers

(a) debt claims rather than capital gain claims if

$$(1-\tau_{ri}) - (1-\tau_{gi})(1-\tau_c) > 0 \tag{4.21}$$

(b) dividend claims rather than capital gain claims if

$$(1-\tau_{ri}) - (1-\tau_{gi}-s\tau_c) > 0 \tag{4.22}$$

(c) debt claims rather than dividend claims if

$$(1-\tau_{ri}) - (1-\tau_c)s > 0 \tag{4.23}$$

Investors now may be partitioned according to their personal tax rate on debt income into three tax groups. Each group is characterized by a preference for a certain kind of income. This result is depicted in figure 4.1.

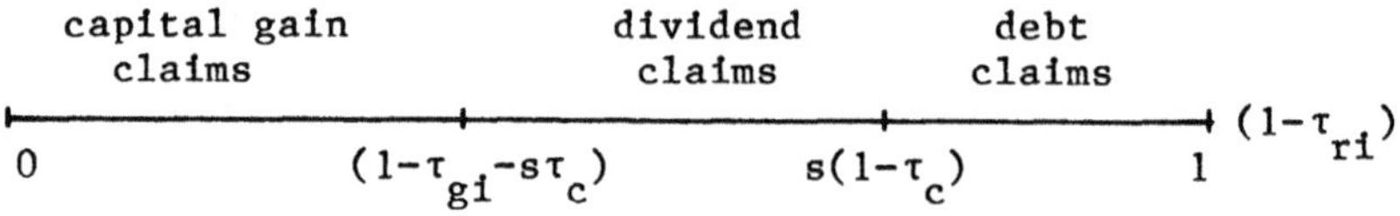

Figure 4.1: Partitioning of investors according to their personal tax rate into claim-preference groups.

The above mentioned partitioning is only feasible if demand for and supply of all security claims simultaneously exist in the market. Supply is guaranteed by the equilibrium condition (4.9). To guarantee the demand for dividend claims in particular, the imputation factor must be such that it will satisfy the condition

$$(1-\tau_{gi}-s\tau_c) < (1-\tau_c)s \tag{4.24}$$

or, equivalently,

$$s > (1-\tau_{gi}) \tag{4.25}$$

Since the personal tax on capital gain mostly is at a rate close to zero, the imputation factor must be around one; that is, investors only will demand positive quantities of dividend claims, if at least the total fraction of the corporate tax paid on dividends is allowed to be substracted from the personal income tax. Note, that under the classical tax system (τ_s=0), condition (4.25) will always be violated; that is, in case investors demand for positive quantities of equity claims, it will be capital gain claims rather than dividend claims.

Finally, in correspondence with (4.17) the choice between debt and capital gain obviously depends on whichever (in)equality holds in

$$(1-\tau_{gi})(1-\tau_c) \gtreqless (1-\tau_{ri}) \tag{4.26}$$

that is, if $(1-\tau_{gi})(1-\tau_c) > (1-\tau_{ri})$ the investor prefers capital gain claims, if the equality-sign holds he takes an indifferent position and otherwise he prefers debt claims.

4.4. Equilibrium market value reconsidered by Gordon

In his 1982 paper Gordon states: "I could not understand how Miller reached this conclusion, and subsequent papers - by Kim, Lewellen and McConnell (1979), Chen and Kim (1979), DeAngelo and Masulis (1980a), and others - which accepted the truth of Miller's conclusion did not clarify Miller's argument to me." [Gordon (1982), p. 483]. In his opinion it is not possible to prove that under Miller's assumptions the equilibrium value of each firm is independent of its leverage rate. Employing the Modigliani-Miller theoretical framework, Gordon claims that only in a special case Miller's conclusion holds. In general, however, the equilibrium value of a firm is found to be a convex function of its leverage rate. Consequently, the optimal (value maximizing) policy for all firms is the maximum possible leverage rate.

Gordon starts his analysis by assuming a zero tax rate on equity income (in agreement with Miller) and a uniform personal income tax rate on debt. Using the work of Arditti, Levy and Sarnat (1977), Gordon then points out that the straight lines V_i, as depicted in figure 4.2, represent the relationship between value and leverage for the case where the personal tax rate of all individuals is τ_{ri} (see also figure 3.2). These personal value functions are given by

$$V_{pi}(L) = V_u + (\tau_{ri} - \tau_c)L \tag{4.27}$$

where

$V_{pi}(L)$: personal value of a firm with leverage L to an investor subject to τ_{ri} and $\tau_d = 0$.

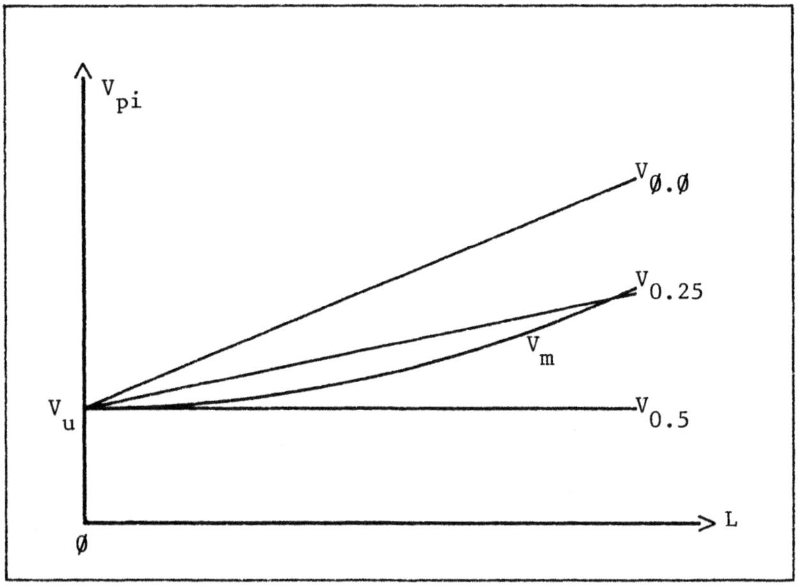

Figure 4.2: Relation between the value of a firm and its leverage rate under a progressive personal tax on debt income and a corporate tax of $\tau_c = 0.5$.

Next, Gordon assumes that the personal tax rate on the proceeds from debt is at a rate which varies with the investor's wealth. In addition, investors are supposed to be distributed over the range of tax rates $\tau_{ri} = 0.0$ to $\tau_{ri} = 0.5$, whereas firms are arbitrarily distributed over the range of leverage rates L_0 to L_{max}. Each V_{pi} in figure 4.2 now represents the equilibrium values of firms for those investors with the indicated tax rate on debt.

Gordon then argues that none of the straight lines in figure 4.2 provides an equilibrium set of values for the firms, since only persons subject to the indicated tax rate will be indifferent to which firm is in his portfolio. Investors subject to lower personal tax rates than the indicated one, will find all firms undervalued and will move into firms with the highest leverage rate in order to maximize their personal gain.

Similarly, investors in higher tax brackets will find all firms overvalued and they will move into unlevered firms in order to minimize their personal loss.

Instead of the individual straight lines V_i, the equilibrium market value of the firms is represented by the upward sloping curve V_m, in figure 4.2, that is, this curve represents the equilibrium relationship between value and leverage. The construction of the V_m-curve is such that the excess demand for shares at each leverage rate is equal to zero. Gordon argues that any investor will move into the shares and corresponding debt of those firms for which the slope of V_m is the same as the slope of his 'personal value'-function V_{pi}. For example, investors subject to $\tau_{ri} = 0.25$ will find that $V_{0.25}-V_m$, the excess of a firm's personal value over its market value, is maximized by holding shares of a firm with the leverage rate of $L_{0.25}$.

To clarify the construction of the line V_m, it is sufficient to describe the solution in case investors are subject to just three tax rates, say $\tau_{ri} = 0.0$, 0.25 and 0.5. Let firms be partitioned according to their leverage rate into three groups as indicated in figure 4.3.

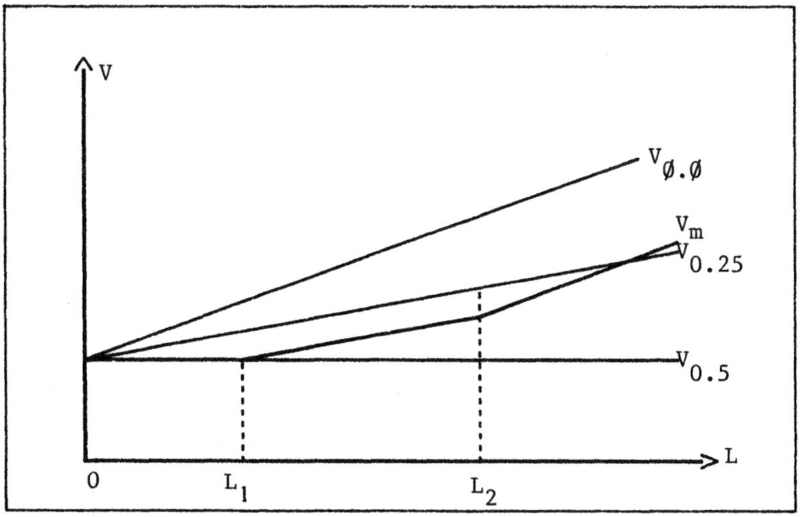

Figure 4.3: Relation between the value of a firm and its leverage rate under progressive personal tax rate on debt at the rates $\tau_{ri} = 0.0$, 0.25 and 0.5, and a corporate tax of $\tau_c = 0.5$.

The partitioning is such that the total share value of the firms in the first group is equal to the share wealth of persons with $\tau_{ri} = \tau_c = 0.5$, for this group of investors is willing to buy shares of firms following a zero or low leverage strategy. Next, investors subject to $\tau_{ri} = 0.25$ fix the equilibrium value of the firm in such way that $V_{0.25}-V_m$ is the same for all shares in the corresponding tax group. Moreover, shares in the other tax group would only provide smaller values for $V_{0.25}-V_m$. The total share value of the firms in the second group is once again equal to the share wealth of persons with $\tau_{ri} = 0.25$.

Similarly, the remaining shares are hold by the remaining investors, those with $\tau_r = 0.0$. So, "with each person's goal the maximization of $V_i - V_m$, the V_m-curve in figure 4.3 results in an equilibrium" [Gordon (1982), p. 490]. Finally, the size of the intervals adjust to make the excess demand for shares in each tax group equal to zero. By extending the number of tax rates and corresponding tax groups the curve V_m tends to the convex curve as depicted in figure 4.2, implying that the equilibrium value of a firm is a convex function of its leverage rate.

Proceeding on this result Gordon then argues that any firm, that has the above knowledge on valuation and that issues debt and equity securities in the proportion that maximizes market value, will adopt a maximum leverage capital structure at which point all firms have the same value.

Gordon concludes that Miller's assumptions do not lead to his explanation of capital structure; that is, the value of the firm is not independent of its capital structure, so that Miller failed to explain the wide range of capital structures that we actually observe.

4.5. Discussion and extension of Gordon's framework

In this chapter we have presented two conflicting views with regard to the after tax equilibrium value of a levered firm. For simplicity, we label the underlying concepts the Miller and Gordon theory respectively.

The Miller theory in particular has been supported by several subsequent contributions [Kim, Lewellen and McConnell (1979), DeAngelo and Masulis (1980a), Kim (1982), Auerbach and King (1983)]. It was Gordon

(1982) who first questioned the correctness of Miller's result. In his opinion Miller's assumptions do not result in a leverage irrelevancy theorem.

In this section we discuss Gordon's criticism by questioning the correctness both of the objective functional Gordon uses to obtain the upwards sloping market value curve (subsection 4.5.1) as well as of the supply adjustment process he describes afterwards (subsections 4.5.2 and 4.5.3). We review some discussion in the literature on the latter topic and add some new arguments, because the results that are known at the moment, are still unsatisfactory. We conclude that on his turn Gordon failed to disprove Miller's explanation of capital structure. Moreover, Gordon's approach is very useful to prove once again the correctness of the Miller leverage irrelevancy theorem.

4.5.1. The investor's objective and the Modigliani-Miller framework

One of Gordon's main objections is the abandonment of the Modigliani-Miller framework by Miller (1977) and subsequent authors. In addition, "they did not reconcile their results with that (M&M) framework." [Gordon, (1982), p. 483]. Therefore, Gordon explores the Modigliani-Miller framework with perfect markets and introduces in sequence: corporate debt, a corporate profit tax, a uniform personal tax and a progressive personal tax on debt income. As soon as progressive personal taxation is included, a distinction can be made between the personal value, which we label by V_{pi}, and the market value of a firm, V_m; that is, maximization of the firm's market value is not longer equivalent to the maximization of the investor's personal values.

To carry out his analysis, Gordon is partitioning the firms according to their leverage rate into different groups in a way, such that the total share value of the firms in each group is equal to the share wealth of investors in the corresponding tax group. Proceeding on the assumption that each investor's goal is the maximization of the excess of the personal value over the market value, Gordon argues that the V_m-curve in figure 4.3 results in an equilibrium "because a person subject to the τ_{ri} -th tax rate finds $V_i - V_m$ the same for all shares in the tax group, and shares in the other tax groups would only provide smaller values for $V_i - V_m$." [Gordon (1982), p. 490].

The maximization of the excess of the personal value over the market value in real terms is a reasonable objective if investors are allowed to lend and borrow unlimited amounts of debt at a constant risk free rate, which is actually the case in the Modigliani-Miller framework. In our opinion, however, Gordon's work does not proceed on the assumption of unlimited liabilities. On the contrary, capital rationing is slumbering into his analysis, which may be illustrated by the next features:

- the assumption that the personal tax rate on the proceeds from debt is a rate which varies only with the investor's initial wealth is a fair assumption if the amount of taxable income is limited. However, in absence of capital rationing investors may lend and borrow unlimited amounts and the personal tax rate, which is assumed to be a progressive one, will thus be affected.
- the partitioning into tax groups, such that the share wealth of the investors equal the share value of the firms in that group is only possible if capital rationing is included.

It is not surprising, that such a capital rationing is slumbering into Gordon's equilibrium analysis, for Auerbach and King have shown "that in a world in which investors face different tax rates, no equilibrium exists unless constraints are imposed". [Auerbach and King (1983), p. 608].

In our opinion, Gordon should have used the Present Value Index, which is a modification of the net present value in order to consider constrained capital budgeting problems with projects that differ with respect to their scale. Due to the limited liabilities, the scale of an investment becomes important and a project will thus be valued according to the return per dollar invested. The present value index, PVI, is defined as the present value of cash inflows divided by the present value of cash outflows [see Copeland and Weston, (1983), p. 56]; that is,

$$PVI = \frac{\text{present value of inflows}}{\text{present value of outflows}} \tag{4.28}$$

Of course, it makes no difference if we would take the net present value index, that is, if we replace the present value of inflows by the net present value. In this way, we are able to say something about the present gain in relation to the present value of outflows, that is, the present rate of return on investment.

Using this latter index, the investor's objective becomes the maximization of $(V_{pi}-V_m)/V_m$. In section 4.6 we carry out the analysis in this way as an example of a more general equilibrium approach we will use later on in this book. For the moment, it is important to know that in the case we use the above criterion, we only obtain quantitative differences with the Gordon result. Although Gordon explores an incorrect criterion, his conclusion, that the equilibrium market value of a firm is a convex function of its leverage rate, still holds.

In the next subsections, we dispute the supply adjustment process that leads to Gordon's second conclusion that any value maximizing firm, that has the above knowledge on valuation, will adopt a maximum leverage capital structure.

4.5.2. Supply adjustment of debt by firms

Gordon argues that any firm, that issues debt and equity securities in the proportion that maximizes market value, will adopt a maximum leverage capital structure. This extravagant supply of debt security claims will also induce value adjustments in the market for security claims, however.

Jaffe and Westerfield (1984) were the first who questioned this conclusion of Gordon. Although they agree with Gordon's treatment concerning a fixed supply of debt and equity, they dispute Gordon's later analysis of supply adjustments. To see their argument, we point at the presence of investors, such as other companies, subject to a tax rate equal to the corporate tax rate in order to argue that the value of a firm is invariant to leverage in such a situation. Jaffe and Westerfield state that "if the value of a totally levered firm is greater than the value of an unlevered firm, individuals with $\tau_{ri} = \tau_c$ desire to purchase stock in unlevered firms but all firms desire to lever" [Jaffe &

Westerfield (1984), p. 493]. Since similar arguments may be used in case the value of a levered firm is less than the value of an unlevered firm, Jaffe and Westerfield conclude that "an equilibrium arises where (1) enough firms lever so that all individuals with $\tau_{ri} < \tau_c$ hold levered stock, (2) the ratio of unlevered stock to levered stock issued to individuals with $\tau_{ri} = \tau_c$ is indeterminate and (3) the value of a firm is invariant to its leverage" [Jaffe & Westerfield (1984), p. 493].

Jaffe and Westerfield clarify their statement by comparing an unlevered and completely levered firm. So, they actually show that $V_U = V_m(L_0) = V_m(L_{max})$. Although they argue that their conclusions would be unchanged if firms are assumed to issue any intermediate amount of debt as well, Gordon disputes their general result when replying: "They should have said that firms at L_0 have the same value as firms at L_{max}" [Gordon (1984), p. 466].

We now obtain this latter result with similar arguments as Gordon uses to argue the existence of the convex value function of the firm. The scarcity of debt providers, Gordon introduces, is still present in the situation in which any firm strives for a maximum leverage position. Since equilibrium requires the absence of any excess demand for or supply of shares at each leverage rate, also investors subject to $\tau_{ri} = \tau_c$ have to demand positive quantities of levered equity securities. However, they are only willing to do so if

$$V_m(L_{max}) = V_i = V_{\tau_c} = V_m(L_0) := V_U \tag{4.29}$$

that is, if market prices adapt itselves to levels at which the value of an unlevered firm equals the value of a completely levered firm.

4.5.3. Value of a firm with interior leverage rate

The analysis of the previous subsection does not clarify, the value of a firm with an interior leverage rate. Jaffe and Westerfield (1984) argue that the equilibrium of the corrected version of Gordon's analysis may lead to an interesting possible polarization. To see their statement, imagine that $\tau_{ri} > \tau_c$ for some investors, $\tau_{ri} < \tau_c$ for others, but $\tau_{ri} = \tau_c$ for no investors. Since low-taxed investors prefer stock from a maximally levered firm while high-taxed investors prefer the unlevered stock, no investor would hold the stock of a firm with an intermediate leverage rate in this situation, unless the value of this latter type of firm were less than the value of the other mentioned types of firms. "Since no firm would issue an intermediate amount of debt, if doing so reducing its value, firms in our corrected version of Gordon's model either lever at the maximum extent or do not lever at all" [Jaffe & Westerfield (1984), p. 494].

Gordon takes this opportunity to strengthen his statement: "Jaffe and Westerfield have shown that firms '... either lever to the maximum extent or do not lever at all' [p. 494]. By implication they also could find no theoretical basis for the Miller conclusion under the relevant assumptions. Also, their analysis provides no basis whatsoever for their statement 'that the value of a firm is invariant to its leverage' [p. 493]." [Gordon (1984), p. 496].

In our opinion this conclusion is, however, besides the mark, for Jaffe and Westerfield's statement is only valid under the absence of investors subject to $\tau_{ri} = \tau_c$. Moreover, in Miller's theory such a situation would neither imply an equilibrium. Corresponding to expression (3.13) of the previous chapter, a supply of debt security claims will be valued either positive or negative, depending on the balance between τ_c and the personal tax rate τ_{ri} of the marginal investor. Consequently, no equilibrium will occur.

Finally, the equality $V_m(L_{max}) = V_m(L_0)$ implies that the value of firms with interior leverages rates equal on their turn the value of firms with polar leverage rates. If this were not true, any investor would be better off when realizing his/her personal leverage by purchasing the shares of a firm with the desired intermediate leverage rather than the corresponding proportion of shares with polar capital structures. That is,

$$V_m(L_\alpha) < \alpha V_m(L_{max}) + (1-\alpha)V_m(L_0) = V_m(L_{max}) = V_m(L_0) \qquad (4.30)$$

where

$V_m(L_\alpha)$: market value of a firm with leverage equal to αL_{max}.

So, with a correct use of the supply adjustment process the Gordon framework confirms the Miller irrelevancy theorem instead of disproving it.

4.5.4. Miller versus Gordon

Comparing the analyses of Miller and Gordon it strikes that both appeal to the scarcity of debt, so that the group of debt providers needs to be subsequently expanded. In Miller's analysis, the existence of a progressive personal tax structure means that the compensation for the personal tax burden, that taxable bonds impose on the investor, must increase as larger quantities of bonds are issued in aggregate. So, in order to enlarge debt capital firms have to attract investors subject to increasing tax rates.

In Gordon's analysis, it looks as if an additional supply of debt requires a demand for it by investors in still lower tax brackets. However, Gordon does not treat the problem in such way that still larger amounts of debt are supplied. Contrary to Miller, he just distributes a fixed supply of debt and equity among investors, who are partitioned into different tax groups.

A second distinction can be made with respect to the return on debt. In Miller's analysis increasing aggregate supply of debt provides decreasing prices. On the contrary, Gordon assumes constant return to scale, that is, when describing the adjustment process of debt supply by firms, he only considers the adaptation of the supplied quantity of debt. Gordon thus neglects the impact an excess supply of debt (that occurs due to the endeavour of firms to obtain a maximum leverage position) imposes on equilibrium market values. In our opinion, this is perhaps the most striking objection and argument in order to disprove Gordon's analysis.

4.6. A corrected equilibrium approach

In this section we describe a corrected version of Gordon's approach to obtain an equilibrium market value function of the firm, when investors are subject to progressive personal tax rates and have limited private means. We elaborate on this approach, because it will turn out to be a valuable tool for the dynamic analysis we carry out in chapter 7.
Let us recall the problem Gordon (1982) puzzles as depicted by the straight lines in figure 4.4.

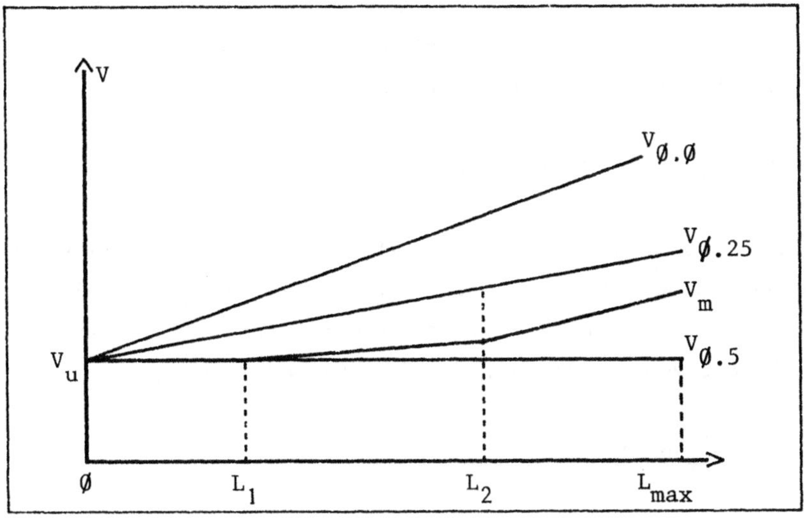

Figure 4.4: Corrected equilibrium value function of the firm under a progressive personal tax.

The analysis, we carry out, is except for the investor's objective, quite similar to that of Gordon. Due to the implicit assumption of limited private liabilities, the investor's objective is changed into the maximization of the return on personal investment net of corporate and personal taxes. Equivalently, we use the net present index rather than the present value rule. The objective of an investor i subject to a personal tax rate on debt τ_{ri} thus is to maximize

$$(V_i - V_m)/V_m = V_i/V_m - 1 \tag{4.31}$$

Similar to Gordon we may now argue that none of the straight lines in figure 4.4 provides an equilibrium set of values for the firm, but that the V_m-curve, which differs from the V_m-curve in figure 4.3, may represent the equilibrium relationship between value and leverage.

To clarify the construction of the V_m-curve, let firms again be partitioned according to their leverage rate into three groups as indicated in figure 4.4 and let this partitioning once again be such that the total share value of the firms in each group is equal to the share wealth of investors in the corresponding tax group. The stock of zero- or low-levered firms will be held by investors subject to $\tau_{ri} = 0.5$. Since $V_{0.5}$ is the lowest personal value function, it may be seen as a lower bound of the equilibrium market value. Hence,

$$V_m(L) = V_{0.5}(L) \qquad \text{if } L \in [L_0, L_1] \tag{4.32}$$

Next, investors subject to $\tau_{ri} = 0.25$ fix the equilibrium value of the firm in such a way that the net present index, $(V_{0.25}-V_m)/V_m$, is at the same maximum level for all shares in the corresponding tax group. This maximum level, denoted by $NPI_{0.25}$, is determined by

$$\frac{[V_{0.25}(L_1) - V_m(L_1)]}{V_m(L_1)} = \frac{V_{0.25}(L_1)}{V_{0.5}(L_1)} - 1 := NPI_{0.25} \tag{4.33}$$

The market value of firms in the second group may now be obtained by rewriting (4.33) into

$$V_m(L) = V_{0.25}(L)/(1 + NPI_{0.25}) \qquad \text{if } L \in [L_1, L_2] \tag{4.34}$$

Finally, the remaining shares are held by the remaining investors those with $\tau_r = 0.0$. Their present value index is fixed by

$$\frac{[V_{0.0}(L_2)-V_m(L_2)]}{V_m(L_2)} = (1 + NPI_{0.25}) \frac{V_{0.0}}{V_{0.25}} - 1 := NPI_{0.0} \tag{4.35}$$

Hence, the market value of the remaining firms is given by:

$$V_m(L) = V_{0.0}(L)/(1 + NPI_{0.0}) \qquad \text{if } L \in [L_2, L_{max}] \qquad (4.36)$$

We have now derived a correct equilibrium market value curve, which makes the excess demand for shares at each leverage rate equal to zero under the assumption of limited private means. It can easily be seen that the equilibrium market value we obtain, always adapts an equal or lower value than the equilibrium values under Gordon's approach. Nevertheless, the approach provides the similar qualitative result that the equilibrium market value of the firm is a convex function of its leverage. However, this result is on its turn disputed in subsection 4.5.2 and sequel.

4.7. Tax induced investment clienteles

In this section we introduce 'tax induced investment clienteles' as a result of the firm's return on net investment, that is, due to the corporate investment policy firms will attract investors in specific tax brackets. Since our analysis is not yet based on an equilibrium framework, we rather indicate than lay claim on the existence of tax-induced return clienteles. For that reason, we did not treat this phenomenon in connection with the dividend and financial leverage clienteles hypotheses. Nevertheless, the inclusion of this topic completes our analysis with respect to the impact of personal taxation on the three issues of corporate behaviour that we consider throughout this book: the financing, dividend and investment policy.

To carry out the analysis we proceed on the basic model of dynamic firm behaviour, which we have presented in chapter two, and we assume a complete separation of management and ownership. So, we study the impact of personal taxation on the behaviour of investors in response to changes in the investment policy of the firm, which is autonomously controlled by its management.

Let us recall the dynamic model of chapter two and its solution. For mathematical convenience we modify the objective by assuming an infinite planning horizon instead of a finite one. Moreover, due to the separation of management and ownership this is a nearly fair assumption. So, the firm's management maximizes the present value of the dividend stream before personal taxes. As we assume that many unknown investors possess shares of the firm, the management uses an estimation of the market time preference rate to fix the discount rate i'. Hence,

$$\underset{D,I,Y}{\text{maximize}} \int_{T=0}^{\infty} D(T)e^{-i'T}dT \tag{4.37}$$

subject to the state equations and constraints as formulated by (2.23) through (2.33). The resulting optimal master trajectories are quite similar to those as depicted in figures 2.3 and 2.4 respectively. Since we assume an infinite planning horizon the final (dividend) policy is of infinite duration. In the case that the manager's discount rate is less than the net cost of debt $i' < (1-\tau_c)r$, we get the master trajectory as depicted in figure 4.5. We now study the reaction of taxable shareholders to this varying policy.

As we deal with certainty it is admissible to assume investor's behaviour to be dependent on three relevant variables: the value of the firm's shares, the net revenue and the net revenue of alternative investment opportunities.

The value of the shares of a firm at time T for investor i, $V_i(T)$, is assumed to be equal to the net discounted value of an infinite stream of constant dividend payments at the firm's net profit level at T, that is

$$V_i(T) = \int_{S=T}^{\infty} (1-\tau_{di})D(T)e^{-r(1-\tau_{ri})(S-T)}dS$$

$$= \frac{(1-\tau_{di})}{(1-\tau_{ri})} \cdot \frac{D(T)}{r} \tag{4.38}$$

We are aware of neglecting the impact of future policies of the firm on the present value. However, this assumption may be justified by pointing at the investor's unconsciousness of the whole future investment policies. In addition, this approach corresponds with the perpetual approach we used to obtain the dividend and financial leverage clienteles effects. In fact, we use a non-dynamic approach.

Note that we propose the time preference rate of the investor to be equal to the market interest rate after taxation. Applying the classical tax system ($\tau_{di} = \tau_{ri}$), the personal value of the firm equals D(T)/r. So the value of the firm V(T), is independent of the investor's tax rates.

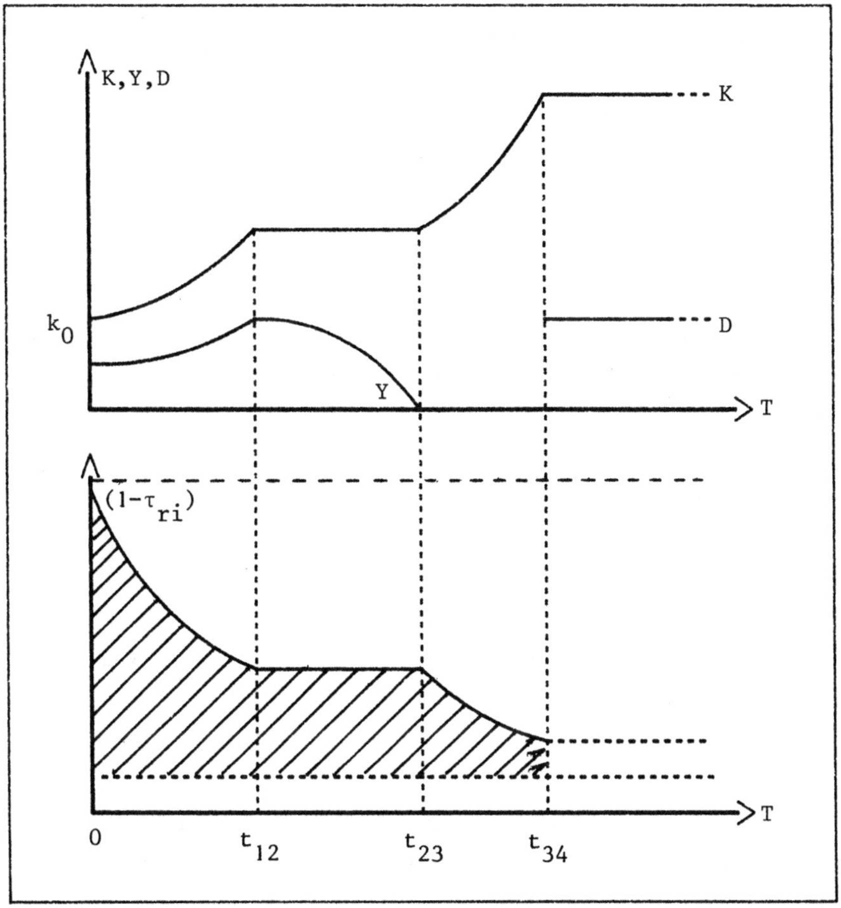

Figure 4.5: Optimal master trajectory if $i' < (1-\tau_c)r$ and the resulting tax induced investment clienteles.

We distinghuish two kinds of share revenue: dividend and capital gain, both taxed in accordance to the corresponding personal tax rate. So the net return per dollar can be expressed by

$$\frac{(1-\tau_{di})D(T) + (1-\tau_{gi})\dot{V}(T)}{V(T)} \tag{4.39}$$

With the help of expression (2.28) and the optimal trajectory presented by figure 4.5 we derive following values:

$$V(T) = (1-\tau_c)(O(K)-rY)/r \tag{4.40}$$

$$\dot{V}(T) = \begin{cases} V(T)(1-\tau_c)(\frac{dO}{dK} + h(\frac{dO}{dK} - r)) & \text{if } 0 \leq T < t_{12} \\ V(T)(1-\tau_c)\frac{dO}{dK} & \text{if } t_{12} \leq T < t_{34} \\ 0 & \text{if } t_{34} \leq T < \infty \end{cases} \tag{4.41}$$

$$D(T) = \begin{cases} 0 & \text{if } 0 \leq T < t_{34} \\ (1-\tau_c)O(K) & \text{if } t_{34} \leq T < \infty \end{cases} \tag{4.42}$$

Based on the above values we can specify the net return per dollar, which will be continuously compared with the revenue of having a bank account. Thus

$$(1-\tau_{gi})(1-\tau_c)(\frac{dO}{dK} + h(\frac{dO}{dK} - r)) \gtreqless (1-\tau_{ri})r \qquad \text{if } 0 \leq T < t_{12}$$

$$(1-\tau_{gi})(1-\tau_c)\frac{dO}{dK} = (1-\tau_{gi})(1-\tau_c)r \gtreqless (1-\tau_{ri})r \qquad \text{if } t_{12} \leq T < t_{23}$$

$$(1-\tau_{gi})(1-\tau_c)\frac{dO}{dK} \gtreqless (1-\tau_{ri})r \qquad \text{if } t_{23} \leq T < t_{34}$$

$$(1-\tau_{di})r = (1-\tau_{ri})r \qquad \text{if } t_{34} \leq T < \infty$$

As operating income O(K) is assumed to be a concave function of the amount of capital goods, which rate of change is determined by state equation (2.23) and which thus is a time- and state-dependent variable, the above expressions not only depend on the level of the personal tax rate τ_{ri}, but also on the state of the firm expressed by the marginal return on new investment.

If net return on new investment exceeds the net market interest rate investors prefer a policy of retaining earnings. Otherwise, dividend income or cash account is more profitable. As during the lifecycle of the firm the financing, dividend and investment policy will be liable to changes, investors' preferences may alter in the course of time. In this way we obtain 'tax induced investment clienteles'.

The declining slope curve as depicted in figure 4.5 satisfies the well known personal equilibrium condition [see e.g. King (1977), p. 90]:

$$(1-\tau_{di})D(T) + (1-\tau_{gi})\dot{V}(T) = (1-\tau_{ri})rV(T) \tag{4.43}$$

Investors subject to a personal tax rate below this curve may agree with a policy of retaining earnings in order to finance new investment with a net return corresponding the state of the firm. Investors in lower tax brackets prefer dividend at that specific state of the firm.

The marked area indicates the tax rates of investors, who may agree to the policy of the firm and may thus have the willingness to hold shares of the firm. As soon as the firm changes its policy from retentions into dividend distribution, all investors will be indifferent between possessing shares or having a bank account of the same size.

4.8. Conclusion

In this chapter the present theory on market equilibrium valuation under personal taxation is discussed and extended. We have explored the Miller 'after tax' theory within the framework of DeAngelo and Masulis (1980b). Thereafter, we have discussed Gordon's criticism on the Miller theory and showed that on his turn Gordon (1982, 1984) failed to disprove the Miller leverage irrelevancy theorem. Moreover, we have described a corrected version of Gordon's approach to obtain a market equilibrium value function of the firm.

We have also discussed the existence of tax induced clienteles, in particular dividend-, financial leverage- and investment clienteles. The former two are explored with in the framework of DeAngelo and Masulis (1980b), which on its turn has been extended by including both the classical and the imputation system. Since we did not yet consider an equilibrium framework, the existence of the latter clientele-effect has only been indicated rather than proved. In addition, we have assumed a complete separation of management and ownership. So, we have studied the behaviour of investors in different tax brackets in response to changes in both the state and investment policy of the firm, which is autonomously controlled by its management.

Proceeding on this assumptions Van Schijndel (1985) has described and solved the investor's dynamic portfolio problem by means of a optimal control model. As we will focus on situations in which investors determine or at least influence the firm's policy we will confine ourselves to refering to the work mentioned.

CHAPTER FIVE

OPTIMAL POLICY STRING OF A SINGLE VALUE MAXIMIZING FIRM UNDER PERSONAL TAXATION

5.1. Introduction

In this and the following chapters we focus on the dynamic modeling of the financing, dividend and investment decisions of firms under both corporate and personal taxation.

As we have stated in the introductory chapter, the aim of this book is the inclusion of corporate and personal taxation into the dynamic theory of the firm. In previous chapters we draw attention to some of the many contributions in finance theory that consider the impact of taxation on corporate and personal policy, and on the financing policy in particular. The purpose of this and the following chapters is the extension of these static results by adding another dimension: time.

In chapter two we already argued that time is of utmost importance with regard to the economic decision process. The survey of Feichtinger (1982b) and the collections of Bensoussan, Kleindorfer and Tapiero (1978) and Feichtinger (1982a, 1985) show very well that many recent contributions extend the theory of the firm by using dynamic optimization techniques to solve dynamic problems analytically. The use of this kind of dynamic models and optimization techniques has turned out to be an excellent tool in order to describe the evolution of characteristic features or variables of the process in the course of time.

Accordingly, this chapter is related to the financial models such as those of Leland (1972), Lesourne (1973), Ludwig (1977), Sethi (1978), Van Loon (1983) and others [see also the survey papers of Lesourne and Leban (1982) and Stepan and Swoboda (1982)]. These papers are dealing with specific problems in finance, dividend and investment optimization.

When discussing the basic model of our dynamic analysis in chapter two, we already pointed out some extensions of this kind of management modeling. Although many authors are aware of the effects of personal taxation their studies in a dynamic setting are lacking this subject, however. Research into this subject has been conducted by Yla-Liedenpohja (1978), but by the assumption of an infinite time horizon and taking debt financing not especially into account, a number of interesting topics were left out of consideration. Also Tuovila (1983) has considered this topic. Although he has derived the optimal policies, he has paid more attention to a numerical solution of the problem; that is, the optimal trajectory, that covers the policy of the firm during the whole planning period, was numerically demonstrated using three oil-product distribution firms rather than analytically derived.

In section 5.2 we will describe a deterministic dynamic model of a single firm which behaves as if it maximizes its value conceived by tax homogeneous shareholders. In fact, we assume no separation of ownership and control. To do so, we modify the basic model of chapter two by including different personal tax rates. We use Optimal Control Theory to provide the analytical solution of the problem, which is indicated in section 5.3 and proved in appendix A1. Section 5.4 presents a further analysis of the economic results. Since we distinguish between personal tax rates on capital gain and dividend, it turns out that in the final stages it could be optimal to retain all earnings in order to finance investment, although the net return is less than the time preference rate of the shareholders. In addition, the firm will at last finance investment with equity only, even in the case of cheap debt financing. Finally, we present in section 5.5 results of a sensitivity analysis concerning parameters that are interesting for economic analysis, such as the personal tax rates and the discount rate.

5.2. The model

In this section we postulate a dynamic control model in order to analyse the impact of both corporate and personal taxation on the optimal dynamic policy of a single shareholder controlled firm. To that end we only need to modify the objective function of the basic model of chapter two.

So, within a deterministic setting we consider a value maximizing firm, which will at some known planning time z stop its activities. This planning horizon may be fixed by e.g. the investor's day of retirement. We may also, however, use another description of the problem: we consider a value maximizing investor who will sell the shares of a particular firm at some known time z. Formulating the problem in this way, the firm is allowed to continue its activities.

The shareholder of the firm is assumed to have personal tax rates on dividend τ_{di} and captial gain τ_{gi}. In agreement with most of the tax systems in use the tax rate on dividend is assumed to exceed the tax rate on capital gain, so that the ratio $(1-\tau_{gi})/(1-\tau_{di})$ exceeds one. Let X(T) be the amount of equity and D(T) the level of dividend payments at time T, then the shareholder has an investment which is valued by

$$\int_{T=0}^{z} (1-\tau_{di})D(T)e^{-iT}dT + X(z)e^{-iz} - \tau_{gi}(X(z)-X(0))e^{-iz} \tag{5.1}$$

where i is the shareholder's discount rate after personal taxes. Formulating the objective in this way, that is, with a separation of dividend income and capital gain, it turns out that not only the difference between the levels of the personal tax rates, but also the time lag valued by the time preference rate i will be of crucial importance.

Furthermore, the inclusion of personal taxation enables us to give another justification and explanation of the additional assumption (2.31), that is

$$i \neq (1-\tau_c)r \tag{5.2}$$

As stated in subsection 2.3.4 the purpose of this assumption is to avoid degenerated solutions. This assumption is justified by means of Van Loon's (1983) argument that only by coincidence an equality occurs, because of the separation of the debt and equity market. The inclusion of personal taxation generates another explanation of this assumption. A deterministic framework with perfect information and without taxation requires an equality between the discount rate and the interest rate. Since the shareholders' discount rate or time preference rate can be seen as the return after personal taxation, we may rewrite in the tradition of Brealey and Myers (1981) expression (5.2) into

$$(1-\tau_{ri})r \neq (1-\tau_c)r \tag{5.3}$$

where τ_{ri} denotes the personal tax rate on debt income of shareholder i. So, in fact only the case $\tau_{ri} = \tau_c$ is excluded by assumption (5.2).

Finally, we explicitly rule out contraction policies by assuming a sufficiently low initial production capacity, that is

$$(1-\tau_c)\frac{dO}{dK}(K(0)) > \max\,(i,\ (1-\tau_c)r) \tag{5.4}$$

In order to avoid confusion, we recall assumption (2.31):

$$(1-\tau_c)\frac{dO}{dK}(0) > \max\,(i,\ (1-\tau_c)r) \tag{5.5}$$

and we remark that the former assumption implies, due to the concavity of O(K), the latter one.

For convenience, we survey the model in its full length. Non relevant variables are omitted however.

$$\underset{D,I,Y}{\text{Maximize}}\ (1-\tau_{di})\int_{T=0}^{z} D(T)e^{-iT}dT + (1-\tau_{gi})X(z)e^{-iz} \tag{5.6}$$

subject to

$$\dot{K} = I - aK \tag{5.7}$$

$$\dot{X} = (1-\tau_c)[O(K)-rY] - D \tag{5.8}$$

$$K = X + Y \tag{5.9}$$

$$Y \leq hX \tag{5.10}$$

$$Y(0) = hX(0) = hx_0 > 0 \tag{5.11}$$

$$D \geq 0,\ I \geq 0,\ Y \geq 0,\ K \geq 0,\ X \geq 0 \tag{5.12}$$

and subject to the additional assumptions (5.2) and (5.4).

The dynamic problem, described by the above formulated model can be solved analytically by using Optimal Control Theory. In appendix A1 the necessary and sufficient conditions for an optimal solution are derived by means of a principle that strongly resembles the standard maximum principle of Pontryagin c.s. (1962), followed by the 'iterative policy connecting' procedure designed by Van Loon (1983) in order to transform the set of necessary conditions into a solution that concerns the optimal policy of the firm over the whole planning period.

5.3. Optimal solution

Applying the procedure of Van Loon (1983) we may discern five different feasible paths or stages, each characterized by the set of restrictions that is active or inactive during the relevant period. These feasible paths result in different policies with regard to capital structure, investment and/or dividend. Since both the two state equations as well as all contraints are the same as in the model of chapter two, we obtain the same policies. It suffices now to summarize the economic interpretation of these policies (see also table 2.1).

Policy 1: maximum growth

The policy is to attract as much debt as possible, to retain all earnings and to use this money to finance new investment in order to realize a maximum increase of the amount of capital goods.

Policy 2: consolidation

The amount of capital goods remains on a constant level K^*_{YX} such that marginal revenue equals marginal net cost of debt. Retentions are used to pay back debt money and investment is put down to replacement level.

Policy 3: growth with equity only

The firm possesses no debt and no dividend is distributed. Retentions are used to finance investment in order to increase the amount of capital goods.

Policy 4: stationary stage with equity only

The amount of capital goods remains on a constant level K_X^* such that marginal revenue equals the time preference rate of the shareholders. Investment is on the corresponding replacement level and remaining earnings are distributed to the shareholders. This policy is only feasible if equity is relatively cheap. That is, if $i < (1-\tau_c)r$.

Policy 5: stationary stage with maximum debt

Again the amount of capital goods is on a constant level K_Y^*, but now such that marginal net revenue equals the weighted sum of the costs of equity and debt. Similar to policy 4 investment is on its corresponding replacement level and remaining earnings are distributed to the shareholders. Contrary to policy 4 this policy is only feasible if $i > (1-\tau_c)r$.

Van Loon's iterative policy connecting procedure enables us to couple two different policies. By applying the necessary testing procedure again and again, we may find a still longer string of subsequent policies. Whether a coupling of two policies will be successful depends among others on the values of the financial and fiscal parameters i, r, τ_c, τ_{di}, τ_{gi} and τ_{ri}. Since all policy strings are subsets of only two different policy strings, we discuss only the 'master string' and corresponding master trajectory of each set.

The first set occurs if $i < (1-\tau_c)r$. Its master trajectory is depicted in figure 5.1 and is a result of the policy string:

policy 1 → policy 2 → policy 3 → policy 4 → policy 3

The sequence and explanation of the first four policies is similar to those of the basic model without personal taxation. The reader may find its description in subsection 2.3.6. However, due to the fixed planning horizon and the non-neutrality of the tax regime with respect to the distribution of corporate profit, it holds for $T > t_{43}$ that one dollar dividend net of taxes is less worth than a net increase of equity at T = z caused by a retention of one dollar:

$$(1-\tau_{di})e^{-iT}\partial X(T) < (1-\tau_{gi})e^{-iz}\partial X(z) \text{ for } T > t_{43} \tag{5.13}$$

Although marginal net revenue $(1-\tau_c)dO/dK$ will fall below the discount rate i, the optimal policy is to stop dividend payment and start expansion investment again, because this loss is counterbalanced by the tax advantage. So, the advantage of the lower tax rate on capital gain ($\tau_{gi} < \tau_{di}$) exceeds the drawback of discounting the salvage value at the planning horizon. Consequently, the discount rate not longer expresses the desired rate of return on equity. In section 5.4 we study this case extensively.

The second set of policy strings occurs if the discount rate exceeds the net cost of debt: $i > (1-\tau_c)r$. The master trajectory starts in the same way as both the previous one and the corresponding trajectory of the basic model without personal taxation: due to the cheapness of debt money it is optimal to borrow the maximum amount that is possible and invest both retentions and debt in capital goods (see figure 5.2). As soon as the production capacity has reached the level K_Y^*, this accelerated growth is cut off at once at $T = t_{15}$. At this level marginal net corporate revenue equals the weighted sum of net costs of debt and equity:

$$(1-\tau_c)\frac{dO}{dK} = \frac{1}{1+h}\, i + \frac{h}{1+h}\,(1-\tau_c)r \tag{5.14}$$

As showed in subsection 2.3.6 this expression implies an equality of marginal return on equity and the discount rate i. Investment falls down to replacement level and remaining earnings are issued to the shareholders.

Corresponding to the previous master policy string a moment occurs at which the firm stops its dividend distribution and starts expansion investment by retaining earnings. Furthermore, it is optimal to borrow as much as possible because borrowing still increases profit and thus raises the rate of growth till $K = K_{YX}^*$ (policy 1). According to the case of relatively expensive debt, the firm now drops debt to save $(1-\tau_c)r$ interest payments per unit (policy 2) and finally it starts growing in a self financing regime till the end of the planning period (policy 3). So we get:

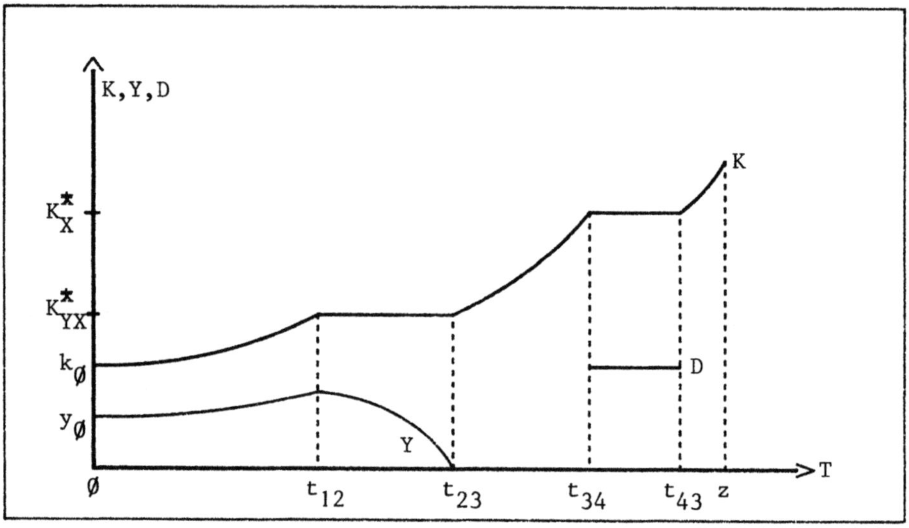

figure 5.1: optimal master trajectory if $i < (1-\tau_c)r$

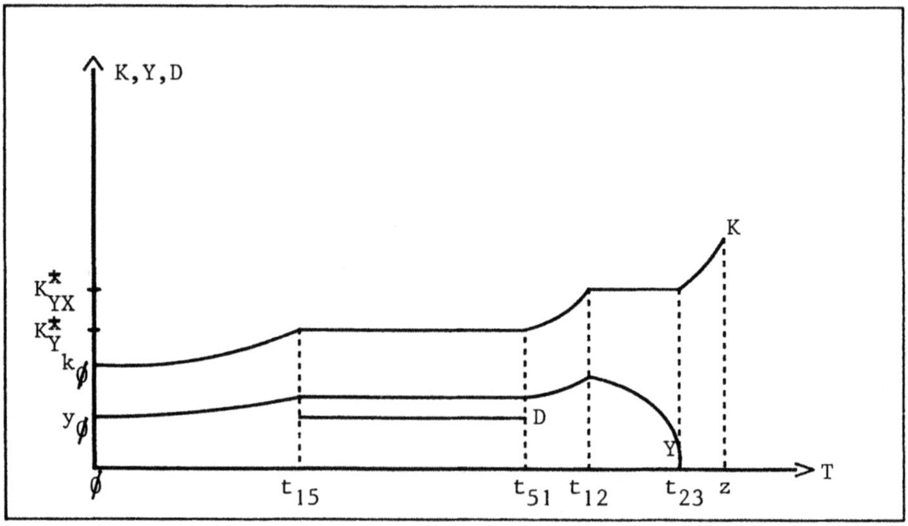

figure 5.2: optimal master trajectory if $i > (1-\tau_c)r$

policy 1 → policy 5 → policy 1 → policy 2 → policy 3

The optimal policy string succeeding policy 5 depends among others on the spread between the personal tax rates, that is, the tax advantage yielded by the shareholders receiving capital gain instead of dividend. A lower value of $(1-\tau_{gi})/(1-\tau_{di})$ will not only alter the final policy, but also postpone the moment $T = t_{51}$ and reduce the number of stages to pass through (see also subsection 5.5.1). Note, that the firm wants to get rid of debt although it is cheap compared to the corporate cost of equity. Altough we will explain this striking result in the next section, we notice that the net corporate marginal revenue $(1-\tau_c)dO/dK$ may fall below the net cost of debt due to the expansion drift of the investor as a result of the non-neutrality of the tax system.

A first comparison of the master trajectories with those of a problem without personal taxation shows two striking differences:

- in final stages it may be optimal to retain all earnings in order to finance expansion investment with a net corporate return less than the shareholder's discount rate, instead of distributing profit at a constant level, which is the optimal policy of our basis model without personal taxation
- the firm will at last finance investment with equity only, that is, the firm may want to get rid of debt, even when $(1-\tau_c)r < i$.

In the next sections we will extensively consider the impact of personal taxation on the optimal decision rules and compare the problems with and without personal taxation with each other.

5.4. Further analysis

In addition to the previous presentation of the optimal policy strings, we modify the two global decision rules, which we have presented in subsection 2.3.6 and which together constitute the optimal policy of the firm.

As we have argued in the above mentioned subsection the financial structure of the firm has two extreme cases: the case that the assets are financed by equity only and the case that the firm is levered at the maximum rate. At each state the firm will try to realize such a financial structure as to maximize marginal return to equity R_X. Since the profit distribution policy of the firm and thus personal taxation has no impact on the present marginal return to equity, we may, given the level of the production capacity, still write

$$R_X = (1-\tau_c)\frac{dO}{dK} + (1-\tau_c)(\frac{dO}{dK} - r)\frac{Y}{X} \tag{5.15}$$

which due to the definition of K^*_{YX}, that is, $(1-\tau_c)dO/dK = (1-\tau_c)r$, implies

$$\text{choose for } \begin{Bmatrix} \text{selffinancing} \\ \text{maximum debt} \end{Bmatrix} \text{ if } K \begin{pmatrix} > \\ < \end{pmatrix} K^*_{YX} \tag{5.16}$$

Consequently, personal taxation has no impact on the financing decision rule of the firm.

With respect to the dividend/investment decision rule, the firm may spend its earnings in two ways: to pay out dividend or to retain it in order to finance investment and/or pay back debt money. The last mentioned decision has been discussed implicitly in the financing decision rule: (5.16) redemption of debt starts as soon as the firm attains the K^*_{YX}-level on which selffinancing becomes optimal. The second situation, financing new investment, is certainly preferable as long as marginal return to equity exceeds the discount of the shareholders, for this rate expresses the rate of return that shareholders can obtain elsewhere. Accordingly, the optimal policy is in general to pay out dividend and invest only on the replacement level as soon as marginal return to equity equals the discount rate.

So far so good, but what happens if the discount rate exceeds marginal return to equity? In absence of personal taxation one can argue that this situation only occurs if the initial amount of capital goods is too high to make production at that level profitable. Van Loon (1983) argues that the optimal policy is a decrease of the capital stock by issuing all revenues. On top of this statement, however, the introduction of personal taxation brings on a second possible situation, which results in an additional dividend/investment decision rule to point out.

On the stationary dividend stages 4 and 5 the firm has to decide whether it will continue dividend distribution or start to retain earnings. If we suppose the firm to hold this earning in cash, so that no additional revenue is obtained, shareholders value the former possibility by $(1-\tau_{di})e^{-iT}$ and the latter one by $(1-\tau_{gi})e^{-iz}$. This means that capital gain on one hand will be more profitable in view of the tax advantage ($\tau_d > \tau_g$), but on the other hand less due to the time lag $z-T > 0$. So, the decision to continue profit distribution or to start retaining earnings and to hold cash money depends on whichever (in)equality holds in

$$(1-\tau_{di})e^{-iT} \gtreqless (1-\tau_{gi})e^{-iz} \tag{5.17}$$

It is obvious that given the values of the tax rates, the discount rate and the planning horizon at only one time instand, $T = t^*_{ex}$ the equality sign of expression (5.17) will hold. Note that in absence of personal taxation the decision always will be in favour of a dividend policy and, consequently, t^*_{ex} equals z.

In spite of the decreasing marginal return to equity, however, expansion investment still acquires positive revenue which can be used again to finance more expansion investment. So, the shareholders will not only receive the dollar of retention but also the total increase of equity during the time interval $[T,z]$. This increase depends on the rate of return on equity during that relevant time interval. The value of time, $T = t^*_{ex}$, therefore, will be determined by

$$(1-\tau_{di})e^{-it^*_{ex}}.\partial X(t^*_{ex}) = (1-\tau_{gi})e^{-iz}.\partial X(z) \tag{5.18}$$

In appendix A2 we will prove that this is equivalent to

$$(1-\tau_{di})e^{-it^*_{ex}} = (1-\tau_{gi})e^{-iz}.\exp\left(\int_{T=t^*_{ex}}^{z} R_X(T)dT\right) \tag{5.19}$$

where R_X denotes the marginal return to equity, which is given by

$$R_X = \begin{cases} (1-\tau_c)\frac{dO}{dK} & \text{if } Y(T) = 0 \\ (1-\tau_c)(\frac{dO}{dK}(1+h)-hr) & \text{if } Y(T) > 0 \end{cases} \qquad (5.20)$$

This discussion thus results in the next dividend/investment decision rule:

- do not pay out dividend and increase the amount of equity

  if $R_X > i$ (5.21)

  or $R_X < i$ and $T > t^*_{ex}$ (5.22)

- invest only on replacement level and pay out all remaining earnings

  if $R_X = i$ (5.23)

- decrease capital stock and pay out all earnings

  if $R_X < i$ and $T < t^*_{ex}$ (5.24)

If we combine the dividend/investment and financing decision rules, we get table 5.1. Since we only need to know the value of the marginal return to equity, this table is very useful to achieve the optimal policy of the firm.

	$R_X > r(1-\tau_c)$	$R_X < r(1-\tau_c)$
$R_X > i$	expansion investment with debt	expansion investment without debt
$R_X = r(1-\tau_c)$	redemption of debt	
$R_X = i$	stationary dividend with debt	stationary dividend without debt
$R_X < i$ $T < t^*_{ex}$	contraction without debt redemption	contraction
$R_X < i$ $T > t^*_{ex}$	expansion investment with debt	expansion investment without debt

Table 5.1: optimal financing, investment and dividend policy where t^*_{ex} satisfies expression (5.20) and R_X denotes the rate of return on equity.

We remark that this table includes, for the sake of completeness, the conditions under which a contraction policy is optimal.

5.5. Sensitivity analysis

In this section we study the influence of environmental changes on six different features of the optimal policy string. This is a sensitivity analysis concerning parameters that are interesting for economic analysis: interest rate r, discount rate i, corporate tax rate τ_c and especially personal tax rates τ_{di} and τ_{gi}. In addition we show the impact of changes in the initial production capacity level K(0) and the planning horizon z.

Features of the policy string are the level of capital goods K^* on stationary stages, speed of growth of equity $\dot{X}$, level of capital gain X(z)-X(0), entry and exit point of the stationary dividend stage, t^*_{en} and t^*_{ex} respectively, and leverage rate Y/X.

Finally, we have to justify the selection of $\dot{X}$ as the speed of growth of the firm. We can measure a firm's size by means of several standards such as sales, employment or equity. Smyth et al (1975) and Shalit & Sankar (1977), have, however, shown that these standards are not simply interchangeable and different conclusions can be drawn depending on the measure chosen. As in our problem, where the shareholder's wealth after taxation has to be maximized, we have chosen equity as a measure of size of the firm, because this standard is relevant for the shareholder.

5.5.1. Influence of the fiscal parameters

a. corporate taxes

A reduction of the corporate tax rate has two direct consequences:

- a rise of the net cost of debt due to the tax decuctibility
- possibilities to increase (expansion) investment in view of lower tax payments.

The first one enables a switch of the inequality in $i \gtrless (1-\tau_c)r$ resulting in a policy switch of the firm in a low leverage strategy. Moreover, according to (5.3) such a reduction of the corporate tax rate implies that still lower taxed investors prefer a low leverage strategy. Contrary to marginal revenue, however, net marginal cost of finance is only partially influenced. Thus, such a reduction results into increasing profit and a larger amount of capital goods at stationary stages. A reduction of the corporate tax rate also increases earnings after tax payments from which (expansion) investment is to be paid. In this way growth accelerates which is demonstrated by

$$-\frac{\partial \dot{X}}{\partial \tau_c} = O(K)-rY > 0 \qquad (5.25)$$

On top of this we find that such a reduction will put forward the finish of the stationary stage, because of the increased value of the marginal return on equity. In addition, the final policy may change [see table 5.2]. No conclusion, however, is possible with respect to the start of dividend stages, because a reduction of the corporate tax rate causes two opposite influences: a rise of the speed of growth and a larger amount of capital goods to be reached. Nevertheless, we conclude that a reduction of the corporate tax rate rises the value of the firm and stimulates enterpreneur's activities.

b. personal taxes

The impact of changes in the value of the personal tax rates on the features, of the firm are obvious: a decrease of the dividend tax rate causes declining interest in capital gain, which results in a postponement of the finish of the stationary stages 4 and 5 respectively. As the speed of growth does not change, the total amount of net dividend payments rises. In addition, the final policy may alter due to the postponement of t^*_{ex}. By means of the transversality conditions we select those policies that may be final ones, that is, feasible at $T = z$ (see appendix A1). Using the features of the several stages we find the conditions that are expressed in table 5.2. We distinguish a financial and a fiscal condition. The first one depends on the financial setting of the firm and is the same as in models without personal taxes. The latter one indicates the investor's attitude towards the desired kind of income: the bigger the difference between the personal tax rates the more he prefers captial gain, that is, a rise of the amount of equity, instead of dividend.

The fiscal condition of table 5.2 is well understandable if we consider that the return on equity net of all taxes of a dividend paying firm is equal to $(1-\tau_{di})i$. So, a policy of retaining earnings e.g. is only optimal at $T = z$ if the net return after all taxes, $(1-\tau_g)(1-\tau_c)dO/dK$, equals at least $(1-\tau_d)i$. Recalling the features of the policies (see e.g. table 2.1), we see e.g. that policy 3 is the optimal final policy if

$$(1-\tau_{gi})(1-\tau_c)r > (1-\tau_{gi})(1-\tau_c)\frac{dO}{dK} = (1-\tau_{di})i \tag{5.26}$$

policy	final policy if
1	$i > (1-\tau_c)r$ and $1 < (1-\tau_{gi})/(1-\tau_{di}) < i/(1-\tau_c)r$
2	$i > (1-\tau_c)r$ and $(1-\tau_{gi})/(1-\tau_{di}) = i/(1-\tau_c)r$
3	$i > (1-\tau_c)r$ and $(1-\tau_{gi})/(1-\tau_{di}) > i/(1-\tau_c)r$
5	$i > (1-\tau_c)r$ and $(1-\tau_{gi})/(1-\tau_{di}) = 1$
3	$i < (1-\tau_c)r$ and $(1-\tau_{gi})/(1-\tau_{di}) > 1$
4	$i < (1-\tau_c)r$ and $(1-\tau_{gi})/(1-\tau_{di}) = 1$

Table 5.2: Conditions for final policies.

So, due to a lower value of the dividend tax rate, net return of a dividend paying policy rises and, accordingly, a policy of retaining earnings remains an optimal policy only if marginal return rises up to the higher level of $(1-\tau_{di})i$. Therefore, policy 2 or even policy 1 becomes a feasible final policy. Consequently, it turns out that the firm not always wants to get rid of debt money.

Finally note that dividend is distributed on a final stage only when the personal tax rates equal each other. This condition shows that similar models without personal taxation (see e.g. Ludwig (1978) or Van Loon (1983)) are in this respect special cases of our model.

If we consider, on the other hand, a rise of the dividend tax rate, the possibility occurs that the stationary dividend stage will disappear, that is, the difference between τ_{di} and τ_{gi} is such that it is never optimal to pay out dividend (see the dividend/investment decision rule, pointed out in section 5.4).

A fall or rise of the tax rate on capital gain gives almost the opposite picture of a change in the dividend tax rate.

5.5.2. Influence of the financial parameters

As earlier research has dealt with a sensitivity analysis in relation to financial parameters (see e.g. Van Loon (1983)) we discuss these results only briefly and refer for a comprehensive discussion to the research mentioned.

A rise of the interest rate causes increasing costs of finance implying a drop in the speed of growth in stages with both debt and equity. In the case of expensive debt the exit point of the stationary dividend stage will be postponed. A switch of inequality in $i \gtrless (1-\tau_c)r$ resulting in a switch of the policy of the firms belongs also to the possibilities.

An increase in the value of the discount rate has no influence on the speed of growth. The level of capital goods in stationary stages will decline and the exit points of these paths will be postponed due to the larger revenue for the investor elsewhere.

The results of an analysis with respect to the opposite changes, that is a fall of the relevant parameters, are summarized in table 5.3.

impact on \ a fall of	τ_c	τ_{di}	τ_{gi}	r	i
level stationar stage K^*	+	0	0	+/-	+
speed of growth $\dot{X}$	+	0	0	+	0
capital gain $X(z)-X(0)$	+	-	+	+	+
entry stationary stage t^*_{en}	?	0	0	?/-	-
exit stationary stage t^*_{ex}	-	+	-	-/0	-
leverage Y/X	-	0	0	+	-

Table 5.3: sensitivity analysis.

where

- $+$: rise of the feature value
- $-$: fall of the feature value
- 0 : no influence on the relevant feature
- ? : no conclusion possible due to opposite influences
- ./.: conclusion before separation sign applies only if $i < (1-\tau_c)r$, after separation sign if $i > (1-\tau_c)r$.

5.5.3. Interaction of fiscal parameters and the time preference rate

As stated before, the time preference rate i expresses the rate of return after taxation, that a shareholder can obtain elsewhere. In a deterministic setting this implies that the time preference rate depends on the market interest rate and the personal tax rate on debt income. As in most of the tax regimes the tax rate on dividends is positively correlated with the tax rate on debt income, we can write

$$i = i(\tau_{di}, r) \qquad (5.27)$$

where

$$\frac{\partial i}{\partial \tau_{di}} < 0 \text{ and } \frac{\partial i}{\partial r} > 0$$

So, a rise of the personal tax rate will generally reduce the discount rate. Considering this dependence we study once more the optimal policy string of the firm by considering two extreme cases.

The results of figure 5.3 are achieved under the assumption that the tax rate on dividend of investor A, τ_{dA}, differs much from the tax rate on capital gain, which is assumed to be a constant τ_g, and has such a value that

$$i_A(\tau_{dA}, r) < (1-\tau_c)r \qquad (5.28)$$

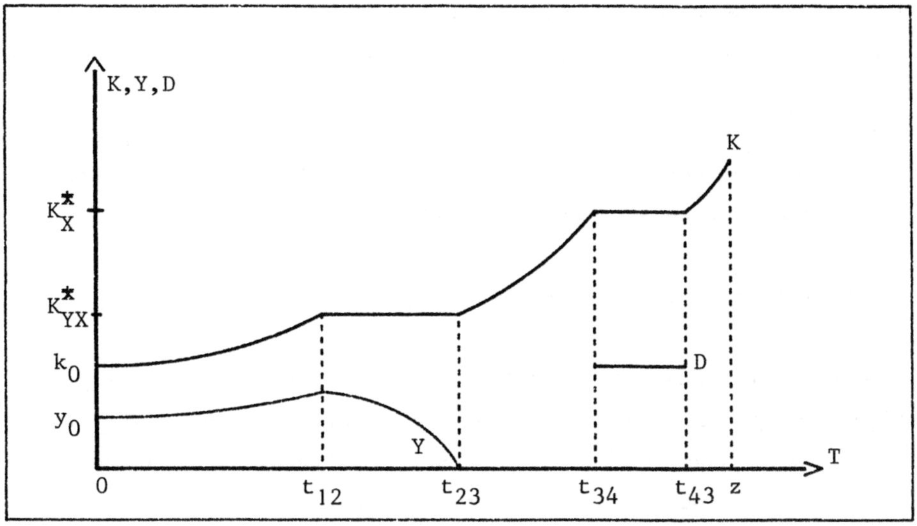

figure 5.3: optimal master trajectory if $i_A < (1-\tau_c)r$

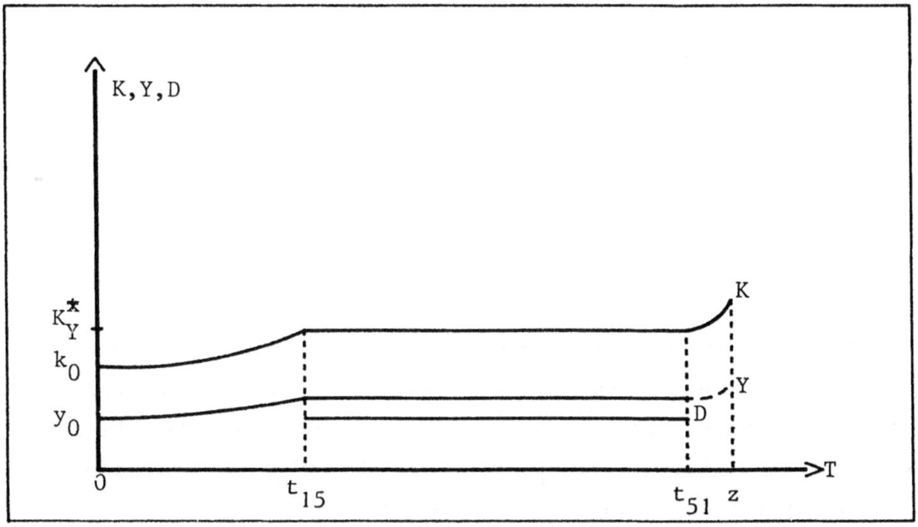

figure 5.4: optimal master trajectory if $i_B > (1-\tau_c)r$ and $(1-\tau_g)/(1-\tau_{dB}) < i_B/(1-\tau_c)r$

According to the Miller hypothesis this investor would prefer firms to follow a low leverage strategy, low dividend payments and high capital gains.

In the second case we assume that the tax rate on capital gain remains the same, but the tax rate on dividend of investors B, τ_{dB}, differs only little from this rate and has such a value that

$$i_B > (1-\tau_c)r \text{ and } (1-\tau_g)/(1-\tau_{dB}) < i_B/(1-\tau_c)r \qquad (5.29)$$

Under these circumstances the optimal evolution of the firm, represented by figure 5.4, will end up with policy 1. In the opinion of investor B the firm has to choose for a high leverage strategy and has to issue as much dividend as possible. These results can be obtained by analyzing tables 5.2 and 5.3.

So, similar to the Miller hypothesis we obtain clear differences between these two policy strings. On top of this similarity the Miller hypothesis is enlarged by the introduction of dynamics: investors in low tax brackets not only prefer a high leverage strategy and dividend rather than capital gain, but they also like to receive earnings as quick as possible, whereas investors in high tax brackets are willing to postpone earnings in view of their tax advantage and low time preference rate.

5.5.4. Switch of tax regime

Until now we have not specified the relation between the personal tax rates, that is, we did not select a specific tax regime. Suppose, however, that we have carried out the previous analyses under the classical tax regime, that is, $\tau_{di} = \tau_{ri}$. Which results will then provide a switch into the imputation system or two-rate system?

The imputation system attempts to give shareholders credit for tax paid by the firm by modifying the personal income tax. So, some fraction of the corporation tax paid on dividends is allowed to be subtracted from the personal income tax. Although this can be done in several ways, the final result is a decrease of the personal tax rate on dividend in relation to the tax rate on debt income: $\tau_{di} < \tau_{ri}$. Hence, the results of a switch from the classical into the imputation system can be achieved by analyzing the impact of a decrease of the personal tax rate on dividend on the optimal policy string of the firm. Recalling the results of table 5.3 we get a postponement of the finish of the stationary dividend policy and a decreasing interest in capital gain. Since the other policies and the level of the amount of capital goods on the stationary dividend stage do not change, the value of the firm's objective function, and thus the value of the firm, sharply rises.

Contrary to the imputation system, the two-rate system relieves the double taxation of dividends by alleviations in the corporate tax sphere rather than the personal tax sphere. When analyzing the results of a switch of tax system into the two-rate system, we are thus forced to modify the underlying dynamic model, in particular expression (5.8). So,

$$\dot{X} = O(K) - rY - [\tau_c(O(K)-rY-D)+\tau_{cd}D]$$

$$= (1-\tau_c)[O(K)-rY] - [1-(\tau_c-\tau_{cd})]D \tag{5.30}$$

where

τ_{cd}: corporate tax rate on distributed profit ($\tau_c > \tau_{cd}$).

Recalling the results of table 5.3 we see that none of the parameters will change due to the introduction of the two-rate system. Therefore, the optimal policy string remains the same. However, since also the production capacity level O(K) on the stationary dividend stage (and the amount of debt) will be unchanged, it turns out that the dividend level will rise (see expression (5.31) and thus the value of the firm.

Finally, we notice that high taxed investors, such as investor A of the previous subsection, profit more by such a switch of tax regime than low taxed investors.

5.5.5. Initial value and planning horizon

Given the initial values of equity x_0 and debt y_0, the planning horizon z must be such that the firm is able to pass through the presented master trajectories. If the planning period is shorter than depicted in figures 5.1 and 5.2, parts of the master trajectories will decay.

Given the values of financial parameters after corporate tax the exit point of the stationary dividend policy depends only on the personal tax rates on dividend and capital gain, τ_{di} and τ_{gi} respectively, and the planning horizon z. A shorter planning period, by putting forward z, thus results in a shorter stationary dividend stage, since the start of this stage will be unaffected.

A change of the initial values of equity and debt has no impact on the evolution pattern after finishing the stationary dividend policy. A rise of the initial values will shorten the first stage through with the start of the dividend policy will put forward. As the finish of this policy will be unchanged, a longer stationary dividend stage occurs.

We conclude that the stationary dividend stage will be very flexible and functions as a buffer in changes of initial values and the planning horizon.

5.6. Conclusion

In this chapter we considered especially the impact of tax systems on the optimal dynamic policy of a value maximizing firm by introducing both corporate and personal taxation. In this way we extended the dynamic theory of the firm. We derived an analytical solution by means of Optimal Control Theory. In addition, we discussed a decision rule in terms of the net return on equity, which constitutes the entire optimal policy string of the firm.

It turns out that the results differ from those of similar dynamic models without personal taxation in three ways:

- in final stages no dividend will be issued
- in some situations the firm wants to get rid of debt, even when debt is relatively cheap
- due to the difference between the tax rate on dividend and capital gain, it may be optimal to start expansion investment with a net return less than the discount rate.

Finally, sensitivity analysis showed the importance of the value of the personal tax rate in providing the optimal (final) policy. Assuming the discount rate to the dependent on the interest rate and the personal tax rate on dividend, we considered especially two extreme optimal policy strings to show the similarities with the Miller hypothesis. Contrary to Miller, however, we did not yet consider market equilibrium situations at which we will pay attention in chapter seven.

CHAPTER SIX

INDIVIDUAL INVESTOR BEHAVIOUR UNDER EQUILIBRIUM CONDITIONS

6.1. Introduction

In this chapter we enlarge the analysis of the previous chapter by allowing investors to sell the shares of the firm under consideration at some unknown point in time. Consequently, the investor's task is not only to determine the optimal policy of the firm during the period he owns and controls the corporation, but also the optimal selling moment of the shares at some market price. Thereafter, the investor may invest his money in the shares of another firm or in other investment opportunities.

In a way we consider an optimal control problem with a free endpoint. In this way we bear up against a possible criticism on the fixed endpoint analysis of the previous chapter: although the controller's aim is to reach the maximum value of his investment, his overall result may be poor, due to the obligation to control the firm until the end of the fixed plan period. In addition, we abandon the implicit assumption that the firm will liquidate at the planning horizon, or, at all events, that the investor will sell the firm at liquidation value. We now take the view that the firm will continue its activities after the actual planning horizon of the initial investor, so that a purchase will take place at market value. When characterizing the above described problem we may say that we consider a single firm that will be subsequently controlled by different value maximizing investors.

The allowance of shareholder-take-overs forces us to consider the market value of the firm at any point in time. This can be done in two ways. In section 6.2 we assume that the market value of the firm is exogeneously determined. That is, we consider the optimization problem of a single taxed investor who may at some unknown point in time sell the shares of the single firm under consideration at a known price. Thereafter, in section 6.3 we explore a model in which the selling price of the shares, that is, the share market value of the firm, is endogeneously determined. This model describes simultaneously the optimal policy problem of both the initial investor as well as of the second investor, who takes over the control of the firm. This second investor will be regarded as a representative of the market. The market value of the firm thus depends on the optimal policy string of the second investor. We will use an optimal control formulation with switching dynamics. Finally, we glance at a differential game approach. We will, however, consider a problem, that slightly differs from the former two analyses, since we assume that the investors will cooperate (section 6.4).

6.2. Free end point approach under equilibrium conditions

In this section we focus on a single value maximizing firm, which is controlled by a single taxed investor. Let $V_m(T)$ be the market value of the shares of the firm under consideration. In general, this value not only depends on the time T but also on the state of the firm. We assume that the market value in all possible situations, that might occur, is known with certainty. The investor thus has an investment which we value by

$$V_j(t) := \int_{T=0}^{t} (1-\tau_{dj})D(T)e^{-i_jT}dT + e^{-i_jt}(1-\tau_{gj})V_m(t) \qquad (6.1)$$

where

V_j: personal value of the firm to investor j which is among others a function of the endpoint t

t : the unknown selling moment

i_j: the investor's time preference rate after taxation

The aim of the investor is to maximize this objective functional by determining simultaneously the dividend, investment and financing policy as well as the optimal selling moment t^*. Since we may adopt the state equations and constraints of the basic model presented in chapter two and used in chapter five, the feasible policies are similar to those of chapter five. Moreover, we may use the results of table 5.1 in order to determine the optimal policy at each state of the firm.

We assume the known market value V_m, to be the result of the also known policy of a second investor, who buys the shares at T = t. For simplicity we propose an infinite planning horizon to the second investor. In the analysis that follows, we distinguish two cases: we first consider the case that the second investor is lower taxed than the initial one. Hereby, we assume for simplicity only that the second investor is tax exempted. Thereafter, we focus on the opposite case.

We may now rewrite the objective functional (6.1) of the initial investor, who is labeled investor 1, into:

$$V_1(0) = \int_{T=0}^{t} (1-\tau_{d1})D_1(T)e^{-i_1 T} dT + (1-\tau_{g1})e^{-i_1 t} \int_{T=t}^{\infty} D_2(T)e^{-i_2(T-t)} dT \quad (6.2)$$

The optimal selling moment t^* may be obtained by means of several methods. A simple way is to take the first derivative of (6.2) with respect to t. Hence,

$$\frac{\partial V_1(t)}{\partial t} = e^{-i_1 t}[(1-\tau_{d1})D_1(t) - (1-\tau_{g1})D_2(t) + (i_2-i_1)(1-\tau_{gi}) \int_{T=t}^{\infty} D_2(T)e^{i_2(T-t)} dT] \quad (6.3)$$

Given the state of the firm and the corresponding policies of both investors we may now analyse the sign of the above derivative. If the first derivative is positive, the investor prefers to keep on the shares of the firm and to postpone the selling moment; if it is equal to zero, the optimal selling moment t^* is found, whereas a negative value implies that the optimal selling moment is passed by.

Similar results may, however, be obtained by means of a more formal method. As we have stated in the introductory section, the problem may be considered as an optimal control problem with a free endpoint. To do so we use (6.1) as objective functional of the initial investor. Since the market value of the firm is assumed to be equal to the present value of investor's 2 dividend policy, that is

$$V_m(T) = \int_{S=T}^{\infty} D_2^*(S)e^{-i_2(S-T)} dS \tag{6.4}$$

we may consider V_m as a state variable which satisfies the additional state equation

$$\dot{V}_m(T) = i_2 V_m - D_2 \tag{6.5}$$

When we adopt furthermore the state equations and constraints of the basic model, presented in chapter two and applied in chapter five, we may formulate the problem as follows:

$$\max\{(1-\tau_{d1}) \int_{T=0}^{t} D_1(T)e^{-i_1 T} dT + e^{-i_1 t} V(t)(1-\tau_{g1})\} \tag{6.6}$$

$$\text{subject to } \dot{V} = i_2 V - D_2 \tag{6.7}$$

$$V(0) = v_0 \tag{6.8}$$

$$\dot{X} = (1-\tau_c)[O(K)-rY] - D_1 \tag{6.9}$$

$$\dot{K} = I - aK \tag{6.10}$$

$$K(0) = (1+h)X(0) = (1+h)x_0 > 0 \tag{6.11}$$

$$K = X + Y \tag{6.12}$$

$$D_1 \geq 0 \quad I \geq 0 \tag{6.13}$$

and subject to the assumptions (5.2) and (5.5), which after modification are expressed by

$$i_1 \neq (1-\tau_c)r \text{ and } i_2 \neq (1-\tau_c)r \tag{6.14}$$

$$(1-\tau_c)\frac{dO}{dK}(K(0)) > \max\{i_1, (1-\tau_c)r\} \tag{6.15}$$

If we apply, in addition to the usual necessary conditions for an optimal solution, the necessary condition to obtain the optimal end point t^* [see e.g. Kamien and Schwartz (1985), p. 148], we get the similar condition as found above by means of the first derivative of the objective functional (6.1). The proof of this derivation is given in the appendix B1. Hence,

$$\text{if } e^{-i_1 t}[(1-\tau_{d1})D_1(t)-(1-\tau_{g1})D_2(t)+(i_2-i_1)(1-\tau_{g1})V_m(t)] \left\{\begin{matrix} < \\ = \\ > \end{matrix}\right\} 0$$

$$\text{then } \left\{\begin{matrix} t^* = 0 \\ 0 < t^* < t \\ t^* = t \end{matrix}\right. \qquad (6.16)$$

Given the state of the firm and the corresponding policies of both investors, we may now analyse the above condition. Note that we may neglect $\exp(-i_1 t)$, because it will not affect the inequality in (6.16). To start our analysis we first recall the five different policies that both investors have to their disposal: growth with or without debt, redemption of debt and stationary dividend with or without debt. However, the final state of the firm produces, due to the policy of the first investor, the initial states of the firm for the second one. Since $i_1 < i_2$, investor 1 prefers higher levels of K than investor 2 and thus the possibility occurs, that the initial state to the second investor will not satisfy the assumption (6.15) after necessary modification. That is,

$$(1-\tau_c)\frac{dO}{dK}(K(t^*)) > \max\{i_2, (1-\tau_c)r\} \qquad (6.17)$$

This assumption was introduced in order to rule out contraction policies. For that reason, we have now to admit contraction policies, which imply a zero investment, so that the amount of capital goods decreases according to the depreciation rate a. All net sales, that is $(1-\tau_c)[O(K)+aK-rY]$, are used either to pay back present debt or to distribute dividend.

Secondly, we emphasize that the left hand side policy at $T = t^*$ is determined by investor 1 and the right hand side policy by investor 2.

So, in order to determine the optimal selling moment of the initial investor, we need to consider only those policies of the two investors, that both are feasible at one and the same state of the firm.

Finally, we note that in particular the dividend policy is of utmost importance with respect to the optimal selling moment. Therefore, we distinguish between three different levels, which can be obtained by recalling the results of table 5.1. When we focus on the dividend policy of investor j, we get the results as presented in table 6.1.

optimal dividend level investor j	condition	label corresponding policy
0	$R_X > i_j$	zero dividend policy
$(1-\tau_c)[O(K)-rY]$	$R_X = i_j$	stationary dividend policy
$(1-\tau_c)[O(K)-rY]+aK$	$R_X < i_j$	contraction policy

table 6.1: Optimal dividend level desired by investor j, given the production capacity level K and the corresponding rate of return R_X [see section 5.4.1].

Since any of both investors has three different kinds of dividend policies to his disposal, we have to check the feasibility and optimality of nine combinations at the end- or switch-point. These combinations are summarized in table 6.2.

combination	policy investor 1	condition	policy investor 2
1	zero dividend	$R_X>i_2>i_1$	zero dividend
2	zero dividend	$i_1<R_X=i_2$	stationary dividend
3	zero dividend	$i_1<R_X<i_2$	contraction
4	stationary dividend	$i_1=R_X<i_2$	contraction
5	stationary dividend	$i_1=R_X=i_2$	stationary dividend
6	stationary dividend	$i_1=R_X>i_2$	zero dividend
7	contraction	$i_1>R_X>i_2$	zero dividend
8	contraction	$i_1>R_X=i_2$	stationary dividend
9	contraction	$i_1>R_X<i_2$	contraction

Table 6.2: combinations of dividend policies at the switching point t^*

However, only the first four mentioned combinations are feasible. Combinations 5 and 6 are not satisfying the condition $i_2 > i_1$, whereas the combinations 7 through 9 are precluded by the initial condition (6.15). We will thus consider the following four feasible switch situations and check whether one of it satisfies the equality sign of the optimality condition (6.16).

Combination 1:
<u>zero dividend policy investor 1 → zero dividend policy investor 2.</u>

Both investors are not paid out any dividend. Whether the investors pursue a growth policy with or without debt or even a redemption policy is not important, since it turns out that the first part of expression (6.16) is always positive:

$$(i_2-i_1)(1-\tau_{g1})V_m(t) > 0 \text{ for all } t \tag{6.18}$$

So, in such a situation and state of the firm it is in favour of the initial investor to continue his policy and to keep the shares of the firm. Notice that this situation contains all states of the firm at which it holds that the marginal return to equity exceeds the time preference rate of both the investors: $R_X > \max\{i_1,i_2\} = i_2$. We may also say that we have considered all states at which both investors will not distribute profit.

Combination 2:
<u>zero dividend policy investor 1 → stationary dividend policy investor 2.</u>

Investor 2 prefers to pursue a stationary dividend policy. This implies that the state of the firm is such that the marginal return to equity is equal to the time preference rate of the second investor: $R_X = i_2$. Since $i_1 < i_2$ it is at such a state optimal for investor 1 to retain earnings instead of paying out dividend. The sign of condition (6.16) is now given by:

$$-(1-\tau_{g1})D_2(t) + (i_2-i_1)(1-\tau_{g1})D_2(t)/i_2 =$$
$$-(1-\tau_{g1})D_2(t)(i_1/i_2) < 0 \tag{6.19}$$

Since the first derivate is negative, postponement of the selling moment harms the initial investor.

Combination 3:

zero dividend policy investor 1 → contraction policy investor 2.

This sequence of policies may occur at any state satisfying $i_1<R_X<i_2$. However, we can conclude that due to the zero dividend policy of investor 1 the sign of (6.16) will always be negative. To that end we first notice that

$$\int_{T=t}^{\infty} D_2(T)e^{-i_2(T-t)}dT < \int_{T=t}^{\infty} D_2(t)e^{-i_2(T-t)}dT =$$
$$\int_{T=t}^{\infty} [(1-\tau_c)(O(K)-rY)+aK]e^{-i_2(T-t)}dT = \frac{(1-\tau_c)(O(K)-rY)+aK}{i_2} \tag{6.20}$$

This result is due to the contraction policy of investor 2, which is succeeded by a stationary dividend policy. Accordingly, D(T) will descend to the stationary level.

If we now substitute the corresponding policies, indicated in table 6.1 into condition (6.16) and if we neglect the exponential function, we get

$$-(1-\tau_{g1})D_2(t) + (i_2-i_1)(1-\tau_{g1})\int_{T=t}^{\infty} D_2(T)e^{-i_2(T-t)}dT <$$

$$-(1-\tau_{g1})[(1-\tau_c)(O(K)-rY)+aK] + (i_2-i_1)(1-\tau_{g1})[(1-\tau_c)(O(K)-rY)+aK]/i_2 =$$

$$-\frac{i_1}{i_2}(1-\tau_{g1})[(1-\tau_c)(O(K)-rY)+aK] < 0 \tag{6.21}$$

The negative sign implies that the optimal end point is already passed by.

Combination 4:
stationary dividend policy investor 1 → contraction policy investor 2.

Investor 1 only distributes profit when the marginal return to equity equals his time preference rate: $R_X = i_1$. Since the time preference rate of the second investor exceeds that of the first one, the second investor prefers at this state a contraction policy. Using (6.21) we now get

$$(1-\tau_{d1})D_1(t) - (1-\tau_{g1})D_2(t) + (i_2-i_1)(1-\tau_{g1}) \int_{T=t}^{\infty} D_2(T)e^{-i_2(T-t)} dT <$$

$$(1-\tau_{d1})(1-\tau_c)(O(K)-rY) - \frac{i_1}{i_2}(1-\tau_{g1})[(1-\tau_c)(O(K)-rY)+aK] \tag{6.22}$$

Let us assume that

$$i_1 = r(1-\tau_{r1}) \text{ and } i_2 = r \tag{6.23}$$

which is in agreement with $i_2 > i_1$. Expression (6.22) is thus negative if

$$[(1-\tau_{d1})-(1-\tau_{g1})(1-\tau_{r1})](1-\tau_c)[O(K)-rY]-(1-\tau_{g1})(1-\tau_{r1})aK < 0 \tag{6.24}$$

Whether this inequality holds or not, depends on the levels of the tax rates and both the constants r and a. However, if we consider e.g. the classical tax regime ($\tau_{d1}=\tau_{r1}$), we get the condition

$$\tau_{g1}[(1-\tau_c)(O(K)-rY)] - (1-\tau_{g1})aK < 0 \tag{6.25}$$

which may hold, since the tax rate on capital gain is often very close to zero.

When studying the above findings, we first note that no sequence of policies exists such that the relevant first derivative equals zero. This is a result from the discontinuity of the dividend policies. Secondly, we observe that the inequality in condition (6.16) switches from negative into positive as soon as the production capacity has reached such a level that the rate of return on equity equals the time preference rate of the second investor. To illustrate this observation, we indicate the locations of the four feasible combinations into the evolution pattern of the firm.

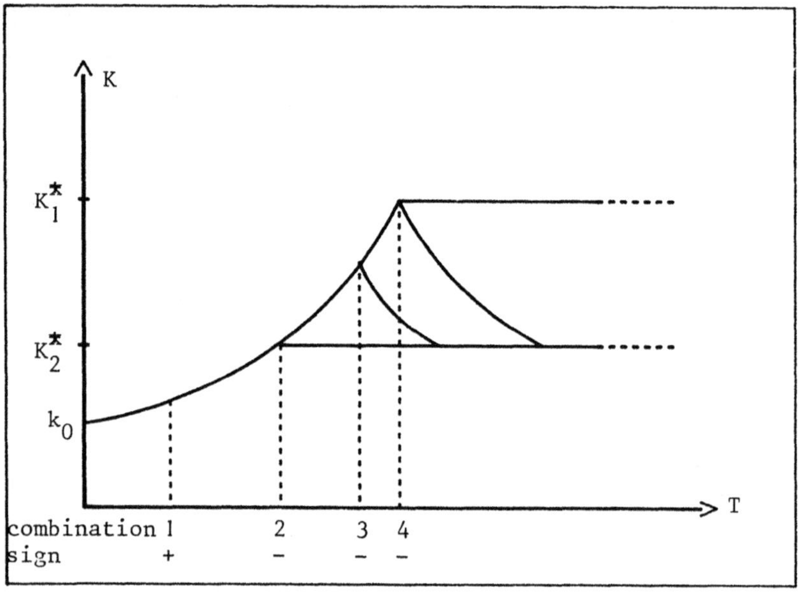

Figure 6.1: location of feasible switching points.

We may summarize the above findings in the following conclusion:

In case of only one buyer, that is investor 2, it is optimal for the initial investor to sell the firm's stock as soon as the state of the firm is such that marginal return to equity equals the time preference rate of the second investor.

The optimal policy string of the firm under consideration will thus be:

zero dividend policy investor 1 → stationary dividend policy investor 2

Whether the zero-dividend policy of investor 1 contains the evolution stages 1 to 3, that is, growth with maximum debt, redemption of debt and growth without debt, or a subset of these policies, depends on the values of the relevant time preference rates and thus of the personal tax rates. To clarify this, we firstly note that this result is derived under the assumption that the initial investor is subject to personal taxation, whereas the second one is tax exempt. However, the result may be extended to all cases in which the tax rates τ_{d1} and τ_{r1} of the initial investor exceed those of the second one. Hence, in case that $i_2 > (1-\tau_c)r$, that is $0 < \tau_{r2} < \tau_c$, the firm's policy string consists of only a maximum growth policy succeeded by a stationary dividend policy, both with maximum debt (see figure 6.2).

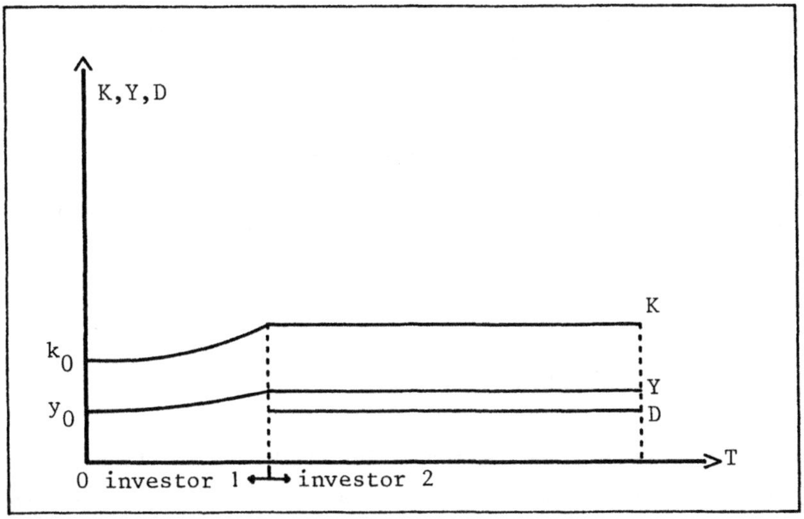

Figure 6.2: the firm's optimal policy string when $0 < \tau_{r2} < \tau_c$.

When $i_2 < (1-\tau_c)r$, or equivalently $\tau_{r2} > \tau_c$, the optimal policy string consists of four different succeeding policies: growth with maximum debt, redemption of debt, growth without debt (all pursued by investor 1) and finally a stationary dividend policy without debt pursued by investor 2 (see figure 6.3).
Finally, the situation $\tau_{r2} = \tau_c$ is excluded, because it will lead to degenerate solutions.

We complete this analysis by considering the situation in which the tax exempt investor is the initial one. It turns out that in case the marginal return to equity exceeds both the time preference rates, that is $R_X > i_2 > i_1$, an immediate switch of investor is optimal, so that we are back to the previous case. If the initial state of the firm is such that investor 2 pays out dividend, that is $R_X < i_2$, he will never surrender the control of the firm.

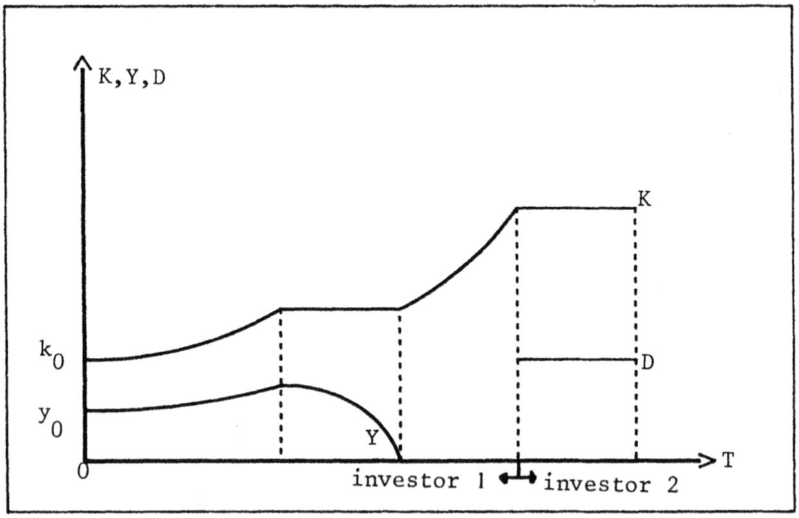

Figure 6.3: the firm's optimal policy string in case $\tau_{r2} > \tau_c$.

6.3. A competitive approach

In this section we explore a model in which the selling price of the shares, that is the share market value of the firm, is endogeneously determined. The model describes simultaneously the optimal policy problem of both the initial investor as well as of the second investor, who may take over the control of the firm at some unknown moment t. The value, that the initial investor receives at the sales moment, will thus depend on the optimal future policy string of the second investor.

In fact we consider two problems, that of investor 1 and 2 respectively, which are connected with each other at the sales moment. We will formulate the problem, however, as a single optimal control problem. For its description we develop a time dependent linear combination of two models with a selection variable S(T), which denotes the actual controller of the firm. We therefore rewrite the objective functional (6.2) into

$$\int_{T=0}^{\infty} [S(T)(1-\tau_{d1})D_1(T)e^{-i_1 T} +$$
$$e^{-i_1 T'(T)}(1-\tau_{g1})(1-S(T))D_2(T)e^{-i_2(T-T'(T))}]dT \tag{6.26}$$

where

S : selection variable, $0 < S(T) < 1$

T': artificial time variable

Due to the linearity of the model the variable S(T) will behave itself as an integer variable. If S(T) = 1, investor 1 controls the firm, whereas S(T) = 0 implies that investor 2 is the manager and owner of the firm.

The artificial time variable T'(T) runs at the same pace as natural time as long as investor 1 manages the firm. As soon as investor 2 will take over the control, the artificial time T'(T) stops and equals the optimal sales moment t^*. So, T'(T) can be considered as a state variable, which movement in time is governed by the control variable S(T). Thus,

$$\dot{T}'(T) = S(T)$$
$$T'(0) = 0 \tag{6.27}$$

Modeling the problem in this way, it has much in common with the 'artificial time'-approach, which has been suggested by Vind (1967) in order to smooth jumps in the state variables. In this line the model may be regarded as the formulation of the second problem investor in order to determine the optimal initial jump $K(t^*) - K(0)$.

We will continue the formulation of the linear combination problem by adopting the state equations and restrictions of the basic model we have presented in chapter two. Of course, these expressions need to be modified, since two decision makers are involved in controlling the firm. We may carry on with a complete separation of the two models by using different state variables for the two investors. Each state variable evolves according to its own state equation, whereas the right hand side limit of the state variable of the first investor must equal the left hand side limit of the corresponding state variable of the second investor in order to guarantee the continuity of the state variable under consideration in the switching point.

Another possibility is the use of only one variable to express the amount of equity and the following description of its evolution:

$$\dot{X} = S[(1-\tau_c)(O(K)-rY_1) - D_1] + (1-S)[(1-\tau_c)(O(K)-rY_2) - D_2] \tag{6.28}$$

$$X(0) = x_0 \tag{6.29}$$

In this way, the problem may also be considered as a sequence of optimal control problems. Luhmer (1982) describes this class of problems, which is labeled 'switching dynamics', and derives the necessary conditions for an optimal solution. However, it is sufficient to include the switch variable S in only the objective functional. This is quite reasonable, since in case that S(T) = 1, positive values of the control variables of the second investors will only reduce the possibilities of the first investor, which is on strained terms with the indicated value of S. Moreover, in appendix B2 we prove that situations, in which, for instance, the first investor is the owner and the control variables of the second investor are non zero, are implicitly ruled out, so that we may neglect additional assumptions to avoid such situations. The following formulation thus describes the problem under consideration. Since K = X + Y, the variable Y has been eliminated.

$$\text{maximize } \left(\int_{T=0}^{\infty} [S(1-\tau_{d1})D_1 e^{-i_1 T} + (1-S)(1-\tau_{g1})e^{-i_1 T'} D_2 e^{-i_2(T-T')}]dT \right. \tag{6.30}$$

subject to

$$\dot{X} = (1-\tau_c)[O(K) - r(K-X)] - D_1 - D_2 \tag{6.31}$$

$$X(0) = x_0 \tag{6.32}$$

$$\dot{K} = I_1 + I_2 - aK \tag{6.33}$$

$$K(0) = k_0 > 0 \tag{6.34}$$

$$\dot{T}' = S \tag{6.35}$$

$$T'(0) = 0 \tag{6.36}$$

$$K - X \geq 0 \tag{6.37}$$

$$(1+h)X - K \geq 0 \tag{6.38}$$

$$D_1 \geq 0 \qquad D_2 \geq 0 \tag{6.39}$$

$$I_1 \geq 0 \qquad I_2 \geq 0 \tag{6.40}$$

$$0 \leq S \leq 1 \tag{6.41}$$

Formulating the problem is this way it looks much like an attempt to find candidates for a so-called 'Pareto-solution' of a dynamic game between two cooperative players. In a dynamic game two or more decision makers will try to control common state variables in a way that their objective functionals are optimized. In case the decision makers cooperate, we seek for a Pareto-solution. Candidates for a Pareto solution may be found by solving a related optimal control problem which formulation is quite similar to the above one [see e.g. Leitmann (1974)], since it is a linear combination of the objective functionals. However, in case of finding condidates for a Pareto solution, the variable S is a constant one, since the two players cooperate and have assigned constant weights S and 1-S to their objective functionals. In our description, S is a time dependent variable, which will actually alternate between zero and one. The two investors do not cooperate in the sense of Pareto, but are maximizing the revenue of their personal investment given the state of the firm and the possibilities of the other player. As stated in the introductory section, we in fact consider the optimization problem of a single taxable investor, who may at some unknown point in time sell the shares of the single firm under consideration at a price, which is determined by a second investor, who on his turn is regarded as a representative of the market.

The optimal solution can be obtained in the same way as those of the chapters two and five: we first derive the necessary conditions for optimality by means of Pontryagin's maximum principle and thereafter we apply Van Loon's policy connecting procedure (see appendix B2).

Considering the given description of the problem it is not surprising that the firm's optimal policy string is the same as derived in the previous section. The only difference between the two problems is the determination of the optimal policy of the second investor, which is exogeneous in section 6.2 and endogeneous in this section. Nevertheless, in both the cases this policy string satisfies the corresponding optimality conditions.

For the sake of convenience we summarize the above findings by indicating the optimal solution in its full length. The derivation of this solution is presented in appendix B2.

We first recall the policies that both the investors have to their disposal:

label	policy
1.j	growth with maximum debt
2.j	redemption of debt
3.j	growth without debt
4.j	stationary dividend without debt
5.j	stationary dividend with debt
6.j	contraction

Table 6.3: disposable policies, where $j = 1,2$ indicates the investor.

The optimal policies strings are now given by:

<u>if $i_2 > i_1 > (1-\tau_c)r$</u>

$K(0) > K^*_{Y1}$: policy 6.1 → policy 5.1

$K(0) = K^*_{Y1}$: policy 5.2

$K^*_{Y2} < K(0) < K^*_{Y2}$: policy 6.2 → policy 5.2

$K(0) = K^*_{Y2}$: policy 5.2

$K(0) < K^*_{Y2}$: policy 1.1 → policy 5.2

<u>if $i_2 > (1-\tau_c)r > i_1$</u>

$K(0) > K^*_{X1}$: policy 6.1 → policy 4.1

$K(0) = K^*_{X1}$: policy 4.1

$K^*_{X2} < K(0) < K^*_{X1}$: policy 6.2 → policy 4.2

$K(0) = K^*_{X2}$: policy 4.2

$K(0) < K^*_{X2}$: policy 1.1 → policy 5.2

<u>if $i_1 < (1-\tau_c)r$, $i_2 < (1-\tau_c)r$ and $i_2 < i_2$</u>

$K(0) > K^*_{X1}$: policy 6.1 → policy 4.1

$K(0) = K^*_{X1}$: policy 4.1

$K^*_{X2} < K(0) < K^*_{X1}$: policy 6.2 → policy 4.2

$K(0) = K^*_{X2}$: policy 4.2

$K(0) < K^*_{X2}$: policy 1.1 → policy 2.1 → policy 3.1 → policy 4.2

where

$$dO(K^*_{Xj})/dK = i_j$$

$$dO(K^*_{Yj})/dK = \frac{1}{1+h}\, i_j + \frac{h}{1+h}\,(1-\tau_c)r$$

Finally we conclude that under the assumption of a sufficiently low initial production capacity level $K(0)$ it is optimal for the initial taxable investor to sell the firm's stock as soon as the state of the firm is such that marginal return to equity equals the time preference rate of the second investor. The optimal policy string of the firm under consideration will thus be:

zero dividend policy investor 1 → stationary dividend policy investor 2

which is in line with the result of the previous section.

6.4. A differential game approach

Looking back at the previous sections we may argue that probably the dynamic game theory will be an excellent tool to obtain the solution of the problem under consideration: in a dynamic setting, we observe two (or more) investors, who are trading to get the shares of a firm in order to pursue the policy that maximizes the return on their investment.

6.4.1. Theory of differential games

The theory of differential games concerns dynamic games, which are games "in which the position of the players develops continuously in time". [Friedman, (1971), p. vii]. Basar and Olsder (1982) refine this statement: "Scientifically, dynamic game theory can be viewed as a child of the parents game theory and optimal control theory. Its character, however, is much more versatile than that of either of its parents, since it involves a dynamic decision process evolving in time, with more than one decision maker, each with his own cost function and possibly having access to different information." [Basar and Olsder (1982), p. 2]. In mathematical sense, the striking feature of a differential game model is the direct or indirect influence of all players on the (common) state variables.

Although it is beyond the scope of this book to elaborate on the theory of differential games, it is for convenience of the reader that we first survey the main lines of this theory. Thereafter we apply the theory on the problem under consideration.

The theory of differential games is by no means easy, not only for mathematical reasons but also because of the number of assumptions necessarily to define the concept of a solution.

Within a continuous time and deterministic setting we firstly distinguish zero-sum and nonzero-sum games. A game is labeled a zero-sum game if the sum of the values of the objective functionals of all players is a constant. So, the gain of one player is the loss of one or more others.

Secondly, as to the choice of the control variables several possibilities are available, depending on the information structure assumed for the players. Let U_i be the control variable of the i-th players and X the common state variable. When we mention just those information structures most commonly used, we may distinguish:

closed-loop : $U_i = U_i(X, T, X(0))$

feedback : $U_i = U_i(X, T)$

open-loop : $U_i = U_i(T, X(0))$

Finally, the concept of a solution is not well defined unless the character or mood of the play has been determined. We distinguish between a cooperative and a non cooperative mood of play. If the players agree to cooperate then they seek for a joint solution that is said to be Pareto optimal. If the players do not cooperate then each player has to consider the problem of what to assume about the other player's decision. The Nash payoff represents a security level when playing against rational players of equal strength. If there are differences in strength or in the amount of information available to the players, then the Stackelberg solution can be used: in a two-person game one player is called the leader and the other the follower. The leader announces his strategy and the follower reacts rationally on it.

For more precise statements and definitions we refer to Leitmann (1974), Basar and Olsder (1982) and Mehlmann (1985). A number of applications of differential games to management science can be found in Feichtinger and Jørgensen (1982), whereas Jørgensen (1982) gives a survey of some differential games in advertising, one of the areas most frequently explored.

6.4.2. Modeling the problem under consideration

The modeling of the problem under consideration depends among others on the assumption with respect to the separability of ownership and control. We may distinguish between three cases.

a. Complete separability of ownership and control: in such a situation the firm is in a way autonomously controlled by the management, which is not the owner of the firm. Such an assumption does not necessarily imply that the management neglects the market circumstances in which the firm is operating. The shareholders have, however, delegated the daily decisions to the management. Differently taxed investors may react to the varying policy of the firm by means of selling and buying shares of the firm. Although the investors' problem may be regarded as a differential game problem, Van Schijndel (1985) used an optimal control approach. Moreover, as stated in the introductory chapter we will only consider those situations in which investors may influence corporate policy.

b. No separability of ownership and control: investors who own the stock of the firm may also control the policy of that particular firm. In this way they are able to pursue a policy that maximizes the net return of their investment. Several solution concepts are available, depending on the assumptions with regard to the problem under consideration.

c. Semi-separability of ownership and control: in this case we assume separation of owner and manager, but both subjects may affect the evolution of the firm, since they both control parts of it; that is, we suppose that the manager controls the investment rate and is in charge of the debt management too. The shareholders, who have different personal tax rates, which, in turn, differ from the corporate tax rate, control the dividend pay-out and are allowed to buy and sell shares from each other. The problem may be considered as a non-cooperative game where the manager acts as a leader in a Stackelberg game, announcing his strategy and the stockholders respond rationally as followers by choosing a dividend policy as well as the amount of internal trade with shares. This problem is subject of current research by Jørgensen, van Schijndel and Kort (1986). Apart from the analytical difficulties they encounter in the analysis of the model (because of the complexity of the problem, a closed-form solution e.g. is not attainable), there are some conceptual difficulties with respect to the division of the roles between the decision makers. In particular the dividend policy deserves some consideration, since it will be determined by the investor who owns the majority of the shares. This majority, however, may change over the horizon as a result of buying and selling shares.

In the next subsection we will briefly consider the second case under the assumption that the two investors cooperate.

6.4.3. A Pareto solution of the problem

In this subsection we develop a deterministic dynamic model of a corporate firm with, for simplicity, only two shareholders. We assume that these shareholders control the firm in a cooperative way. Due to these assumptions we may adopt the state equations of the basic model presented in chapter two.

$$\dot{K} = I - aK \tag{6.42}$$

$$K(0) = k_0$$

$$\dot{X} = (1-\tau_c)[O(K) - rY] - D$$

$$X(0) = x_0 \tag{6.43}$$

State equation (6.42) describes the impact of gross investment I(T) on the amount of capital goods K(T), whereas (6.43) points out that the operating income O(K) less the interest payment rY after corporate taxes may be used either to increase the amount of equity through retentions or to pay out dividend.

Now we turn to the division of the stock. Let Z_j be the fraction of the stock that the j-th investor possesses. Hence,

$$Z_1 + Z_2 = 1 \tag{6.44}$$

Both investors may trade in order to increase or decrease their fraction. To limit the number of control variables we assume that the investors have the following contractual agreement: if one investor wants to sell, then the other must buy. Hence a shareholder has always the option to leave the company. On the other hand, no stockholder can be forced to sell, that is, nobody can be forced to give up a majority position or to leave the firm. This implies that only the selling rates are controls. Since $\dot{Z}_1 = -\dot{Z}_2$ we only need one state equation with respect to division of shares:

$$\dot{Z}_1 = S_2 - S_1 \tag{6.45}$$

$$Z_1(0) = z_{10} > 0$$

where

S_j: the selling rate of the j-th investor/shareholder, j = 1,2

Also for the sake of simplification, we may fix the price at which buying and selling takes place at p, where p is a positive constant. This rather strong assumption could be relaxed by letting the share prices be determined by bargaining between the two shareholders or by letting the price be a function of the amount of equity. However, it will turn out that this assumption is less crucial than expected, because under our propositions the buy and sell prices will cancel out. So, we do not need to make any assumption with respect to the prices.

To construct the payoffs of the investors we adopt the usual tax rates τ_{dj} and τ_g. So, the tax rate on capital gain is assumed to be the same for both the investors. We further assume that share transaction between investors are not taxed; this does not seem to be a crucial assumption if such transactions are taxed according the tax rate on capital gain. The payoff functionals are now given by:

$$V^1 = \int_{T=0}^{z} [p(S_1-S_2) + (1-\tau_{d1})DZ_1]e^{-i_1 T} dT +$$

$$Z_1(z)[X(z) - \tau_g(X(z)-X(0))]e^{-i_1 z} \tag{6.46}$$

$$V^2 = \int_{T=0}^{z} [p(S_2-S_1) + (1-\tau_{d2})D(1-Z_1)]e^{-i_2 T} dT +$$

$$[1-Z_1(z)][X(z) - \tau_g(X(z)-X(0))]e^{-i_2 z} \tag{6.47}$$

Finally, we include the usual restrictions: debt is limited in the same way as in chapter two, all variables are assumed to be nonnegative and, finally, all control variables have an upper bound in order to avoid impulse controls.

In order to find candidates for a Pareto solution, let us consider the simplest problem of maximizing $V^1 + V^2$, assuming $i_1 = i_2$ and $\tau_{d1} > \tau_g = \tau_{d2}$. We now get the following objective functional:

$$\int_{T=0}^{z} [(1-\tau_{d1})DZ_1 + (1-\tau_{d2})D(1-Z_1)]e^{-i_1 T} dT + [X(z) - \tau_g(X(z)-X(0))]e^{-i_1 z} \tag{6.48}$$

The problem can be considered as an optimal control problem, which can be solved by means of Pontryagin's maximum principle followed by Van Loon's iterative policy connecting procedure [see appendix B3].

The solution of the above problem has not any surprise in it. Since we have in fact only one time preference rate, only one desired equilibrium level of the amount of capital goods exists, which is such that the net return on equity equals the time preference rate [see results of chapter two and five and in particular table 5.1]:

$$K = K^* \text{ such that } R_X(K^*) = i_1 = i_2 \qquad (6.49)$$

where R_X is defined by [see also section 5.4]:

$$R_X = (1-\tau_c)dO/dK + (1-\tau_c)(dO/dK - r)\frac{Y}{X} \qquad (6.50)$$

Furthermore, we recall that the level of K^* depends on the sign of $i_1 - (1-\tau_c)r$, that is:

$$\text{if } i_1 > (1-\tau_c)r \text{ then } K^* = K_Y^*$$

$$\text{if } i_1 < (1-\tau_c)r \text{ then } K^* = K_X^*$$

The optimal policy string now depends on the initial values of K and Z_1. We get the next three main possibilities:

a. if $K(0) < K^*$: zero dividend policy investor 1 and 2 → stationary dividend policy investor 2.

The policy string starts with a zero dividend policy. Since both investors completely agree with this policy, the value of Z_1 is indefinite. However, this evolution path needs to end up with a zero value of Z_1, because on the succeeding stationary dividend policy the second investor will own all the firm's shares. Finally, the role of debt is determined by the level of the time preference rate in relation to the net costs of debt, $(1-\tau_c)r$. As a consequence, the firm's master evolution trajectories are exactly the same as depicted in the figures 2.1 and 2.2 in chapter two.

b. if $K(0) = K^*$: stationary dividend policy investor 2 in principle.

The firm's optimal master evolution consists of only one policy and that is a stationary dividend policy. The second investor owns in principle the shares of the firm. Because the initial value of Z_1 is positive, that is, the first investor possesses shares of the firm at the initial moment, he will sell his part of the stock instantaneously to the second investor: $\dot{Z}_1 = -S_1 = -S_{max}$.

c. if $K(0) > K^*$: contraction policy investor 2 in principle $\rightarrow$ stationary dividend policy investor 2.

Similar to the previous case $\dot{Z}_1$ will be negative at the maximum level if the initial value of Z_1 is not equal to zero. The firm's evolution is in first instance determined by the contraction policy succeeded by the stationary dividend policy. Whether debt will be adopted or not depends once again on the balance of the time preference rate and the net cost of debt.

The main result of the above considerations is that the optimal policy string of the firm always ends up with a stationary policy of paying out dividend to the second, that is, lowest taxed, investor. Moreover, this result was predictable, since the first investor has always to pay over an equal or greater fraction of his earnings for tax purposes than the second one. This loss is not counterbalanced by a gain due to a lower time preference rate. Hence, in that case, the problem will be analytically hard to solve, since the results will depend on accidental values of some variables. For that reason, it will be very difficult or perhaps impossible to obtain analytical results in the case that the investors do not cooperate and thus play Nash-strategies.

6.5. Conclusion

In this chapter we enlarged the analysis of the previous chapter by allowing investors to trade the shares of the firm under consideration. In first instance we considered the problem of a single taxable investor, who has to determine the optimal policies with respect to dividend, investment and finance, and in addition the optimal moment to sell the shares of the firm at some known price. Thereafter, we relaxed the assumption of the known price and known policy after the take-over by considering a model that simultaneously described the optimal policy problem of both the initial investor as well as of the second investor, who takes over the control of the firm. To these purposes we used optimal control theory approaches. Finally, we considered a differential game approach and discussed the implications of a cooperative strategy for the two investors.

With respect to the firm's evolution a general conclusion may be that the optimal policy string always ends up with a stationary dividend policy and the firm's stock is owned by the investor subject to the lowest personal tax rates. Investors subject to high personal tax rates will sell the shares of the firm as soon as the amount of capital goods has reached such a value that the low taxed investor prefers a constant amount of dividend.

In the next chapter we will study the implications of these strategies in an equilibriuim framework.

CHAPTER SEVEN

A TIME DEPENDENT EQUILIBRIUM APPROACH UNDER A PROGRESSIVE PERSONAL TAX

7.1. Introduction

The purpose of this chapter is an attempt to justify the thesis that during each stage of their evolution firms will be controlled by investors in different tax brackets. To that end, we consider in a dynamic setting the impact of personal taxation on the optimal policy string of value maximizing firms and the equilibrium portfolio selection of investors, both under the assumption of no separation of ownership and control.

In chapter five we have studied the case of a single investor who owned and managed a single value maximizing firm. We have showed that the optimal evolution pattern consists of subsequent policies concerning investment, dividend and finance, and that it strongly depends on the personal tax structure of the investor. So, different personal tax rates, that is different investors will induce different optimal policy strings. In fact, this analysis has been carried out under the assumption of no real alternative investment opportunities, because the investor was forced to own and control the firm during a fixed planning period.

In chapter six we have enlarged this analysis by considering cases in which the investor has the opportunity to sell the stock of the firm to another investor. In particular, we explored a model with one firm and two value maximizing investors.

In this chapter we focus on the dynamic market equilibrium problem of many investors and many shareholder controlled firms. So, investors have actually the opportunity to select and control at any time firms in a particular state in order to maximize the value of their investment.

As stated above the aim of this chapter is the justification of the thesis that during each stage of their evolution firms will be controlled by investors in different tax brackets. To do so, we firstly recall the impact of personal taxation on the optimal investment/dividend policy of value maximizing firms. In section 7.2 we therefore consider a dynamic model of firm behaviour that is appropriate for our purpose. All variables, that for the moment being are beyond our scope, such as corporate debt, are left out of consideration in order to simplify the problem and model formulation. In this way we are able to concentrate on the main contribution of the chapter. Thereafter we compute the values of firms, which are continuously distributed over a range of feasible production capacity levels, to investors in different tax brackets (section 7.3). Next, we evolve an equilibrium valuation and portfolio theory under personal taxation in section 7.4. Finally, we summarize the findings in section 7.5.

7.2. Optimal behaviour of an equity financed firm

In this section we recall the deterministic dynamic model of a shareholder controlled value maximizing firm that we have explored in chapter five. However, we introduce some modifications with regard to the personal tax system, the planning horizon and the use of corporate debt.

The objective of each investor is to maximize the value of any firm under control. Investors may sell a firm's stock and thus surrender the control of firms. We assume, however, that all firms will continue after the take-over. So, the value of a firm may be expressed as the present value at T of the net dividend stream over an infinite plan period:

$$V_p(T) := \int_{S=T}^{\infty} (1-\tau_p)D_p(S)e^{-i_p(S-T)}\,dS \tag{7.1}$$

where

$V_p(T)$: personal value of a firm at time T to investor p

i_p : time preference rate after personal taxation of investor p

τ_p : personal tax rate of investor p

$D_p(T)$: dividend at T when investor p is the manager of the firm

As stated before the time preference rate reflects the alternative rate of return after personal taxation. Within our deterministic framework we may therefore assume the time preference rate to be dependent on the market interest rate r and the personal tax rate τ_p. For simplicity we define in particular:

$$i_p := r(1-\tau_p) \tag{7.2}$$

Since we use only the tax rate on personal income, we actually impose the classical tax system ($\tau_{dp} = \tau_{rp} = \tau_p$). In addition we have taken tax exempt capital gain for granted when reproducing the investor's objective functional (7.1). However, we would obtain a similar type objective functional if we had assumed that capital gain tax is paid at each T and that for every investor the after tax yield on money investment must be equal to the dividend plus the capital gain both net of taxes. Hence,

$$r(1-\tau_p)V_p(T) = (1-\tau_p)D_p(T) + (1-\tau_{gp})\dot{V}_p(T) \tag{7.3}$$

This personal capital market equilibrium condition (see King (1977) is a differential equation for V, which is in its integral form at T = 0:

$$V_p(0) = \frac{(1-\tau_{dp})}{(1-\tau_{gp})} \int_{T=0}^{\infty} D_p(T).e^{-r((1-\tau_{rp})/(1-\tau_{gp}))T} dT \tag{7.4}$$

Under the classical tax system, $\tau_{rp} = \tau_{dp} := \tau_p$, and the definition of τ_p by

$$(1-\tau_p) := (1-\tau_{dp})/(1-\tau_{gp}) \tag{7.5}$$

the objective functional, which is used by e.g. Yla-Liedenpohja (1978), is similar to that of expression (7.1). Hence, with respect to the objective we assume an infinite time horizon instead of a finite one, and impose the classical tax system with tax exempt capital gain. The latter assumptions, however, do not affect the results of the analysis, but are put forward only for sake of simplicity.

The final modification concerns the firm's financial structure, which is assumed to exist entirely of internal equity; that is, the firm may not attract debt and issues of new shares are prohibited. Consequently, the initial state assumption that guarantees the existence of alternatives that are profitable from the start on, becomes: if $K(T) = 0$, then $(1-\tau_c)dO/dK > i_p$.

Since all remaining assumptions of the chapter two and five models are adopted, we may now formulate the firm's optimization problems as follows:

$$\underset{D_p,\, I_p}{\text{maximize}} \left\{ \int_{T=0}^{\infty} (1-\tau_p)D_p(T)e^{-i_pT}dT \right\} \tag{7.6}$$

$$\text{subject to } \dot{K}(T) = I_p(T) - aK(T) \tag{7.7}$$

$$\dot{X}(T) = (1-\tau_c)O(K) - D_p(T) \tag{7.8}$$

$$K(T) = X(T) \tag{7.9}$$

$$D_p(T) \geq 0 \qquad I_p(T) \geq 0 \tag{7.10}$$

$$K(T) \geq 0 \qquad X(T) \geq 0 \tag{7.11}$$

$$K(0) = X(0) = k_0 > 0 \tag{7.12}$$

Notice that $O(K)$ may now be considered as the corporate profit before taxation.

Equality (7.9) enables us to simplify the model by eliminating both $X(T)$ and $I_p(T)$. The model in its reduced form can then be solved analytically by applying optimal control theory. So, we first derive the necessary and sufficient conditions for an optimal solution by means of the standard maximum principle of Pontryagin c.s. (1962), and afterwards we apply the 'iterative policy' connecting procedure designed by Van Loon (1983), which is a convenient procedure in order to determine from the set of necessary conditions a solution for the optimal policy of the firm over the whole planning period. Since the model under consideration has much in common with the chapter five model, the optimal solution can be easily obtained by setting some variables of the latter mentioned model to zero. Therefore, we do not elaborate on the derivation of the optimal policy string, neither in this chapter nor in an appendix.

The optimal evolution patterns are very simple and consist at most of two subsequent policies. Two of these patterns are depicted in the figures 7.1 and 7.2.

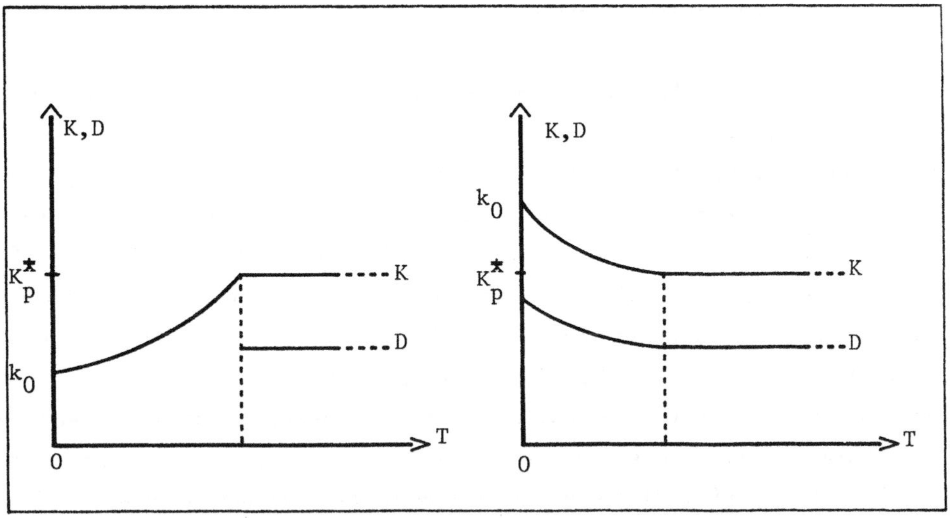

Figure 7.1: optimal policy string when $K(0) < K_p^*$

Figure 7.2: optimal policy string when $K(0) > K_p^*$

Due to the assumption of an infinite planning horizon, both evolution patterns end up with a stationary dividend policy: the production capacity $K(T)$ remains on a constant level K_p^*, such that marginal revenue equals the shareholder's time preference rate: $(1-\tau_c)dO/dK = i_p$. Notice that the desired stationary level K_p^* depends on the investor's personal tax rate.

Depending on the initial value K_0 this policy is preceded by a maximum growth (figure 7.1) or a contraction policy (figure 7.2). Due to the decreasing return to scale, marginal revenue of values of $K(T)$ below K_p^* exceeds marginal cost of equity, that is $(1-\tau_c)dO/dK > i_p$, if $K(T) < K_p^*$. The optimal policy, therefore, is to retain earnings and use this money to finance expansion investment in order to realize a maximum increase of the production capacity and with that of the firm's profit.

If the production capacity is above the desired level K_p^* the optimal policy is to cut down the capital stock at the maximum rate that is allowed for, that is at depreciation rate a, for, due to the nonnegativety constraint on investment, the firm cannot divest. All profit is paid out to the shareholder.

The reader can imagine that a firm having an initial production capacity just on the optimal level K_p^*, will keep on that level during the whole planning period by investing at such a level as necessary only to replace absoleted capital goods.

Finally, we survey the main results and features of the problem in an appropriate way:

- the desired level K_p^* is fixed by the time preference rate i_p, such that $(1-\tau_c)dO/dK = i_p$. So, due to the concavity of $O(K)$ a higher level of i_p results in a lower desired equilibrium level of $K(T)$. A far reaching consequence of this dependence can be shown by considering two values of i_p such that $K_{p1}^* < K_0 < K_{p2}^*$. If $i_p = i_{p1}$ the shareholder prefers a contraction policy, whereas in the case of $i_p = i_{p2}$ a maximum growth policy is the optimal one. Moreover, since i_p depends on its turn on the personal tax rate τ_p, investors in different tax brackets may prefer different policies at one and the same state K_0.

- The optimal dividend policy, and with that the resulting state trajectory $K^*(T)$, depends on only the present state of the firm $K(T)$ and the desired stationary level K_p^*, which on its turn is fixed by τ_p. The optimal dividend policy is thus given by

$$D_p^*(T) = \left\{\begin{matrix} 0 \\ O(K)-aK \\ O(K) \end{matrix}\right\} \text{ if } K(T) \left\{\begin{matrix} < \\ = \\ > \end{matrix}\right\} K_p^* \tag{7.13}$$

Consequently, the optimal (future) policy of the firm depends on the present production capacity level and the level of the personal tax rate of the shareholder, who owns and controls the firm under consideration.

7.3. Valuation of the firm's policy string

The final result of the previous section with regard to the dependence of the optimal policy string on the firm's present state K and the personal tax rate τ_p forces us to evolve an equilibrium valuation and portfolio theory. To that end, we firstly analyse the value of firms, continuously distributed over the range of production capacity levels K_0 to K^*_{pmax}, to investors in different tax brackets. K^*_{pmax} is determined by $(1-\tau_c)dO/dK = r(1-\tau_{pmax})$ where τ_{pmax} is the personal tax rate of investors in the highest tax bracket. So, K^*_{pmax} is the maximum desired stationary production capacity level, whereas K denotes the minimum level necessary to enter the market. The range K_0 to K^*_{pmax} thus covers all relevant values for K.

According to (7.13) the optimal (future) policy of a firm is uniquely determined by the present production capacity level and the level of the personal tax rate of the present shareholder. Using the objective functional (7.1) this implies that the value of a firm may be expressed as a function of only state and personal tax rate. In order to construct such personal value functions we first consider the optimal policy string of a particular investor. In this way, any arbitrary value of K in the range K_0 to K^*_{pmax} (with exception for K^*_p), say k, can be uniquely attached to a moment t_{kp} of the master policy string of the investor subject to the personal tax rate τ_p. Thereafter we are able to determine the personal value of the firm by substituting both t_{kp} and $D^*_p(T)$ into expression (7.1). Because t_{kp} corresponds to one and only one value of K, we have finally found the value of a firm with state k to an investor subject to τ_p: $V_p(k)$. If $K = K^*_p$ all points in the range t_{kdp} to infinity of the master policy string of the investor subject to the personal tax rate τ_p can indeed be attached, but all these points provide nevertheless one and the same value.

Summarizing the above procedure for an arbitrary value k in a diagram, we get:

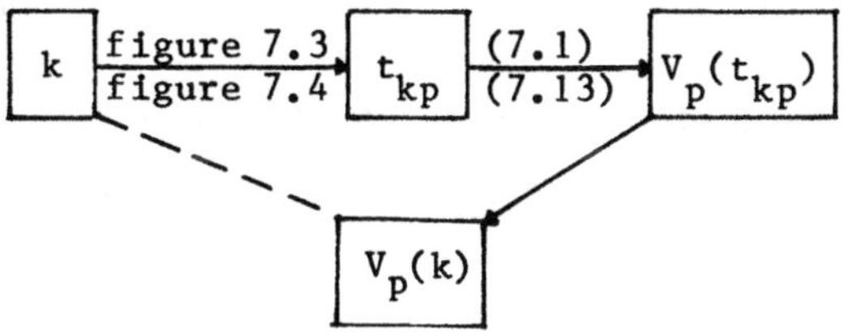

In correspondence to the above preview we start with the consideration of the optimal policy string of one particular investor. We need two of these master strings, one of both starting at K_0 and the other at K^*_{pmax}. We label these evolutions the personal master patterns. The personal policy strings and corresponding master trajectories, together constituting the master patterns, of an investor in the τ_p-th tax bracket are depicted in the figures 7.3 and 7.4. With the help of these figures we are able to attach an arbitrary value of K, over the range K_0 to K^*_{pmax}, to a corresponding moment of one of the two master patterns. The arbitrary values k_1 and k_2 are e.g. attached to t_{k_1gp} and t_{k_2cp}. In this way we are able to determine the time lag between the start of the stationary dividend policy and the current moment. It will turn out that such a time lag is of utmost importance with regard to the determination of the personal value of a firm. Note, that the corresponding moments t_{k_1gp} and t_{k_2cp} not only depend on the state of the firm, but also on the tax rate of the investor, who is valueing the firm.

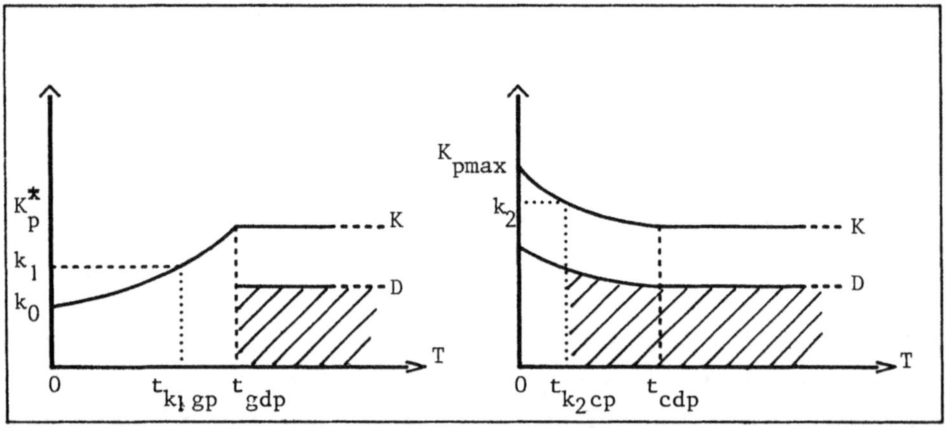

Figure 7.3: personal master trajectory of investor in τ_p-th tax bracket starting at K_0.

Figure 7.4: personal master trajectory of investor in τ_p-th tax bracket starting at K_{pmax}.

Using the value expression (7.1) we obtain the personal value of a firm with state k_1 and k_2 respectively to an investor subject to τ_p:

$$V_p(t_{k_1gp}) = \int_{T=t_{k_1gp}}^{\infty} (1-\tau_p)D_p(T)e^{-i_p(T-t_{k_1gp})}\,dT \quad \text{if } k_1 < K_p^*$$

$$V_p(t_{k_2cp}) = \int_{T=t_{k_2cp}}^{\infty} (1-\tau_p)D_p(T)e^{-i_p(T-t_{k_2cp})}\,dT \quad \text{if } k_2 > K_p^* \qquad (7.14)$$

where

t_{k_1gp}: corresponding point in time on the personal master trajectory of the τ_p-th investor in case $k_1 < K_p^*$ so that $K(t_{k_1gp}) = k_1$

t_{k_2cp}: corresponding point in time on the personal master trajectory of the τ_p-th investor in case $k_2 > K_p^*$ so that $K(t_{k_2cp}) = k_2$.

Let $V_p(k)$ denote the value of a firm with an arbitrary production capacity level k to an investor in the τ_p-th tax bracket. Because any value of the production capacity level with exception for K_p^* corresponds to a unique point of one of the master trajectories of an investor in the τ_p-th tax bracket, we may finally rewrite (7.14) in a more general expression.

Recalling the expression of the alternative rate of return (7.2) and still proceeding on the assumption that ownership and control coincide, we now find following expressions by substituting (7.13) in (7.14):

$$V_p(k) = \begin{cases} (D_p^*/r).e^{-i_p(t_{gdp}-t_{kgp})} & \text{if } k < K_p^* \\ D_p^*/r & \text{if } k = K_p^* \\ (D_p^*/r).e^{-i_p(t_{cdp}-t_{kcp})} + \\ \int_{T=t_{kcp}}^{t_{cdp}} (1-\tau_p)D_p(T)e^{-i_p(T-t_{kcp})}\,dT & \text{if } k > K_p^* \end{cases} \qquad (7.15)$$

where

t_{gdp}: switching point on personal master trajectory from growth into dividend policy to investor in τ_p-th tax bracket

t_{cdp}: switching point on personal master trajectory from contraction into dividend policy to investor in τ_p-th tax bracket

D_p^* : desired level of stationary dividend policy to investor in τ_p-th tax bracket (corresponding K_p^*-level: $(1-\tau_c)dO/dK = i_p$).

Be aware of the notion that the time lags $t_{gdp}-t_{kgp}$ and $t_{cdp}-t_{kcp}$, that is, the time lags between and the current moment the start of the stationary dividend policy, are of utmost importance and may be considered as functions of only K and τ_p.

We may clarify the results of (7.15) as follows. If $k = K_p^*$ the investor will immediately start to pay out dividend at the D_p^*-level and continue this policy for many a long day. Using (7.1) and (7.2) we then get:

$$\int_{T=0}^{\infty} (1-\tau_p)D_p^* . e^{-r_p T} dT = \frac{(1-\tau_p)D_p^*}{(1-\tau_p)r} = \frac{D_p^*}{r} \tag{7.16}$$

If $k < K_p^*$ the shareholder will yield the same amount of dividend payments. Since the dividend distribution only starts as soon as the production capacity has reached the K_p^*-level, the value of this dividend stream need to be discounted according the time lag $t_{gdp}-t_{kgp}$.

Finally, if the present production capacity is above the desired level the shareholder not only yields the discounted value of the constant dividend payments, but in addition the entire distributed profit due to the initial contraction policy.

We have now found an expression to determine the value of a firm with state k to an investor subject to a personal tax rate τ_p. Substitution of all values of k over the range K_0 to K_{pmax}^* results into personal value curves.

We illustrate the above result graphicly in the case of two investors, p1 and p2 respectively, subject to tax rates such that $\tau_{p1} > \tau_{p2}$ and thus $i_{p1} < i_{p2}$.

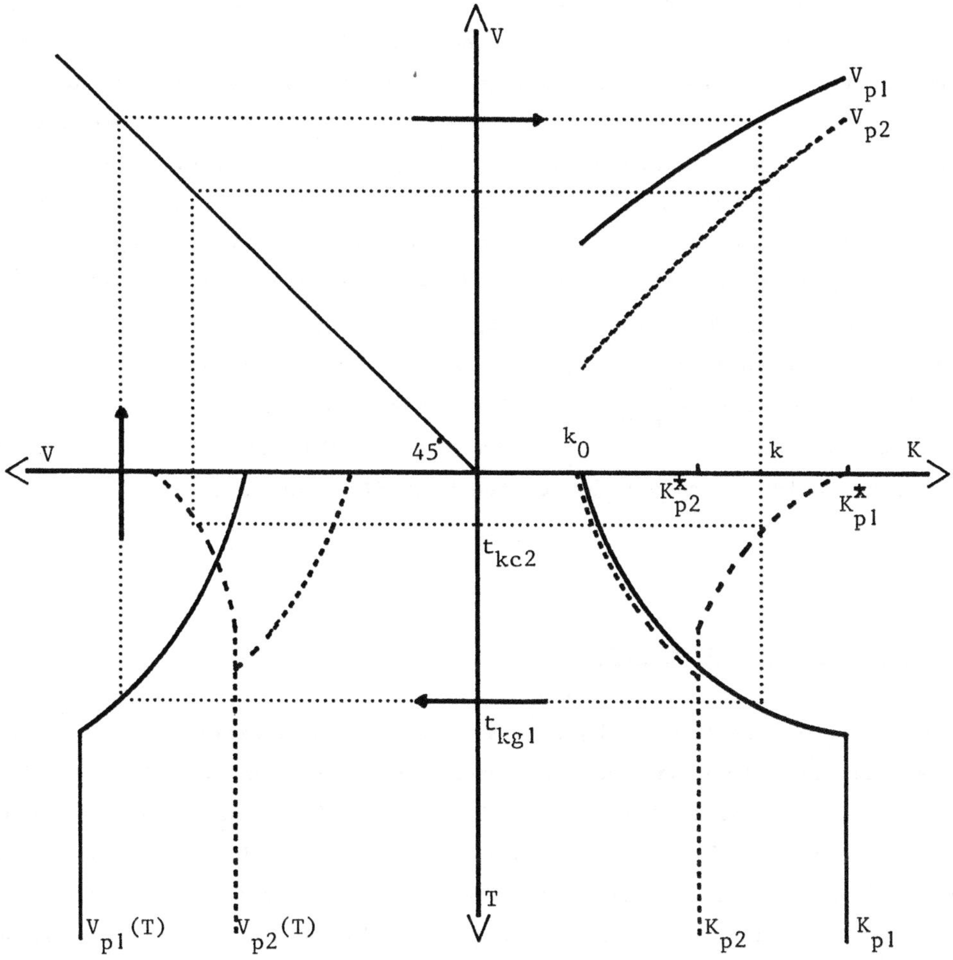

Figure 7.5: Personal value of firms with a production capacity level k to investors subject to $\tau_{p1} := \tau_{pmax}$ and τ_{p2} respectively.

The K-T-plane of figure 7.5, which is comparable with the figures 7.3 and 7.4, pictures both the locations t_{kg1} and t_{kc2} corresponding to a production capacity level of k and the optimal policy of the investors. Investor p1 will pursue a maximum growth policy, whereas the second investor prefers a contraction policy in order to decrease the production capacity. So, given state k investors may control the firm in varying ways and, consequently, attach different values to the same firm. These values are depicted in the V-T-plane, which is a graphical reproduction of expression (7.14). The V-K-plane, finally, pictures the personal value curves $V_p(K)$. We observe that V_{p1} exceeds V_{p2} for all values of K over the range K_0 to K^*_{p1}, where the latter, for simplicity only, is assumed to be equal to K^*_{pmax}. Generally speaking we conclude that low taxed investors attach lower values to a particular firm than high taxed investors, which is mainly due to the high discount rate.

7.4. Market equilibrium approach

In the previous section we have shown that due to a progressive personal income tax investors may have different opinions with regard to the future policy and value of the firm. Given these different taxes and valuations, we now explore how adjustments in the demand for shares of the firms affect the equilibrium value and future policy string of firms. As the problem under consideration has much in common with the problem Gordon elaborated on [see section 4.4], we use the corrected version of Gordon's approach to derive the equilibrium value function of the firm [see section 4.6].

To deal with the equilibrium problem, let us at first consider two groups of investors: wealthy organizations such as fully tax exempt, which are pension funds, and private investors with limited and constant private liabilities. Similar to previous sections their private income is taxed at rate τ_p, which varies with the investors initial wealth, whereas capital gain is tax exempt. Firms are continuously distributed over the range of production capacity levels K_0 to K^*_{pmax}. Furthermore, all firms are assumed to face the same environment and to dispose of the same production techniques, organization structure, etcetera, so that we may use the model (7.6)-(7.12) to describe the evolution of any firm. New firms may enter the market at level k_0 and evolve according to state equation (7.7): $\dot{K} = I - aK$.

Before continuing the analysis we define following variables:

V_m: equilibrium market value of a firm

V_i: personal value of a firm to any investor i, $i = \{p,e\}$

V_p: personal value of a firm to private investors subject to tax rate τ_p

V_e: personal value of a firm to tax exempt investors.

All V_p and V_e-curves in figure 7.6 now represent the personal equilibrium values of firms for those investors with the indicated tax rate. If the values of all firms are on a particular curve, say V_e, tax exempt investors will be indifferent to which firm is in his/her portfolio. However, similar to the problem Gordon had to tackle, none of the per-

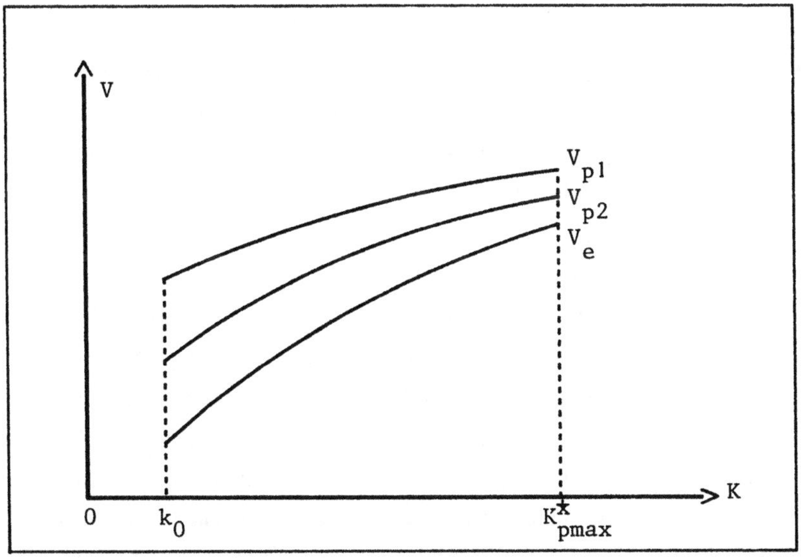

Figure 7.6: personal values of firms.

sonal value curves in figure 7.6 provides an equilibrium set of values for the firms. We will show, however, the existence of a V_m-curve, that makes the excess demand for shares at each production capacity level to zero.

To that end, it is sufficient to describe the equilibrium in case investors are subject to just two tax rates, that is, we consider tax exempt investors and private investors subject to a particular tax rate τ_p, say τ_{pmax}. Let firms be partitioned according to their production capacity level into two groups, that is k_0 to k_{bp} and k_{bp} to K^*_{pmax} (see figure 7.7).

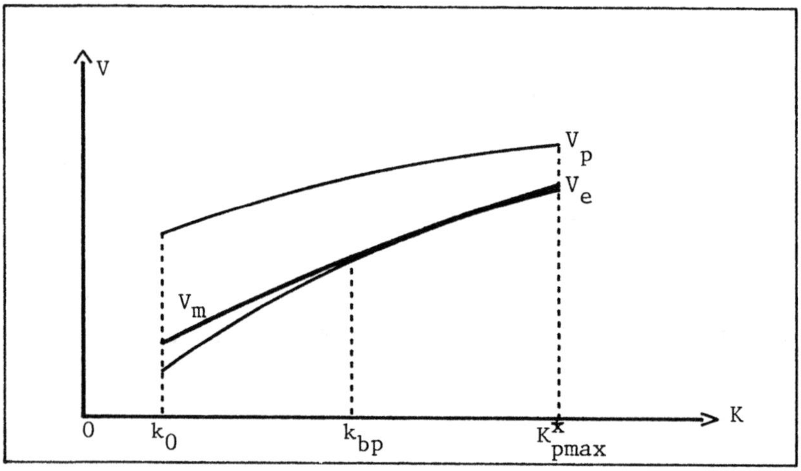

Figure 7.7: personal and market value of firms in case of two groups of investors subject to $\tau_p = 0$ and $\tau_p = \tau_{pmax}$ respectively.

The partitioning is such that the total share value of firms in the first group is equal to the share wealth of the private investors, and the total share value of the remaining firms is equal or less to the share wealth of the tax exempt investors. Due to the limited liabilities investors strive at the maximization of $(V_i - V_m)/V_m$, which is equivalent to the maximization of V_i/V_m. So, we use the Present Value Index, PVI, that is introduced in subsection 4.5.1 and defined by (4.28). We now clarify that, the V_m-curve provides an equilibrium. In the sketch of figure 7.7 V_e denotes the lowest personal value and thus fixes the lower bound of V_m. Private investors, who intend to buy shares, have to pay at least V_e in order to buy out tax exempt investors. With goal the maximization of the rate of return $V_p/V_m = V_p/V_e$ private investors intend to buy shares of firms with low production capacity levels, because of the negative derivative of the rate of net return with respect to K (a proof of this statement is given in appendix C). So, firms distributed over the range k_0 to k_{bp} are controlled by private investors subject to tax rate τ_p. Consequently, the net rate of return of a production capacity level k_{bp}, denoted c_p, is fixed by

$$c_p := V_p(k_{bp})/V_m(k_{bp}) = V_p(k_{bp})/V_e(k_{bp}) \tag{7.17}$$

where

$$\int_{K=k_0}^{k_{bp}} V_m(K)dK = \text{budget investor p} \tag{7.18}$$

The constant c_p has a similar meaning as the constants $NPT_{0.25}$ and $NPI_{0.0}$ used in the expressions (4.33) and (4.36) of section 4.6. To prevent excess demand for shares at lower production levels market value will adjust such that V_p/V_m is constant over the range under consideration; that is, an investor subject to tax rate τ_p finds V_p/V_m the same for all firms in the first group whereas shares in the second group will only provide smaller values of V_p/V_m. So, the equilibrium value curve V_m is given by:

$$V_m(K) = \begin{cases} V_p(K)/c_p & \text{if } k_0 \leq K \leq k_{bp} \\ V_e(K) & \text{if } k_{bp} < K \leq K^*_{pmax} \end{cases} \tag{7.19}$$

Finally, the size of the intervals k_0 to k_{bp} and k_{bp} to K^*_{pmax} adjust to make the excess demand for shares in each group equal to zero.

Contrary to the leverage problem Gordon (1982) considers, firms may now not adopt that production capacity level, which maximizes market value. So, firms may not instanteneously adjust their production capacity, because its evolution is determined by state equation (7.7). Moreover, we wonder whether the firm's incentive is still to adopt that production capacity level that maximizes the market value, since the market value depends on the present shareholders and adjustments of production capacity lead to changes in the group of shareholders.

The above described problem may, of course, be extended to more than one private investor. The derivation of the equilibrium market value curve will be similar to the one used above. The partitioning of the firms into groups need to be adjusted to the number of tax groups of private investors. The result of a problem with two groups of taxable investors, such as illustrated in the figures 7.5 and 7.6, is depicted in figure 7.8. We observe a succession of investors subject to decreasing personal tax rates.

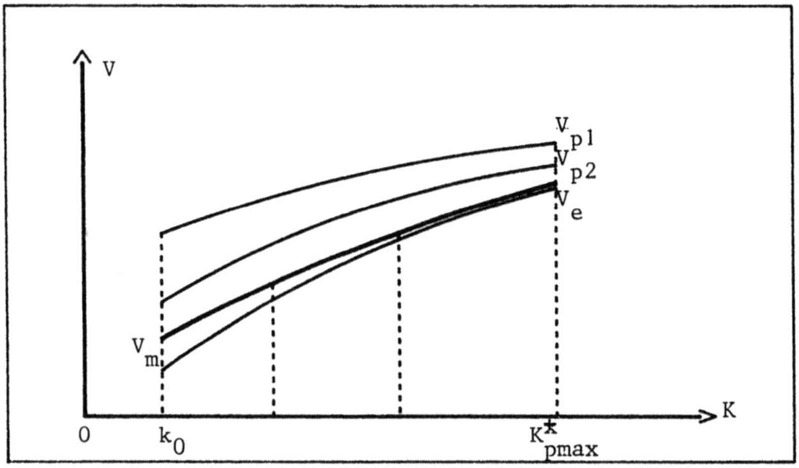

Figure 7.8: personal and market equilibrium value in case of one (group of) tax exempt investor(s) and two (groups of) taxable private investors.

7.5. Final results and conclusion

In this chapter we have examined the impact of personal taxation on the optimal policy string of value maximizing firms and the portfolio selection of investors. We may summarize the contribution of the chapter by following conclusions.

The optimal policy string of shareholder-controlled-companies depends on only the state of the firm and the personal tax rate of the shareholder. Due to the progressive personal tax rates investors attach values which vary along their tax rates. Nevertheless, we have been able to show the existence of the V_m-curve that makes the excess demand for shares at each production capacity level equal to zero.

Each investor will move into the shares and corresponding production capacity level of those firms for which the rate of return is maximized. Investors subject to high tax rates prefer firms at low production levels in order to pursue a maximum growth policy. Consequently, new firms enter the market at k_0 on the initiative of private investors. Tax exempt investors, on the contrary, absorb going companies and exert themselves to pursue a stationary dividend policy as soon as possible.

In case private share wealth is of minor importance, no firm will exceed the K_e^*-level, desired by tax exempt investors. Accordingly, the optimal policy of each firm consists under absense of debt of a maximum growth policy succeeded by a stationary dividend policy. This result is shown in figure 7.9, where k_{bp} denotes the total share wealth of all private investors. With regard to the 'investor string' we observe a succession of investors subject to decreasing tax rates.

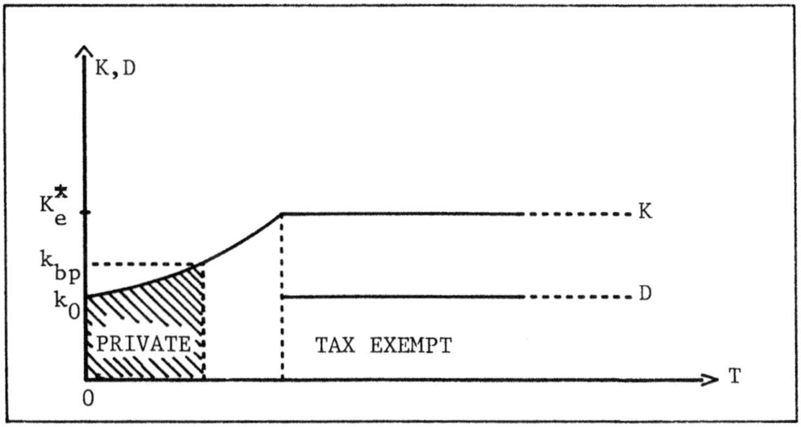

Figure 7.9: optimal equilibrium policy string.

Finally we have found a justification of the thesis that during each stage of their evolution firms will be controlled by investors subject to varying tax rates, because each investor will move into the shares and corresponding production capacity level of those firms for which his rate of return is maximized. Consequently, in the case that all firms start at the same initial value k_0 and face the same environment, each investor's portfolio consists of the shares of firms with capital sizes comprised within a narrow range of levels.

CHAPTER EIGHT

CONCLUSIONS

In this book we paid attention to the inclusion of progressive personal taxation into the deterministic dynamic theory of the firm. We considered the impact of both corporate and personal taxation on three important features of the firm: the financing, the dividend and the investment policy. Moreover, we inserted ourselves to generalize the dynamic theory of the firm by exploring an equilibrium framework. We now summarize the main results and findings in this concluding chapter.

The impact of both corporate and personal taxation on the optimal policy of the firm and the behaviour of investors is still an important issue in finance theory. The inclusion of a progressive personal tax, in particular, brings on interesting features with respect to the equilibrium market value of a firm and the resulting phenomenon of 'tax induced clienteles'. Both topics are considered in this book.

With regard to the equilibrium valuation theory we distinguish between a 'before tax' and an 'after tax' theory. Exploring the latter theory Miller (1977) argued that even in a world with progressive personal taxation the value of a firm could be independent of its leverage. Although many subsequent papers accepted and clarified the thruth of Miller's result, it was Gordon (1982) who first questioned the correctness of Miller's hypothesis. However, in our opinion Gordon's conclusion, that the market value of a firm is a convex function of its leverage, is not correct. We question both the objective functional Gordon uses to obtain an upwards sloping market curve as well as the supply adjustment process he describes afterwards. In our opinion Gordon on his turn failed to disprove Miller's explanation of capital structure. Moreover, we show that Gordon's approach is very usefull to prove once again the correctness of the Miller leverage irrelevancy theorem.

Personal taxes induce tax clienteles: due to its policy a firm will attract investors in specific tax brackets. In the literature on finance theory this notion has been discussed with respect to the dividend and financing policy of the firm. We add 'tax induced investment clienteles': generally speaking we may say that the willingness to accept investments with a low rate of return is negatively correlated to the level of the personal tax rate. So, firms that invest in low return projects could only attract investors in high tax brackets. Under the assumption that the operating income is a concave function of the production capacity level, this result implies that ceteris paribus large expanding firms could only attract high taxed investors.

The framework of DeAngelo and Masulis (1980a) may fruitfully be applied to explain the nature of dividend and financial leverage clienteles. The existence of these phenomena, however, depend strongly on the kind of equity claim as well as on the tax system under consideration. We show that in the case in which firms are supplying dividend claims only, no single investor facing the classical tax system, neither subject to personal taxation nor tax exempt, will demand a positive quantity of equity claims. In addition to the introduction of a dividend tax shelter [DeAngelo and Masulis (1980a)] a reform of the tax system into an imputation system may establish such a positive demand.

Furthermore, we explore a model in which we consider the dividend and the financing decisions as well as the resulting clienteles simultaneously. Under the imputation tax system we achieve a partitioning of investors according to their personal tax rate on debt income into three tax groups, each characterized by a preference for a certain kind of income. Extremely high taxed investors always prefer capital gain claims, whereas other investors subject to a tax rate above the level of the corporate tax rate prefer dividend claims. The remaining investors are only willing to buy debt claims. This partitioning is only attainable if the imputation factor is close to one, that is, investors will only demand positive quantities of dividend claims, if at least the total fraction of the corporate tax paid on dividends is allowed to be substracted from the personal income tax.

Personal taxation has a strong impact on the optimal dynamic policy of a value maximizing firm. We show that the optimal policy string of a shareholder controlled firm depends on both the state of the firm as well as on the personal tax rate of the shareholder. In the case of a fixed finite planning horizon we obtain in particular striking differences with the results of similar dynamic problems without personal taxation, viz.

- in final stages no dividend will be issued
- in some situations the firm wants to get rid of debt, even when debt is relatively cheap
- due to the gap between the levels of the tax rates on dividend and capital gain, it may be optimal to start expansion investments with a net return less than the time preference rate.

Investors in low tax brackets not only prefer a high leverage strategy and dividend income rather than capital gain, but they also like to collect earnings as soon as possible, whereas investors in high tax brackets are willing to postpone this collection in view of their tax advantage ad low time preference rate. Moreover, firms controlled by high taxed investors, are forced to reach higher production levels than firms controlled by low taxed investors.

A switch of tax system from the classical into the imputation system results in a sharp rise of the market value of a firm. In addition, firms are less forced to expand the production capacity level, that is, to invest in projects with low rates of return. Consequently, firms may more easily attract providers of equity.

From the sensitivity analysis, we carry out, we find a striking impact of the corporate tax rate. A reduction of the corporate tax rate stimulates enterpreneur's activities and raises the profit, the stationary production capacity level and thus the value of the firm. In addition, such a reduction may cause a policy switch of the firm into a low leverage strategy, that is, a low corporate tax rate favours the providers of equity.

In the situation of two differently taxed investors, the optimal policy string of a shareholder controlled firm, facing an infinite planning horizon, always ends up with a stationary dividend policy pursued by the investor subject to the lowest personal tax rate. Investors subject to high personal tax rates will sell the shares of the firm as soon as the amount of capital goods has reached such a level that the low taxed investor will pay out a constant amount of dividend.

In the case of many shareholder controlled firms and many differently taxed and budget constrained investors, we show the existence of an equilibrium value function that makes the excess demand for shares at each production capacity level equal to zero. Since each investor will move into the shares and corresponding production capacity level of those firms for which the rate of return is maximized, it turns out that investors subject to high tax rates prefer the stock of firms at low production capacity levels in order to pursue a maximum growth policy. Consequently, new firms enter the market at the initial production capacity level on the initiative of private investors, whereas tax exempt investors, such as pension funds, absorb the going companies and exert themselves to pursue a stationary dividend policy as soon as possible.

In case private share wealth is of limited and minor importance, the optimal level of firms is determined by tax exempt investors.

During its evolution a firm will be succesively controlled by investors subject to varying, that is, in the course of time declining, tax rates. Consequently, each investor's portfolio consists of the shares of firms with capital sizes comprised within a narrow range of levels.

APPENDIX A1

THE SOLUTION OF THE OPTIMAL CONTROL PROBLEMS FORMULATED IN THE CHAPTERS TWO AND FIVE

In this appendix we derive the optimal solution of the problem, that is formulated in chapter five [eqs. (5.7)-(5.13)]. Since the basic problem of chapter two is a special case of the more general problem formulated in chapter five (that is $\tau_d = \tau_r = \tau_g = 0$) we consider only the latter one.

In order to simplify the solution procedure, we will first eliminate the variable Y(T). We, therefore, substitute (5.10)

$$Y = K - X \tag{A.1}$$

into (5.7) - (5.13) and thus obtain the following optimal control model:

$$\max \left\{(1-\tau_d) \int_{T=0}^{z} D(T)e^{-iT}dT + (1-\tau_g)X(z)e^{-iz}\right\} \tag{A.2}$$

subject to $\dot{X} = (1-\tau_c)[O(K) - r(K-X)] - D$

$$X(0) = X_0 > 0 \tag{A.3}$$

$$\dot{K} = I - aK$$

$$K(0) = k_0 > 0 \tag{A.4}$$

$$K - X \geq 0 \tag{A.5}$$

$$(1+h)X - K \geq 0 \tag{A.6}$$

$$D \geq 0 \tag{A.7}$$

$$I \geq 0 \tag{A.8}$$

$$X \geq 0 \tag{A.9}$$

We assume the conditions (5.2) and (5.6) to be valid.

(5.2): $i \neq (1-\tau_c)r$

(5.6): if $K(T) = 0$ then $(1-\tau_c)\frac{dO}{dK} > \max\{i, (1-\tau_c)\}$

As a negative value of X will not satisfy the constraints (A.5) and (A.6) simultaneously, constraint (A.9) is thus superfluous. Therefore, we will leave it out.

Since the control variables D and I appear linear in the above formulation of the problem and have no upperbound in addition, jumps in the state variables may occur. One way to avoid such jumps is to restrict the control region by putting artificial boundaries to dividend and investment. However, due to the linearity of the model with respect to both the control variables, we obtain either singular or corner solutions. So, omitting the artificial boundaries implies the allowance of instantaneous adjustments to the optimal level, that in fact may occur at the initial moment. At other moments, such an adjustment is not feasible because of the financial restrictions. The above is in line with the proposition of Arrow and Kurz, that gives an indication that with our model formulation and assumptions a jump will never be optimal except possibly at the initial time point [Arrow and Kurz (1970), p. 57]. So, in addition to the proposition to consider only continuous solutions, the above provides an argument to omit the boundaries on the control variables with exception of the lower bound on dividend.

The constraints (A.5) and (A.6) are pure state constraints. In general, it may, therefore, happen that the corresponding co-state variables will be discontinuous in the entry or exit points of the boundary arcs of such a state constraint, that is, in the points in which the state constraint becomes active respectively inactive. To avoid such discontinuities we could apply the maximum principle designed by Russak (1970) [see also Van Loon (1983), pp. 107-113]. Geerts (1985), however, showed that with our assumptions the co-state variables in our model formulation will be continuous. In particular, he has proved the following even more general theorem (Geerts (1985), p. 155):

Theorem

Given an optimal control problem with two linearly appearing control variables and one state constraint of the first order (its time derivative contains a non vanishing control term).

Lets define J_1 and J_2 to represent the optimal control variable(s) that is (are) not respectively is (are) actual on one of its boundaries within the interior of the boundary arc.

Assuming J_1 is not empty, the costate variables (in the formulation of the necessary conditions for optimality given by Jacobson, Lele and Speyer (1971) are continuous in the entry point of the boundary arc if

- at least one of the optimal control variables within J_1 is not on its boundaries just before the entry point, or if

- all optimal control variables within J_1 are on one of their boundaries just before the entry point and at least one of all optimal controls i.e. the aggregation of J_1 and J_2 is discontinuous in the entry point.

Remarks

- this theorem is also valid in the exit point of the boundary arc
- the theorem can be applied to problems with more than one state constraint if at most one of them is active at any time
- the result also holds in the case of more than two linearly appearing control variables.

In this way Geerts (1985) has provided a contribution to the existing theory on this topic (see e.g. Hartl (1984)) which often requires regularity of the Hamiltonian function to ensure the costate variables' continuity (see Feichtinger and Hartl (1986)). In our situation the necessary conditions of Jacobson, Lele and Speyer (1971) thus coincide with the maximum principle of Pontryagin et. al. (1962) by using the 'direct adjoining approach'.

Let the Hamiltonian be

$$H = (1-\tau_d)De^{-iT} + \psi_1[(1-\tau_c)(O(K)-rK+rX)-D] + \psi_2[I-aK] \tag{A.10}$$

and let the Langrangian or extended Hamiltonian be

$$L = H + \lambda_1(K-X) + \lambda_2[(1+h)X-K] + \lambda_3 D \tag{A.11}$$

where

ψ_j: adjoint variables or co-state variables which denote the marginal contribution of the j-th level state variable to the performance level

λ_s: dynamic Lagrange multipliers representing the dynamic 'shadow price' or 'opportunity costs' of the s-th restriction.

For an optimal control history $\{D^*, I^*\}$ of the problem formulated by (A.2) through (A.9) with a resulting state trajectory $\{K^*, X^*\}$, it is necessary that there are functions $\psi_j(T)$ and $\lambda_s(T)$ such that

$$H_{optimal} := H(K^*, X^*, D^*, I^*, \psi_j, T)$$

$$= \max_{D,I} \{H(K^*, X^*, D, I, \psi_j, T)\} \text{ for all } T,\ 0 < T < z$$

Except at points of discontinuity of (D^*, I^*) we thus have:

optimality of control

$$\frac{\partial L}{\partial D} = (1-\tau_d)e^{-iT} - \psi_1 + \lambda_3 = 0 \tag{A.12}$$

$$\frac{\partial L}{\partial I} = \psi_2 = 0 \tag{A.13}$$

Euler-Lagrange equations

$$-\dot{\psi}_1 = \psi_1(1-\tau_c)r + (1+h)\lambda_2 - \lambda_1 \tag{A.14}$$

$$-\dot{\psi}_2 = \psi_1(1-\tau_c)(dO/dK - r) - a\psi_2 - \lambda_2 + \lambda_1 \tag{A.15}$$

transversality conditions

$$\psi_1(z) = \frac{\partial S(K,X,z)}{\partial X} = e^{-iz}(1-\tau_g) \tag{A.16}$$

$$\psi_2(z) = \frac{\partial S(K,X,z)}{\partial K} = 0 \tag{A.17}$$

where

S(K,X,z): terminal value of objective functional, that is
$$S(K,X,z) = (1-\tau_g)X(z)e^{-iz}$$

complementary slackness conditions

$$\lambda_1[K - X] = 0 \tag{A.18}$$

$$\lambda_2[(1+h)X - K] = 0 \tag{A.19}$$

$$\lambda_3 D = 0 \tag{A.20}$$

In addition

$\psi_j(T)$ are continuous with piecewise continuous derivatives (A.21)

$\lambda_s(T)$ are nonnegative and continuous on intervals of continuity of (D,I) (A.22)

From these conditions we derive that $\psi_1(T)$ is a continuous function if and only if $\lambda_3(T)$ is continuous. As $\psi_2(T)$ always equals zero, it is also continuous (see expressions (A.12), (A.13) and (A.27)).

For the sake of convenience we further derive from (A.13) and (A.15)

$$\psi_1(1-\tau_c)(dO/dK - r) - \lambda_2 + \lambda_1 = 0 \tag{A.23}$$

This result will be used later on.

We now apply the iterative policy-connecting procedure designed by Van Loon (1983, pp. 115-117) in order to transform the set of necessary conditions into a solutions which covers the optimal policy of the firm over the whole planning period. This procedure consists of four steps.

step 1: Based on the complementary slackness conditions (A.18)-(A.20) we may discern $2^3 = 8$ different policies, each characterized by active and inactive states of the restrictions. This number will be reduced, however, to five by assumptions (2.31) and (2.32), or, equivalently, (5.2) and (5.6). The properties of these policies are summarized in table 2.1.

step 2: The second step is the selection of those policies that may be a final policy, that is, policies feasible at T = z. A feasible final policy satisfies the transversality conditions (A.16) and (A.17). Using the features of the policies we derive conditions as presented in table 5.2. From this table we easily observe that in case we consider the basic problem, that is, the problem without personal taxation, only the policies 4 and 5 satisfy all the conditions necessary to be a final policy.

step 3: To couple a feasible preceding policy with a final policy we use the continuity properties of relevant variables. Therefore we test each policy whether coupling with the final policy will or will not violate the (necessary) continuity properties of the state variables K and X and the co-state variables ψ_1 and ψ_2. If the set of feasible preceding policies appears to be empty, then the relevant final policy is the description of the optimal trajectory of the firm for the whole planning period, supposing that the initial state constraints mentioned in (A.3) and (A.4) are fulfilled (step 4). If the set is not empty we apply the testing procedure again. In this way we find a still longer string of policies constituting an optimal policy string.

step 4: If the set of feasible preceding policies is empty we stop the iterative procedure of step 3 and, finally, check whether the initial state constraints mentioned in (A.3) and (A.4) are fulfilled. In the case that the answer to this question is positive, we have found an optimal policy string; in the other case we have to start the procedure once again with another final policy.

We now apply the above described procedure on the problem under consideration. We will illustrate the procedure by means of examples only, because the derivations are both quite straight forward as well as similar to those presented in other publications [see e.g. Van Loon (1983) and Van Schijndel (1986)].

step 1: feasible and infeasible policies

Based on the complementary slackness conditions we may now discern eight different policies. The next three are infeasible, however.

a. infeasibility of $\lambda_1 = \lambda_2 = \lambda_3 = 0$.

From (A.12) we get $\psi_1(T) = (1-\tau_d)e^{-iT}$ and so $-\dot{\psi}_1 = i(1-\tau_d)e^{-iT}$. Substitution of this result into (A.14) gives $i = (1-\tau_c)r$, which is excluded by assumption (5.2).

b. infeasibility of $\lambda_1 > 0$, $\lambda_2 > 0$, $\lambda_3 = 0$.

$$\left.\begin{array}{l}\lambda_1 > 0 \rightarrow K = X \\ \lambda_2 > 0 \rightarrow (1+h)X = K\end{array}\right\} \rightarrow K = X = 0$$

The addition sum of (A.14) and (A.15) gives

$$-\dot{\psi}_1 = h\lambda_2 + \psi_1(1-\tau_c)dO/dK$$

From (A.12) we once again get $\dot{\psi}_1 = i\psi_1$, which results in:

$$i\psi_1 = \psi_1(1-\tau_c)dO/dK + h\lambda_2$$

As $h\lambda_2 > 0$ this implies $(1-\tau_c)dO/dK < i$, which is excluded by assumption (5.6).

c. infeasibility of $\lambda_1 > 0$. $\lambda_2 > 0$, $\lambda_3 > 0$.

In addition to the previous case we get the next result:

$\lambda_3 > 0 \rightarrow D = 0$

so that

$K = X = I = D = 0.$

So, the firm is in a stationary state with initial value $X(t_0) = 0$. This state is infeasible, however, because

- no feasible evolution exists that ends up with a zero amount of equity;
- the above state does not satisfy the initial state constraints mentioned in (A.3) and (A.4), so that this state can not be an initial state as well.

The five remaining policies are feasible and have the characteristic features that are presented in table 2.1 and which we derive now.

Policy 1: $\lambda_1 = 0$, $\lambda_2 > 0$, $\lambda_3 > 0$

from (A.18): $\lambda_1 = 0$: $K > X$ from (A.19): $\lambda_2 > 0$: $K = (1+h)X$ from (A.20): $\lambda_3 > 0$: $D = 0$	maximum amount of debt no dividend
from (A.23): $\psi_1(1-\tau_c)(dO/dK-r)-\lambda_2=0$ from (A.12): $\psi_1=(1-\tau_d)e^{-iT} + \lambda_3 > 0$ $dO/dK > r$	$K(T) < K^*_{YX}$
from (A.3) : $\dot{X} = (1-\tau_c)(O(K) - \frac{h}{1+h} rK)$. As $O(K)$ is a concave function of K and $dO/dK > r$ this implies $O(K) > rK > \frac{h}{1+h} rK$ and thus $\dot{X} > 0$, $\dot{K} > 0$ and $\dot{Y} > 0$.	increasing equity, debt and amount of capital goods

Policy 2: $\lambda_1 = \lambda_2 = 0,\ \lambda_3 > 0.$

from (A.18): $\lambda_1 = 0 \rightarrow K > X$	indefinite
$\rightarrow X < K < (1+h)X$	amount of
from (A.19): $\lambda_2 = 0 \rightarrow K < (1+h)X$	debt
from (A.20): $\lambda_3 > 0 \rightarrow D = 0$	no dividend
from (A.23): $\psi_1(1-\tau_c)(dO/dK - r) = 0$	
$\rightarrow dO/dK = r$	$K(T) = K^*_{YX}$
from (A.12): $\psi_1 = (1-\tau_d)e^{-iT}+\lambda_3 > 0$	
differentiating (A.23) gives $\frac{d^2O}{dK^2}\dot{K} = 0$ and	investment on
so: $I = aK$	replacement
	level
from (A.3) : $\dot{X} = (1-\tau_c)[O(K) - r(K-X)]$	
As $O(K)$ is a concave function of K and	increasing
$dO/dK = r$, this implies $O(K) > dO/dK\ K =$	equity and
rK and therefore $\dot{X} > (1-\tau_c)rX > 0$.	decreasing
Since $\dot{K} = 0 \rightarrow \dot{Y} < 0$.	debt.

Policy 3: $\lambda_1 > 0,\ \lambda_2 = 0,\ \lambda_3 > 0$

from (A.18): $\lambda_1 > 0 \rightarrow K = X$	no debt
from (A.19): $\lambda_2 = 0 \rightarrow K < (1+h)X$	
from (A.20): $\lambda_3 > 0 \rightarrow D = 0$	no dividend
from (A.23): $\psi_1(1-\tau_c)(dO/dK-r)+\lambda_1=0$	
$\rightarrow dO/dK < r$	$K(T) > K^*_{YX}$
from (A.12): $\psi_1 = (1-\tau_d)e^{-iT}+\lambda_3 > 0$	
from (A.3) : $\dot{X} = (1-\tau_c)O(K) > 0$	K and X are increasing

Policy 4: $\lambda_1 > 0,\ \lambda_2 = 0,\ \lambda_3 = 0$

from (A.18): $\lambda_1 > 0 \rightarrow K = X$	no debt
from (A.19): $\lambda_2 = 0 \rightarrow K < (1+h)X$	
from (A.20): $\lambda_3 = 0 \rightarrow D > 0$	positive dividend
from (A.14) + (A.15): $-\dot{\psi}_1 = \psi_1(1-\tau_c)dO/dK$	
from (A.12) : $\psi_1 = (1-\tau_d)e^{-iT}$ and thus	
$-\dot{\psi}_1 = i\psi_1$ which implies	
$(1-\tau_c)dO/dK = i$	$K(T) = K_X^*$
from (A.14) + (A.15) and (A.12) we get $\psi_1(1-\tau_c)\frac{d^2O}{dK^2}\dot{K} = 0 \rightarrow \dot{K} = 0$	investment on replacement level
from (A.14): $-\dot{\psi}_1 = \psi_1(1-\tau_c)r - \lambda_1$ or	
$i\psi_1 = \psi_1(1-\tau_c)r - \lambda_1 \rightarrow i < (1-\tau_c)r$	only feasible if $i < (1-\tau_c)r$

Policy 5: $\lambda_1 = 0,\ \lambda_2 > 0,\ \lambda_3 = 0$

from (A.18): $\lambda_1 = 0 \rightarrow K > X$	maximum debt
from (A.19): $\lambda_2 > 0 \rightarrow K = (1+h)X$	
from (A.20): $\lambda_3 = 0 \rightarrow D > 0$	positive dividend
from $(1+h)\cdot$(A.14) + (A.15): $-\dot{\psi}_1=\psi_1(1-\tau_c)[(1+h)\frac{dO}{dK} - hr]$	
from (A.12): $\psi_1 = (1-\tau_d)e^{-iT}$ and thus $-\dot{\psi}_1 = i\psi_1$, which implies	
$(1-\tau_c)dO/dK = \frac{1}{1+h}\,i + \frac{h}{1+h}\,(1-\tau_c)r$	$K(T) = K_Y^*$
from $(1+h)\cdot$(A.14) + (A.15) and (A.12): $\dot{K} = 0 \rightarrow I = aK$	investment on replacement level

from (A.14): $-\dot{\psi}_1 = \psi_1(1-\tau_c)r + \lambda_2$ or
$i\psi_1 = \psi_1(1-\tau_c)r + \lambda_2 \rightarrow i > (1-\tau_c)r$ | only feasible if $i > (1-\tau_c)r$

step 2: final policies

A feasible final policy satisfies the transversality conditions (A.16) and (A.17). Due to (A.13) the condition (A.17) will always hold. Substitution of (A.16) into the first order condition (A.12) gives at T=z:

$$(1-\tau_d)e^{-iz} - (1-\tau_g)e^{-iz} + \lambda_3(z) = 0 \qquad (A.24)$$

or

$$\lambda_3(z) = (\tau_g - \tau_d)e^{-iz}. \qquad (A.25)$$

This expression points out that under different personal taxes a dividend policy $[\lambda_3 = 0]$ can never be an optimal final policy. On the other hand, under absence of personal taxation $\lambda_3(z) = 0$ holds, so that the amount of distributed dividend may be positive.

A policy may be a final policy if it satisfies (A.25). Because $\lambda_3(t_{ex}) = 0$, this condition is equivalent with

$$\lambda_3(z) = \int_{T=t_{ex}}^{z} \dot{\lambda}_3(T)\, dT \qquad (A.26)$$

where

t_{ex}: exit point of dividend policy.

Due to (A.13) we may also write

$$\lambda_3(z) = \int_{T=t_{ex}}^{z} [\dot{\psi}_1(T) + i(1-\tau_d)e^{-iT}]dT \qquad (A.27)$$

Using (A.14), (A.15) and the expression of the marginal return on equity (5.16), this expression is equivalent with

$$\lambda_3(z) = \int_{T=t_{ex}}^{z} [-\psi_1(T)R_X(T) + i(1-\tau_d)e^{-iT}]dT \tag{A.28}$$

From (A.25) we derive

$$\frac{d\lambda_3(z)}{dz} = -i\lambda_3(z) \tag{A.29}$$

which needs to equal the derivative of (A.26) with respect to z. Hence,

$$-i\lambda_3(z) = \hat{\lambda}_3(t_{ex})\frac{dt_{ex}}{dz} + \hat{\lambda}_3(z) + \int_{T=t_{ex}}^{z} [d\hat{\lambda}_3(T)/dz]dT$$

$$= \psi_1(t_{ex})i - i(1-\tau_d)e^{-it_{ex}} - \psi_1(z)R_X(z) + i(1-\tau_d)e^{-iz} +$$

$$+ \int_{T=t_{ex}}^{z} [-i\hat{\lambda}_3(T)]dT$$

$$= (1-\tau_d)e^{-it_{ex}}i - i(1-\tau_d)e^{-it_{ex}} - (1-\tau_g)e^{-iz}R_X(z)$$

$$+ i(1-\tau_d)e^{-iz} - i\lambda_3(z) \tag{A.30}$$

Hence,

$$i(1-\tau_d)e^{-iz} - (1-\tau_g)e^{-iz}R_X(z) = 0 \tag{A.31}$$

or

$$\frac{(1-\tau_g)}{(1-\tau_d)} = i/R_X \tag{A.32}$$

Using the properties of the policies, we get

policy	property	final policy if
1	$R_X > (1-\tau_c)r$	$1 < (1-\tau_g)/(1-\tau_d) < i/(1-\tau_c)r$
2	$R_X = (1-\tau_c)r$	$(1-\tau_g)/(1-\tau_d) = i/(1-\tau_c)r$
3	$R_X < (1-\tau_c)r$	$(1-\tau_g)/(1-\tau_d) > i/(1-\tau_c)r$
4	$R_X = i$	$(1-\tau_g)/(1-\tau_d) = 1$
5	$R_X = i$	$(1-\tau_g)/(1-\tau_d) = 1$

step 3: coupling of feasible policies to master policy strings

We consider two master policy strings, both ending up with policy 3, that according to table 5.2 can be a final policy if

$$i < (1-\tau_c)r \text{ and } (1-\tau_g)/(1-\tau_d) > 1$$

or

$$i > (1-\tau_c)r \text{ and } (1-\tau_g)/(1-\tau_d) > i/(1-\tau_c)r.$$

Which policy can precede policy 3? To give an answer to this question we will concentrate on the continuity properties of the state and co-state variables. We will denote the coupling moment between the policies a and b by t_{ab} and the left hand side limit of a variable by an arrow to the right. So,

$$\vec{K}(t_{ab}) = \lim_{T \uparrow t_{ab}} K(T)$$

which is the final value of K at the state described by policy a.

policy 1 → policy 3

K and X can not be simultaneously continuous, because

$$\vec{K}(t_{13}) = (1+h)\vec{X}(t_{13}),\ h > 0$$

$$\vec{K}(t_{13}) = \vec{X}(t_{13})$$

<u>policy 2 → policy 3</u>

Because the same expression for ψ_1 will hold under both policy 2 and policy 3, ψ_1 can be continuous [see (A.12)].

$$\vec{K}(t_{23}) > \vec{X}(t_{23}) \text{ and } \vec{K}(t_{23}) < (1+h)\vec{X}(t_{23})$$

$$\vec{K}(t_{23}) = \vec{X}(t_{23})$$

So, K and X can be simultaneously continuous if $\vec{K}(t_{23}) = \vec{X}(t_{23})$. Furthermore, K can be continuous, since

$$\vec{K}(t_{23}) = K^*_{YX}$$

$$\vec{K}(t_{23}) > K^*_{YX} \text{ and } \dot{K} > 0 \text{ under policy 3.}$$

Later on it will turn out that this combination of policies with policy 3 as a final policy, will only be feasible if $i > (1-\tau_c)r$, since policy 5 will be one of the precessors.

<u>policy 4 → policy 3</u>

Under both the policies the firm's assets are financed by equity only. So, if K is continuous then X is continuous too.

$$\vec{K}(t_{43}) = K^*_X$$

$$\vec{K}(t_{43}) > K^*_{YX}$$

K can thus be continuous if $K_X^* > K_{YX}^*$, that is, if $i < (1-\tau_c)r$.

Furthermore we have to check the continuity of the co-state variable ψ_1.

$$\overset{\rightarrow}{\psi}_1(t_{43}) = (1-\tau_d)e^{-it_{43}}$$

$$\overset{\leftarrow}{\psi}_1(t_{43}) = (1-\tau_d)e^{-it_{43}} + \overset{\leftarrow}{\lambda}_3(t_{43})$$

So, ψ_1 is continuous if $\overset{\leftarrow}{\lambda}_3(t_{43}) = 0$, that is, if $\dot{\lambda}_3 > 0$ when $\lambda_3 = 0$ under policy 3. From (A.12) we derive with the use of (A.14) and (A.23) that

$$\dot{\lambda}_3 = \dot{\psi}_1 + i(1-\tau_d)e^{-it_{43}}$$

$$= -[\lambda_3 + (1-\tau_d)e^{-it_{43}}](1-\tau_c)\frac{dO}{dK} + i(1-\tau_d)e^{-it_{43}}$$

So, if $i > (1-\tau_c)\ dO/dK$, that is, if $K(T) > K_X^*$ under policy 3, the above expression is positive and ψ_1 can therefore be continuous.

<u>Policy 5 → policy 3</u>

K and X can not be simultaneously continuous, because

$$\vec{K}(t_{53}) = (1+h)\vec{X}(t_{53}) \text{ and } \overset{\leftarrow}{K}(t_{53}) = \overset{\leftarrow}{X}(t_{53})$$

Moreover, even K single can not be continuous, because

$$\vec{K}(t_{53}) = K_Y^* \text{ and } \overset{\leftarrow}{K}(t_{53}) > K_{YX}^*.$$

Continuity of K requires $K_{YX}^* < K_Y^*$, or, equivalently,

$$(1-\tau_c)r > \frac{1}{1+h}\, i + \frac{h}{1+h}\,(1-\tau_c)r$$

which is only possible when $i < (1-\tau_c)r$. However, policy 5 is only feasible if $i > (1-\tau_c)r$, so that the above inequality will not hold and K will be discontinuous.

When we summarize the above described results, we get:

selection of policies preceding final policy 3

policy 1	no	X discontinuous
policy 2	yes	if $i > (1-\tau_c)r$
policy 4	yes	if $i < (1-\tau_c)r$
policy 5	no	X discontinuous

So, we have to distinguish two cases. However, we only survey the results of these remaining analyses.

a. The case $i > (1-\tau_c)r$ and $(1-\tau_g)/(1-\tau_d) > i(1-\tau_c)r$

selection of policies preceding policy 2 → policy 3

policy 1	yes	
policy 3	no	K discontinuous
policy 4	no	only feasible if $i < (1-\tau_c)r$
policy 5	no	K discontinuous

selection of policies preceding policy 1 → policy 2 → policy 3

policy 2	no	K discontinuous
policy 3	no	K and X not simultaneously continuous
policy 4	no	only feasible if $i < (1-\tau_c)r$
policy 5	yes	

selection of policies preceding policy 5→policy 1→policy 2→policy 3

policy 1	yes	
policy 2	no	K discontinuous
policy 3	no	K discontinuous
policy 4	no	only feasible if $i < (1-\tau_c)r$

b. The case $i < (1-\tau_c)r$ and $(1-\tau_g)/(1-\tau_d) > 1$.

selection of policies preceding policy 4 → policy 3

policy 1	no	K discontinuous
policy 2	no	K discontinuous
policy 3	yes	
policy 5	no	only feasible if $i > (1-\tau_c)r$

selection of policies preceding policy 3 → policy 4 → policy 3

policy 1	no	K and X not simultaneously continuous
policy 2	yes	
policy 4	no	K discontinuous
policy 5	no	only feasible if $i > (1-\tau_c)r$

selection of policies preceding policy 2→policy 3→policy 4→policy 3

policy 1	yes	
policy 3	no	K discontinuous
policy 4	no	K discontinuous
policy 5	no	only feasible if $i > (1-\tau_c)r$

Summarizing the above tables we get the next optimal master policy strings under personal taxation:

if $i < (1-\tau_c)r$ and $(1-\tau_g)/(1-\tau_d) > 1$:

policy 1 → policy 2 → policy 3 → policy 4 → policy 3

if $i > (1-\tau_c)r$ and $(1-\tau_g)/(1-\tau_d) > i/(1-\tau_c)r$:

policy 1 → policy 5 → policy 1 → policy 2 → policy 3

In absense of personal taxation we get a subset of the above strings, viz. [see also table 5.2 for the selection of the final policy] if $i < (1-\tau_c)r$:

policy 1 → policy 2 → policy 3 → policy 4

if $i > (1-\tau_c)r$:

policy 1 → policy 5

APPENDIX A2

DERIVATION OF A PARTICULAR EXPRESSION IN CHAPTER FIVE

In this appendix we prove the similarity of the expressions (5.19) and (5.20) of chapter five by means of the necessary conditions for an optimal solution. To that end, we firstly recall expression (5.19):

$$(1-\tau_{di})e^{-t_{ex}^{*}}\partial X(t_{ex}^{*}) = (1-\tau_{gi})e^{-iz}\partial X(z) \tag{A.33}$$

where

t_{ex}^{*}: the optimal exit point of the stationary dividend stage.

For any optimal solution of a control problem it holds that

$$\psi_j(t_1)\partial X_j(t_1) = \psi_j(t_2)\partial X_j(t_2) \tag{A.34}$$

Substitution of the corresponding values of $\psi_1(t_{ex}^{*})$ and $\psi_1(z)$ gives the above statement.

Expression (5.20) also points out a relation between the revenues at $T = t_{ex}^{*}$ and $T = z$:

$$(1-\tau_{di})e^{-it_{ex}^{*}} = (1-\tau_{gi})e^{-iz}.\exp(\int_{T=t_{ex}^{*}}^{z} R_X(T)dT) \tag{A.35}$$

This statement can be proved by solving the differential equations for ψ_1.

To that end we recall the expressions (A.14) and (A.15). Using (A.13) we get:

$$\begin{aligned} &(A.14) + (A.15) &&: -\dot{\psi}_1 = \psi_1(1-\tau_c)dO/dK + h\lambda_2 \\ &(A.14) + (1+h)*(A.15) &&: -\dot{\psi}_1 = \psi_1(1-\tau_c)[dO/dK(1+h) - hr] + h\lambda_1 \end{aligned} \tag{A.36}$$

Using the features of the policies as described in Appendix A1 and the expressions for the marginal return to equity, that is

$$\lambda_1 = 0,\ \lambda_2 > 0 \rightarrow Y = hX \qquad R_X = (1-\tau_c)(dO/dK(1+h)-hr)$$

$$\lambda_1 = 0,\ \lambda_2 = 0 \rightarrow 0 < Y < hX \qquad R_X = (1-\tau_c)r = (1-\tau_c)dO/dK$$

$$\lambda_1 > 0,\ \lambda_2 = 0 \rightarrow Y = 0 \qquad R_X = (1-\tau_c)dO/dK$$

we may write

$$-\dot{\psi}_1 = \psi_1 R_X \tag{A.37}$$

Solving this differential equation we get

$$\psi_1(t^*_{ex}) = \exp\left(\int_{T=t^*_{ex}}^{z} R_X dT\right).\exp(c) \tag{A.38}$$

After determining exp(c) by means of the transversality condition (A.16) we get

$$\psi_1(t^*_{ex}) = (1-\tau_{gi})e^{-iz} \exp\left(\int_{T=t^*_{ex}}^{z} R_X(T)dT\right) \tag{A.39}$$

From (A.12) we derive that on the stationary dividend stage it holds that

$$\psi_1(T) = (1-\tau_{di})e^{-iT} \tag{A.40}$$

and thus we get

$$(1-\tau_{di})e^{-it^*_{ex}} = (1-\tau_{gi})e^{-iz}.\exp\left(\int_{T=t^*_{ex}}^{z} R_X(T)dT\right). \tag{A.41}$$

APPENDIX B1

DERIVATION OF OPTIMAL SWITCHING POINT

Let us firstly rewrite the model as described in section 6.2 by eliminating the control variable Y.

$$\max\{(1-\tau_{d1}) \int_{T=0}^{t} D_1(T)e^{-i_1 T}\,dT + (1-\tau_{g1})e^{-i_1 t}\,V_m(t) \tag{B.1}$$

$$\text{subject to } \dot{V}_m = i_2 V_m - D_2 \tag{B.2}$$

$$V_m(0) = V_{m0} \tag{B.3}$$

$$\dot{X} = (1-\tau_c)(O(K) - r(K-X)) - D_1 \tag{B.4}$$

$$X(0) = x_0 \tag{B.5}$$

$$\dot{K} = I - aK \tag{B.6}$$

$$K(0) = k_0 > 0 \tag{B.7}$$

$$K - X \geq 0 \tag{B.8}$$

$$(1+h)X - K \geq 0 \tag{B.9}$$

$$\text{all variables nonnegative} \tag{B.10}$$

In order to determine the optimal end point t^* of the above problem, we need only the Hamiltonian and the transversality conditions.

Let the Hamiltonian be

$$H = (1-\tau_{d1})D_1 e^{-i_1 T} + \psi_0[i_2 V_m - D_2] + \psi_1[(1-\tau_c)(O(K)-rK+rX)-D] + \psi_2[I-aK] \tag{B.11}$$

The transversality conditions are given by

$$\psi_0(t) = (1-\tau_{g1})e^{-i_1 t} \tag{B.12}$$

$$\psi_1(t) = 0 \tag{B.13}$$

$$\psi_2(t) = 0 \tag{B.14}$$

We now use the usual condition to derive the optimal end-point [see e.g. Feichtinger & Hartl (1986)]:

$$\text{if } H(t^*) \left\{\begin{matrix} < \\ = \\ > \end{matrix}\right\} -\frac{dS}{dt} \text{ then } \left\{\begin{matrix} t^* = 0 \\ 0 < t^* < t \\ t^* = t \end{matrix}\right\} \tag{B.15}$$

where

S: the salvage value of the objective functional.

Substitution of the above results yields:

$$(1-\tau_{d1})D_1(t)e^{-i_1 t} + (1-\tau_{g1})e^{-i_1 t}[i_2 V_m(t) - D_2(t)] \left\{\begin{matrix} < \\ = \\ > \end{matrix}\right\} i_1(1-\tau_{g1})V_m(t)e^{-i_1 t}$$

or

$$e^{-i_1 t}[(1-\tau_{d1})D_1(t) - (1-\tau_{g1})D_2(t) + (i_2-i_1)(1-\tau_{g1})V_m(t)] \left\{\begin{matrix} < \\ = \\ > \end{matrix}\right\} 0$$

which is after substitution of (6.14) similar to (6.3).

APPENDIX B2

SOLUTION OF THE OPTIMAL CONTROL PROBLEM FORMULATED IN CHAPTER SIX

In this appendix we derive the optimal solution of the problem described by the expressions (6.30) through (6.41) in chapter six.

Firstly, we present the necessary conditions for an optimal solution by means of a method that strongly resembles Pontryagin's Maximum Principle. According to the theorem of Geerts (1985) [see appendix A1] we may use the direct adjoining approach. In line with the argumentation used in appendix A1, we omit the artificial boundaries on the control variables.

Secondly, we apply Van Loon's iterative policy connecting procedure in order to obtain optimal policy strings.

Since the derivation of this solution has much in common with the one presented in the appendix A1, it suffices to give only the main expressions and lines.

Let the Hamiltonian be

$$\begin{aligned} H = {} & S(1-\tau_{d1})D_1 e^{-i_1T} + (1-S)(1-\tau_{g1})e^{-i_1T'} D_2 e^{-i_2(T-T')} \\ & + \psi_1[(1-\tau_c)(O(K)-r(K-X))-D_1-D_2] \\ & + \psi_2[I_1+I_2-aK] \\ & + \psi_3 S \end{aligned} \tag{B.17}$$

and the Lagrangian

$$L = H + \lambda_1 D_1 + \lambda_2 D_2 + \lambda_3 I_1 + \lambda_4 I_2 + \lambda_5(K-X) + \lambda_6[(1+h)X-K]$$

$$+ \lambda_7 S + \lambda_8(1-S) \tag{B.18}$$

For an optimal control history of the problem formulated by (6.30) through (6.41) with a resulting state trajectory, it is necessary that there are co-state variables $\psi_j(T)$ and Langrange parameters $\lambda_s(T)$ such that

$$H_{optimal} = \max H \tag{B.19}$$

Except at points of discontinuity of $(D_1^*, D_2^*, I_1^*, I_2^*, S^*)$ we thus get:

$$\frac{\partial L}{\partial D_1} = S(1-\tau_{d1})e^{-i_1 T} - \psi_1 + \lambda_1 = 0 \tag{B.20}$$

$$\frac{\partial L}{\partial D_2} = (1-S)(1-\tau_{g1})e^{(i_2-i_1)T'} e^{-i_2 T} - \psi_1 + \lambda_2 = 0 \tag{B.21}$$

$$\frac{\partial L}{\partial I_1} = \psi_2 + \lambda_3 = 0 \tag{B.22}$$

$$\frac{\partial L}{\partial I_2} = \psi_2 + \lambda_4 = 0 \tag{B.23}$$

$$\frac{\partial L}{\partial S} = (1-\tau_{d1})D_1 e^{-i_1 T} - (1-\tau_{g1})e^{-i_1 T'} D_2 e^{-i_2(T-T')} + \psi_3$$

$$+ \lambda_7 - \lambda_8 = 0 \tag{B.24}$$

$$-\dot{\psi}_1 = \psi_1(1-\tau_c)r - \lambda_5 + \lambda_6(1+h) \tag{B.25}$$

$$-\dot{\psi}_2 = \psi_1(1-\tau_c)(\frac{dO}{dK} - r) - a\psi_2 + \lambda_5 - \lambda_6 \tag{B.26}$$

$$-\dot{\psi}_3 = (i_2-i_1)e^{(i_2-i_1)T'} e^{-i_2 T}(1-S)D_2 \tag{B.27}$$

$$\lambda_1 D_1 = 0 \qquad \lambda_2 D_2 = 0 \tag{B.28}$$

$$\lambda_3 I_1 = 0 \qquad \lambda_4 I_2 = 0 \tag{B.29}$$

$$\lambda_5(K-X) = 0 \qquad \lambda_6((1+h)X-K) = 0 \tag{B.30}$$

$$\lambda_7 S = 0 \qquad \lambda_8(1-S) = 0 \tag{B.31}$$

$$\lim_{T\to\infty} \psi_1(T)X(T) = 0 \tag{B.32}$$

$$\lim_{T\to\infty} \psi_2(T)K(T) = 0 \tag{B.33}$$

$$\lim_{T\to\infty} \psi_3(T)T'(T) = 0 \tag{B.34}$$

$\psi_j(T)$ are continuous with piecewise continuous derivatives (B.35)

$\lambda_s(T)$ are nonnegative and continuous on intervals of continuity of $\{D_1, D_2, I_1, I_2, S\}$ (B.36)

Remarks

1. Note that due to the positive initial value of K, the state equation of K and the upperbound on debt, that is, the expressions (6.34), (6.33) and (6.38) of chapter six respectively, it holds that both K and X are always positive, so that the transversality conditions (6.36) and (6.37) may be simplified.

2. If one particular investor is the owner of all the firm's shares, then the control D_j of the other investor will be equal to zero.

   example: Let $S(T) = 1$, and so $\lambda_7 = 0$ and $\lambda_8 > 0$. Substitution of $S(T) = 1$ in (B.21) gives

$$\psi_1(T) = \lambda_2(T) \tag{B.37}$$

   Substitution in (B.20) gives

$$\psi_1(T) = (1-\tau_{d1})e^{-i_1 T} + \lambda_1 > 0 \tag{B.38}$$

From (B.37) and (B.38) we get $\lambda_2 > 0$ and thus $D_2(T) = 0$.

3. This derivation starts with investor 1 as initial investor and decision maker. Analogous we may consider the problem with investor 2 as initial decision maker.

We now apply the policy connecting procedure designed by Van Loon (1983), which consists of four steps as described in the appendix A1.

The policies we derive in the first step are almost similar to those derived in the appendix A1. In addition, however, we have to consider contraction policies as described in chapter six. So, an investor j has to his disposal the six policies that are indicated in table 6.3.

In the second step we check which policy may be a feasible final policy. Using the modified versions of the transversality condition (B.32) and the optimality conditions (B.20) and (B.21) it turns out that the final policy is always a dividend policy, pursued either by investor 1 or 2. That is,

$$\lim_{T\to\infty} [S(T)(1-\tau_{d1})e^{-i_1T} - \psi_1(T) + \lambda_1(T)] = 0 \text{ if } \lim_{T\to\infty} \lambda_1(T) = 0 \tag{B.39}$$

$$\lim_{T\to\infty} [(1-S(T))(1-\tau_{g1})e^{(i_2-i_1)T'} e^{-i_2T} - \psi_1(T) + \lambda_2(T)] = 0$$

$$\text{if for any constant } T'\text{: } \lim_{T\to\infty} \lambda_2(T') = 0 \tag{B.40}$$

Only policies with $\lambda_1 = 0$ or $\lambda_2 = 0$ satisfy these conditions, which implies that a dividend policy will be final policy.

In the case that the final policy is pursued by investor 1, we get the next results:

Because no switch of investor occurs it holds that $S(T) = 1$ for all feasible T, which implies:

(B.27): $-\dot{\psi}_3 = 0$

(B.34): $\lim_{T\to\infty} \psi_3(T) = 0$, because $T'(T) = T > 0$

Hence, $\psi_3(T) = 0$ for all feasible T.

In the case that the final dividend policy is pursued by investor 2, it holds that

$$\text{(B.24)}: \psi_3 = (1-\tau_{g1})D_2 e^{(i_2-i_1)T'} e^{-i_2T} - \lambda_7$$

$$\text{(B.27)}: -\dot{\psi}_3 = (i_2-i_1)e^{(i_2-i_1)T'} e^{-i_2T} D_2 > 0$$

$$\text{(B.34)}: \lim_{T\to\infty} \psi_3(T) = 0 \text{ if } T'(T) > 0$$

The transversality condition (B.34) may be fulfilled if $\psi_3(T) > 0$ at the final dividend policy. (B.42)

Step 3 connects the feasible policies to optimal policy strings. To that end we use the continuity properties of relevant variables. We mostly summarize the findings in tables only, because the analysis is quite straight on.

We have to consider six cases, which are summarized in the next table.

case	condition	final policy	a property
a	$i_2 > i_1 > (1-\tau_c)r$	5.1	$K^*_{Y2} < K^*_{Y1}$
b	$i_2 > (1-\tau_c)r > i_1$	4.1	$K^*_{Y2} < K^*_{YX1} < K^*_{X1}$
c	$i_2 < (1-\tau_c)r > i_1$	4.1	$K^*_{X2} < K^*_{X1}$
d	$i_2 > i_1 > (1-\tau_c)r$	5.2	$K^*_{Y2} < K^*_{Y1}$
e	$i_2 > (1-\tau_c)r > i_1$	5.2	$K^*_{Y2} < K^*_{YX1} < K^*_{X1}$
f	$i_2 < (1-\tau_c)r > i_1$	4.2	$K^*_{X2} < K^*_{X1}$

where

$$(1-\tau_c)\,\frac{dO(K^*_{Xj})}{dK} = i_j,\quad (1-\tau_c)\,\frac{dO(K^*_{YXj})}{dK} = (1-\tau_c)r \text{ and}$$

$$(1-\tau_c)\frac{dO(K^*_Y)}{dK} = \frac{i_j}{1+h} + \frac{h}{1+h}\,(1-\tau_c)r$$

a) Final policy: stationary dividend with maximum debt in the case $i_2 > i_1 > (1-\tau_c)r$.

Selection of policies preceding final policy 5.1

1.1	no	ψ_3 discontinuous
2.1	no	K and ψ_3 discontinuous
3.1	no	K and ψ_3 discontinuous
4.1	no	only feasible if $i_1 < (1-\tau_c)r$
6.1	yes	
1.2	no	ψ_3 discontinuous
2.2	no	K and ψ_3 discontinuous
3.2	no	K and ψ_3 discontinuous
4.2	no	only feasible if $i_2 < (1-\tau_c)r$
5.2	no	K discontinuous
6.2	no	ψ_1 discontinuous

If we repeat the same procedure once again, we find no feasible policy that can precede the above string. We now apply the fourth step of the iterative procedure: under which conditions may the initial state constraints be satisfied? We find the next results:

$K(0) = K^*_{Y1}$: stationary dividend policy 5.1

$K(0) > K^*_{Y1}$: contraction policy 6.1 → stationary dividend policy 5.1

b) Final policy: stationary dividend without debt pursued by investor 1 in the case $i_2 > (1-\tau_c)r > i_1$.

Analogous to case a) we find only a contraction policy pursued by investor 1 as a feasible and thus optimal preceding policy of the stationary dividend policy. Since $i_1 < (1-\tau_c)r$ both the contraction and the dividend policy are financed by equity only. The following strings also satisfies the initial state constraints of step 4:

if $K(0) = K^*_{X1}$: stationary dividend policy 4.1

if $K(0) > K^*_{X1}$: contraction policy 6.1 → stationary dividend policy 4.1

c) Final policy: stationary dividend policy 4.1 without debt in the case $i_1 < (1-\tau_c)r$, $i_2 < (1-\tau_c)r$, $i_1 < i_2$.

The results of this case are similar to that of the previous one, to which we for convenience sake refer.

d) Final policy: stationary dividend policy 5.2 with debt in the case $i_2 > i_1 > (1-\tau_c)r$.

Selection of policies preceding final policy 5.2

1.1	yes	
2.1	no	K discontinuous
3.1	no	K and X not continuous simultaneously
4.1	no	only feasible if $i_1 < (1-\tau_c)r$
5.1	no	K and ψ_1 discontinuous
6.1	no	ψ_1 discontinuous
1.2	no	ψ_3 discontinuous
2.2	no	K and ψ_3 discontinuous
3.2	no	K-X and ψ_3 discontinuous
4.2	no	only feasible if $i_2 < (1-\tau_c)r$
6.2	yes	

We illustrate the above selection by means of two examples. We denote the coupling (or switching) point by t.

The string policy 1.1 → policy 5.2

continuity of $\psi_1(t)$: $\overset{\rightarrow}{\psi}_1(t) = (1-\tau_{d1})e^{-i_1 t} + \overset{\rightarrow}{\lambda}_1(t)$

$$\overset{\leftarrow}{\psi}_1(t) = (1-\tau_{g1})e^{-i_1 t}$$

ψ_1 may be continuous since $0 < (1-\tau_{g1})e^{-i_1 t} - (1-\tau_{d1})e^{-i_1 t} = \lambda_1(t)$.
Continuity of ψ_2 is no problem, because $\lambda_3 = \lambda_4 = 0$.
Continuity of $\psi_3(t)$: $\overset{\rightarrow}{\psi}_3(t) = \overset{\rightarrow}{\lambda}_8(t) > 0$

$$\overset{\leftarrow}{\psi}_3(t) = (1-\tau_{g1})e^{-i_1 t}D_2 - \lambda_7(t) > 0 \text{ due to (B.42)}$$

So, the continuity of all the co-state variables is possible.

String policy 1.2 → policy 5.2

Continuity of $\psi_3(t)$: $\overset{\rightarrow}{\psi}_3(t) = -\overset{\rightarrow}{\lambda}_7 < 0$

$$\overset{\leftarrow}{\psi}_3(t) = (1-\tau_{g1})e^{(i_2-i_1)T'}e^{-i_1 T}D_2 - \overset{\leftarrow}{\lambda}_7(t) > 0$$

Hence, ψ_3 will not be continuous, so that this coupling is not possible.

We can show in a similar way that no policy can precede the two strings we found above. So, we get the next strings, that also satisfy the initial state constraints:

if $K(0) > K^*_{Y2}$: contraction policy 6.2 → stationary dividend policy 5.2

if $K(0) = K^*_{Y2}$: stationary dividend policy 5.2

if $K(0) < K^*_{Y2}$: growth policy with debt 1.1 → stationary dividend policy 5.2

e) Final policy: stationary dividend policy 5.2 with debt in the case

$$i_1 < (1-\tau_c)r < i_2.$$

The results of this case are similar to those of the previous one, to which we for convenience sake refer.

f) Final policy: stationary dividend policy 4.2 without debt in the case

$$i_1 < (1-\tau_c)r,\ i_2 < (1-\tau_c)r \text{ and } i_1 < i_2.$$

Selection of policies preceding final policy 4.2

1.1	no	K discontinuous
2.1	no	K discontinuous
3.1	yes	
4.1	no	K and ψ_1 discontinuous
5.1	no	only feasible if $i_1 > (1-\tau_c)r$
6.1	no	ψ_1 discontinuous
1.2	no	K and ψ_3 discontinuous
2.2	no	K and ψ_3 discontinuous
3.2	no	ψ_3 discontinuous
5.2	no	only feasible if $i_2 < (1-\tau_c)r$
6.2	yes	

So, we have two substrings:

f1: policy 3.1 → policy 4.2

f2: policy 6.2 → policy 4.2

ad f1: <u>selection of policies preceding policy 3.1 → policy 4.2</u>

Because we know the switch-point, only policies pursued by investor 1 can precede this string (otherwise ψ_3 will be discontinuous). So, we may apply the analysis of appendix A1, which results in:

growth policy 1.1 with debt → redemption of debt 2.1 →
growth policy 3.1 without debt → stationary dividend 4.2

ad f2: selection of policies preceding policy 6.2 → policy 4.2

We find no policy that may precede this string.

Summarizing and combining the above findings we get the results that are presented in the final part of section 6.3.

APPENDIX B3

A PARETO SOLUTION OF A DIFFERENTIAL GAME

In this appendix we look for candidates for a Pareto solution of the model presented in chapter six by the expressions (6.42) through (6.47). We solve the related optimal control model of maximizing V^1+V^2 under the assumptions: $i = i_1 = i_2$ and $\tau_{d1} > \tau_g = \tau_{d2}$.

We simplify the model by defining $A(T) := S_2(T) - S_1(T)$ and by eliminating the variable $Y(T)$. For the sake of convenience we present the problem in its full length.

$$\text{maximize } \{ \int_{T=0}^{z} D(T)[(1-\tau_{d1})Z_1 + (1-\tau_{d2})(1-Z_1)]e^{-iT}dT$$

$$+ [X(z) - \tau_g(X(z)-X(0))]e^{-iz}\} \tag{B.43}$$

$$\text{subject to } \dot{X} = (1-\tau_c)[O(K) - r(K-X)] - D$$

$$X(0) = x_0 > 0 \tag{B.44}$$

$$\dot{K} = I - aK$$

$$K(0) = k_0 > 0 \tag{B.45}$$

$$\dot{Z}_1 = A$$

$$Z_1(0) = z_{10} \text{ and } z_{10} < 1 \tag{B.46}$$

$$D \geq 0 \tag{B.47}$$

$$I \geq 0 \tag{B.48}$$

$$K - X \geq 0 \tag{B.49}$$

$$(1+h)X - K \geq 0 \tag{B.50}$$

$$A_{max} - A \geq 0$$

$$A - A_{min} \geq 0 \tag{B.51}$$

$$Z_1 \geq 0 \qquad 1 - Z_1 \geq 0 \tag{B.52}$$

Due to (B.45), (B.48) and (B.50) the state constraints $X \geq 0$ and $K \geq 0$ are always satisfied, so we omit them.

Formulating the problem in this way we have to solve an optimal control problem. The procedure, we apply, is once again similar to that of appendix A1: firstly we derive the necessary conditions for an optimal solution and thereafter we apply the iterative policy-connecting procedure designed by Van Loon. Moreover, we use the direct adjoining approach and omit artificial upper bounds on the control variables $D(T)$ and $I(T)$.

Let the Hamiltonian be

$$H = [(1-\tau_{d1})DZ_1 + (1-\tau_{d2})D(1-Z_1)]e^{-iT} +$$

$$\psi_1[(1-\tau_c)(O(K) - r(K-X)) - D] +$$

$$\psi_2[I - aK] +$$

$$\psi_3 A \tag{B.53}$$

and the Lagrangian

$$L = H + \lambda_1 D + \lambda_2 I + \lambda_3[K-X] + \lambda_4[(1-h)X-K] +$$

$$\lambda_5[A_{max}-A] + \lambda_6[A-A_{min}] + \lambda_7 Z_1 + \lambda_8[1-Z_1] \tag{B.54}$$

For an optimal control history of the problem formulated by (B.43) through (B.51) with resulting state trajectory, it is necessary that there are co-state variables $\psi_j(T)$ and Lagrange parameters $\lambda_s(T)$ such that

$$H_{optimal} = \underset{D,I,A}{\text{maximum}}\ H \tag{B.55}$$

Except at points of discontinuity of (D^*, I^*, A^*) we have:

$$\frac{\partial L}{\partial D} = [(1-\tau_{d1})Z_1 + (1-\tau_{d2})(1-Z_1)]e^{-iT} - \psi_1 + \lambda_1 = 0 \tag{B.56}$$

$$\frac{\partial L}{\partial I} = \psi_2 + \lambda_2 = 0 \tag{B.57}$$

$$\frac{\partial L}{\partial A} = \psi_3 - \lambda_5 + \lambda_6 = 0 \tag{B.58}$$

$$-\dot{\psi}_1 = \psi_1(1-\tau_c)r - \lambda_3 + \lambda_4(1+h) \tag{B.59}$$

$$-\dot{\psi}_2 = \psi_1(1-\tau_c)(\frac{dO}{dK} - r) - a\psi_2 + \lambda_3 - \lambda_4 \tag{B.60}$$

$$-\dot{\psi}_3 = D(\tau_{d2} - \tau_{d1})e^{-iT} + \lambda_7 - \lambda_8 \tag{B.61}$$

$$\psi_1(z) = (1-\tau_g)e^{-iz} \tag{B.62}$$

$$\psi_2(z) = 0 \tag{B.63}$$

$$\psi_3(z) = 0 \tag{B.64}$$

$\psi_j(T)$ are continuous with piecewise continuous derivatives (B.65)

$\lambda_s(T)$ are nonnegative and continuous on intervals of continuity of $\{D, I, A\}$ (B.66)

and, in addition, the usual complementary slackness conditions.

According to the derivations of chapters two and five, we have to distinghuish two cases:

a) $i > (1-\tau_c)r$ and b) $i < (1-\tau_c)r$

Because the derivations of both cases run in the same way, we consider only the former one and leave the derivation of the latter one to the reader. As stated before, we apply an iterative solution procedure, that consists of four steps.

step 1: The disposable policies are the same as used until now in this book. However, because each policy may be pursued by either investor 1 or investor 2, or even by both investors together, we will summarize the policies with its features and labels in the next table.

investor(s)	1	2	1 and 2	1 and 2	1 and 2	1 and 2
Z_1	1	0	+	+	+	+
$\dot{Z}_1$	0	0	0	−	−	+
A	0	0	0	−	A_{min}	−
growth with debt	1.1	1.2	1.0	1.12	1.12m	1.21
redemption	2.1	2.2	2.0	2.12	2.12m	2.21
growth without debt	3.1	3.2	3.0	3.12	3.12m	3.21
dividend without debt	4.1	4.2	4.0	4.12	4.12m	4.21
dividend with debt	5.1	5.2	5.0	5.12	5.12m	5.21
contraction	6.1	6.2	6.0	6.12	6.12m	6.21

step 2: We select the candidates for a final policy by substituting the transversality conditions (B.62)-(B.64) into the first order conditions (B.56)-(B.58):

$$[(1-\tau_{d1})Z_1 + (1-\tau_{d2})(1-Z_1)]e^{-iz} - (1-\tau_g)e^{-iz} + \lambda_1(z) = 0 \quad (B.67)$$

$$\lambda_2(z) = 0 \quad (B.68)$$

$$-\lambda_5(z) + \lambda_6(z) = 0 \quad (B.69)$$

Using the assumption $\tau_{d2} = \tau_g$ we may rewrite (B.67) into:

$$[\tau_{d2} - \tau_{d1}]Z_1(z)e^{-iz} + \lambda_1(z) = 0 \qquad (B.70)$$

Because $\lambda_5 = \lambda_6 > 0$ implies that A is on its lower and upper bound at one and the same moment, which is impossible, a final policy need to satisfy the following conditions:

* $Z_1(z) = 0$ and $\lambda_1(z) = 0$ or (B.71)
  $Z_1(z) > 0$ and $\lambda_1(z) > 0$ (B.72)

* $\lambda_2(z) = 0 \rightarrow I(z) > 0$ (B.73)

* $\lambda_5(z) = \lambda_6(z) = 0 \rightarrow A_{min} < A < A_{max}$ (B.74)

We are able to eliminate many policies by means of these conditions.

* Because we consider only the case $i > (1-\tau_c)r$ we may eliminate all policies 4.number, which are only feasible if $i < (1-\tau_c)r$.
* Condition (B.71) eliminates the policies 1.1, 2.1 and 3.1, which are characterized by $\lambda_1 > 0$.
* Due to (B.73) all contraction policies may be left out of consideration.
* (B.74) implies that there is no need to consider policies with A on one of its boundaries.
* Condition (B.72) eliminates those dividend policies in which investor 1 is involved, that is, the policies 5.1, 5.0, 5.12 and 5.21.

After these eliminations only 10 policies are left, which may be divided into two groups:

1. stationary dividend policy 5.2, pursued by only investor 2;
2. zero dividend policies, pursued by both the investors.

The existence of the second group of policies can be clarified by recalling the results of chapter five and the corresponding appendix A1: due to the lower tax rate on capital gain than on dividend, it may be in favour to the investor to pursue a zero dividend policy at decision moment close to the planning horizon.

<u>step 3</u>: The selection of preceding is based on some relevant continuity properties, in particular with respect to the state and co-state variables.

We first consider the selection of preceding policies of the second group of final policies. We know from chapter five that in the case that a zero dividend policy is a final policy, the marginal return on equity is below the time preference rate. Furthermore, such a policy (string) will generally by preceded by a stationary dividend policy. We now show that the problem under consideration prevents such a succession.

On the dividend stage it holds that

$$-\dot{\psi}_3 = D(\tau_{d2}-\tau_{d1})e^{-iT} \tag{B.75}$$

Since ψ_3 (z) = 0 and $\dot{\psi}_3(T) = 0$ on the (final) growth policies, this implies that $\psi_3(T) < 0$ during the dividend policy. Substitution of this result into (B.58) gives $\lambda_6(T) > 0$ and thus A(T) = A_{min}, which implies that the final value of Z_1 on the dividend stage is rather zero than positive.
We thus conclude that no policy can precede a growth policy as final policy. This result implies that such a policy (string) need to satisfy the initial state constraints in order to be a feasible policy (string).
When we consider the final policy 5.2 we know form the analysis of chapter two that we may eliminate in the case that $i > (1-\tau_c)r$ and $K(0) < K^*_{Y2}$ all the policies with 2., 3. and 6., as first index. Furthermore, the continuity of Z_1 requires that investor 2 forms part of the preceding policy. We thus concentrate on the next policies:

selection of preceding policies of final policy 5.2

5.12	no	a non feasible policy
5.12m	yes	
1.2	no	a non feasible policy
1.12m	no	ψ_3 discontinuous
1.12	yes	

Policy 5.12 is non feasible policy, because $\lambda_5 = \lambda_6 = 0$, which implies $\psi_3 = 0$, whereas $-\dot{\psi}_3 = D(\tau_{d2}-\tau_{d1})e^{-iT} < 0$.
Policy 1.2 turns out to be a non feasible policy too, because $\lambda_5 = \lambda_6 = 0$ implies $\psi_3 = 0$, whereas $-\dot{\psi}_3 = \lambda_7 > 0$.

The string 1.12m → 5.2 is not possible because of the discontinuity of ψ_3. On policy 1.12m it holds that $\psi_3 = -\lambda_6$ and $-\dot{\psi}_3 = 0$, so that $\psi_3(t) < 0$, whereas $\psi_3 = 0$.

Until now we found two strings ending up with policy 5.2. If we apply once again the selection procedure, it turns out that no policy can precede the first string 5.12m → policy 1.2, and that only policy 1.0 may precede the second string.

step 4: We check whether the above strings may satisfy the initial state constraints. We find the following results:

$K(0) = K^*_{Y2}$: policy 5.12m → policy 5.2

$K(0) < K^*_{Y2}$: policy 1.0 → policy 1.12 → policy 5.2

If we allow an initial value K(0) such that $K(0) > K^*_{Y2}$ we can analogously prove that the next string is optimal:

$K(0) > K^*_{Y2}$: policy 6.12m → policy 6.2 → policy 5.2

APPENDIX C

DERIVATION OF A PARTICULAR EXPRESSION IN CHAPTER SEVEN

To prove $d(V_p/V_e)/dK < 0$ we distinguish two cases.

<u>case 1</u>: $K < K_e^* < K_p^*$.

According to (7.15) it holds that for any $k < K_e^* < K_p^*$ that

$$V_p(k) = (D_p^*/r)\exp(-r(1-\tau_p)(t_{gdp}-t_{kp})) \tag{C.1}$$

$$V_e(k) = (D_e^*/r)\exp(-r(t_{gde}-t_{ke})) \tag{C.2}$$

Hence,

$$V_p/V_e = (D_p^*/D_e^*)\exp(-r(1-\tau_p)(t_{gdp}-t_{kp}) + r(t_{gde}-t_{ke})) \tag{C.3}$$

Since the derivative with respect to K can generally be expressed by

$$d(V_p/V_e)/dK = d(V_p/V_e)/dT \;.\; dT/dK \tag{C.4}$$

we find that

$$d(V_p/V_e)/dK = [(\dot{V}_p V_e - \dot{V}_e V_p)/V_e^2].dT/dK \tag{C.5}$$

After substitution of the derivatives with respect to time of both (C.1) and (C.2), that is with respect to t_{kp} and t_{ke} respectively, this results in:

$$d(V_p/V_e)/dK = \underbrace{r[(1-\tau_p) - 1]}_{< 0} \;.\; \underbrace{V_p/V_e}_{> 0} \;.\; \underbrace{dT/dK}_{> 0} < 0 \tag{C.6}$$

case 2: $K_e^* < k < K_p^*$.

According to (7.15) the value of $V_e(k)$ is now given by

$$V_e(t_{ke}) = D_e^*/r.\exp(-r(t_{cde}-t_{ke})) + \int_{T=t_{ke}}^{t_{cde}} D(T)\exp(-r(T-t_{ke}))dT \qquad (C.7)$$

Hence, for any t_{ke} it holds that

$$dV_e/dt_{ke} = rV_e(t_{ke}) - D(t_{ke}) \qquad (C.8)$$

We now get with respect to t_{ke}

$$\frac{d(V_p/V_e)}{dk} = [V_e(dV_p/dk) - V_p(dV_e/dk)]/V_e^2$$

$$= [V_e \frac{dV_p}{dt_{kp}} \cdot \frac{dt_{kp}}{dK} - V_p \frac{dV_e}{dt_{ke}} \cdot \frac{dt_{ke}}{dK}]/V_e^2 \qquad C.9)$$

which with the use of (7.7)-(7.9) and (7.13) results in

$$\frac{d(V_p/V_e)}{dk} = [V_e \frac{dV_p}{dt_{kp}} / (1-\tau_c)O(K) - V_p \frac{dV_e}{dt_{ke}} / aK]/V_e^2 \qquad (C.10)$$

Substitution of (C.8) and the derivative with respect to time of (C.1) into (C.10) gives:

$$\frac{d(V_p/V_e)}{dk} = V_p[V_e r(1-\tau_p)/(1-\tau_c)O(K) - (rV_e-D)/aK]/V_e^2 \qquad (C.11)$$

Due to $D_e^* < (1-\tau_c)O(K(t_{ke}))$ it holds that

$$V_e(t_{ke}) < \frac{(1-\tau_c)O(K(t_{ke}))}{r} < \frac{(1-\tau_c)O(K(t_{ke}))}{r(1-\tau_p)} \qquad (C.12)$$

implying

$$V_e r(1-\tau_p)/(1-\tau_c)O(K) < 1 \qquad (C.13)$$

In addition it holds due to (7.13) and (C.12) that

$$(rV_e - D)/aK = [rV_e - (1-\tau_c)0(K) - aK]/aK$$

$$= [rV_e - (1-\tau_c)0(K)]/aK - 1 < -1 \qquad (C.14)$$

Putting these results together we get

$$V_e r(1-\tau_p)/(1-\tau_c)0(K) + (rV_e - D)/aK < 1 + (-1) = 0 \qquad (C.15)$$

which proves that the derivative of (C.7) is negative.

LIST OF SYMBOLS

B : retention rate, inflow of debt

B_L : market value debt of levered firm

C : cash outlays

$C(L)$: leverage related costs

CF : cash flow

C_Y : marginal costs of debt

D : dividend

E : total corporate profit

F_j : acceptence indicator j

G : capital gain

I : gross investment

K : production capacity, amount of capital goods

L : labour

NPI : net present index

NPV : net present value

$O(K)$: operating income

P_J : current market price per dollar J, J = D, G, Y

Q : production level

R : revenue project, marginal return to total capital

a : depreciation rate

b : retention rate, redemption rate

g : rate of growth

h : debt to equity rate

i : time preference rate of shareholders

l : labour to capital rate

n : number of projects

q : capital productivity

r : market interest rate

r' : net return on capital

r_d : demand interest rate

r_o : tax free interest rate

r_s : supply interest rate

s : imputation factor

t : free end point

t_{en}: entry point dividend stage

t_{ex}: exit point dividend stage

w : wage rate

z : planning horizon

R_X : marginal return to equity

S : selection variable

S_j : selling rate investor j

S(K): sales level

S_D : market value dividend claims

S_G : market value capital gain

S_L : market value equity of levered firm

S_U : market value equity of unlevered firm

T : time

T' : artificial time

TTL : total tax liability

V : value of a firm

V_e : personal value of a firm to a tax exempt investor

V_L : value of a levered firm

V_m : market value of a firm

V_{pi} : personal value of a firm to an investor subject to τ_{ri}

V_U : value of an unlevered firm

X : equity

Y : debt

Z_j : fraction of the stock that the j-th investor possesses

τ_c : corporate profit tax

τ_{cd}: corporate tax rate on distributed dividend

τ_d : personal tax rate on dividend

τ_g : personal tax rate on capital gain

τ_p : personal tax rate private investor

τ_r : personal tax rate on debt

τ_s : rate of imputation

Small letters are constants, capitals are variables.

REFERENCES

APPELS A.W.C., (1986), Political Economy and Enterprise Subsidies, (Tilburg University Press, Tilburg)

ARDITTI F.D., H. LEVY & M. SARNAT, (1977), Taxes, capital structure and the cost of capital: some extensions, Quarterly Review of Economics and Business 17, pp. 89-95

ARROW K.J. & M. KURZ, (1970), Public Investment, the Rate of Return and Optimal Fiscal Policy, (John Hopkins Press, Baltimore)

ATKINSON A.B. & J.E. STIGLITZ, (1980), Lectures on Public Economics, (McGraw Hill, New York)

AUERBACH A., (1979), Wealth maximization and the cost of capital, Quarterly Journal of Economics 93, pp. 433-446

AUERBACH A.J. & M.A. KING, (1983), Taxation, portfolio choice and debt-equity ratios: a general equilibrium model, Quarterly Journal of Economics 97, pp. 587-609

BASAR T. & G.J. OLSDER, (1982), Dynamic Noncooperative Game Theory, (Academic Press, New York)

BELLMAN R., (1957), Dynamic Programming, (Princeton University Press, Princeton)

BENSOUSSAN A., E.G. HURST jr. & B. NASLUND, (1974), Management applications of modern control theory, (North Holland, Amsterdam)

BENSOUSSAN A., P.R. KLEINDORFER & C.S. TAPIERO, (1978), Applied Optimal Control, TIMS Studies in Management Science 9, (North Holland, Amsterdam)

BRENNAN M.J., (1970), Taxes, market valuation and corporate financial policy, National Tax Journal 23, pp. 417-427

BREALEY R. & S. MYERS, (1981), Principles of Corporate Finance, (McGraw Hill, New York)

BRENNAN M.J. & E.S. SCHWARTZ, (1978), Corporate income taxes, valuation and the problem of optimal capital structure, Journal of Business 51, pp. 103-114

CHEN A. & E.H. KIM, (1979), Theories of corporate debt policy: a synthesis, Journal of Finance 34, pp. 371-384

COPELAND Th.E. & J.F. WESTON, (1983), Financial Theory and Corporate Policy, (Addison Wesley, Reading)

DEANGELO H. & R. MASULIS, (1980a), Optimal capital structure under corporate and personal taxation, Journal of Financial Economics 8, pp. 3-29

DEANGELO H. & R. MASULIS (1980b), Leverage and dividend irrelevancy under corporate and personal taxation, Journal of Finance 35, pp. 453-467

EKMAN E.V., (1978), Some Dynamic Economic Models of the Firm, ph.d. thesis EFI, (Stockholm School of Economics, Stockholm)

FARRAR D. & L. SELWYN, (1967), Taxes, corporate financial policies and returns to investors, National Tax Journal 20, pp. 444-454

FEICHTINGER G., (1982a), Optimal Control Theory and Economic Analysis, (North Holland, Amsterdam)

FEICHTINGER G., (1982b), Anwendungen des Maximumprinzips im Operations Research, Teil 1 und 2, OR Spektrum 4, pp. 171-190 and 195-212

FEICHTINGER G. & R.F. HARTL, (1986), Optimale Kontrolle Oekonomischer Prozesse, Anwendungen des Maximumprinzips in den Wirtschaftswissenschaften, (de Gruyter, Berlin)

FEICHTINGER G. & S. JØRGENSEN, (1982), Differential game models in management science, European Journal of Operational Research 14, pp. 137-155

FEICHTINGER G. & M. LUPTACIK, (1983), Optimal employment, wage and price policies of a firm, Forschungsbericht 62, (TU Wien)

FEICHTINGER G., (1985), Optimal Control Theory and Economic Analysis 2, (North Holland, Amsterdam)

FRIEDLAENDER A.F. & A.F. VANDENDORPE, (1978), Capital taxation in a dynamic general equilibrium setting, Journal of Public Economics 10, pp. 1-

FRIEDMAN A., (1971), Differential Games, (John Wiley and Sons, New York)

GEERTS A.H.W., (1985), Optimality Conditions for Solutions of Singular and State Constrained Optimal Control Problems in Economics, Master thesis, (Eindhoven University of Technology, Eindhoven)

GORDON M.J., (1962), The Investment, Financing and Valuation of the Corporation, (Homewood, Illinois)

GORDON M.J., (1982), Leverage and the value of a firm under a progressive personal income tax, Journal of Banking and Finance 6, pp. 482-493

GORDON M.J., (1984), Leverage and the value of a firm under a progressive personal income tax: reply, Journal of Banking and Finance 8, pp. 495-497

HALEY C.W. & L.D. SCHALL, (1979), The Theory of Financial Decisions, (McGraw Hill, New York)

HAMADA R.S. & M.S. SCHOLES, (1985), Taxes and corporate financial management, in E. ALTMAN & M. SUBRAHMANYAM (eds.): Recent Advances in Corporate Finance, (Irwin, Homewood), pp. 187-226

HARRIS J.M., (1981), Personal Income Taxes and Capital Structure, (University Microfilms International, Michigan)

HARTL R.F., (1984), A survey of the optimality conditions for optimal control problems with state variable inequality constraints, in J.P. BRANS (ed): Operational Research '84, (North Holland, Amsterdam), pp. 423-433

JAFFE J.F. & R. WESTERFIELD, (1984), Leverage and the value of a firm under a progressive personal income tax: a correction and extension, Journal of Banking and Finance 8, pp. 491-494

JENSEN M. & W. MECKLING, (1976), Theory of the firm managerial behaviour, agency costs and ownership structure, Journal of Financial Economics 4, pp. 305-360

JØRGENSEN S., (1982), A survey of some differential games in advertising, Journal of Economic Dynamics and Control 4, pp. 341-369

JØRGENSEN S., G.J.C.Th. van SCHIJNDEL & P.M. KORT, (1986), Optimal investment, financing and dividends: a Stackelberg differential game, workingpaper Copenhagen School of Economics and Business Administration

JORGENSON D.W., (1963), Capital theory and investment behaviour, American Economic Review 52, pp. 247-259

JORGENSON D.W., (1967), The theory of investment behaviour, in R. FERBER (ed): Determinants of Investment Behaviour, National Bureau of Economic Research, (Columbia University Press, New York)

KAMIEN M.I. & N.L. SCHWARTZ, (1985), Dynamic Optimization, the Calculus of Variations and Optimal Control in Economics and Management, (North Holland, New York), 4th reprint

KIM E.H., (1978), A mean variance theory on optimal capital structure and corporate debt capacity, Journal of Finance 35, pp. 45-64

KIM E.H., (1982), Miller's equilibrium, stockholders leverage clienteles and optimal capital structure, Journal of Finance 37, pp. 301-323

KIM E.H., W.G. LEWELLEN & J.J. McCONNELL, (1979), Financial leverage clienteles, Journal of Financial Economics 7, pp. 83-109

KING M., (1977), Public Policy and the Corporation, (Chapmann and Hall, London)

KORT P.M., (1986), Adjustment costs in a dynamic model of the firm, in L. STREITFERDT et al. (eds): Operations Research Proceedings 1985, (Springer, Berlin), pp. 497-505

KORT P.M., (1987), Optimal investment policy under financial restrictions and adjustment costs, to be published in European Economic Review.

KROUSE C.G. & W.Y. LEE, (1973), Optimal equity financing of the corporation, Journal of Financial and Quantitative Analysis, pp. 539-561

LEBAN R., (1982), Employment and wage strategies of the firm through a business cycle, Journal of Economic Dynamics and Control 4, pp. 371-394

LEITMAN G., (1974), Cooperative and Noncooperative Differential Games, Courses and Lectures 90, (International Centre for Mechanical Science, Udine)

LELAND H.E., (1972), The dynamics of a revenue maximizing firm, International Economic Review 13, pp. 376-385

LESOURNE J., (1973), Modeles de Croissance des Entreprises, (Dunod, Paris)

LESOURNE J. & R. LEBAN, (1982), Control theory and the dynamics of the firm: a survey, OR Spektrum 4, pp. 1-14

LOON P.J.J.M. van, (1983), A Dynamic Theory of the Firm: Production, Finance and Investment, Lecture Notes in Economics and Mathematical Systems 218, (Springer, Berlin)

LOON P.J.J.M. van, (1985), Investment grants and alternatives to stimulate industry and employment, in G. FEICHTINGER (ed): Optimal Control Theory and Economic Analysis 2, (North Holland, Amsterdam), pp. 331-340

LORIE J.H. & L.J. SAVAGE, (1955), Three problems in capital rationing, Journal of Business, pp. 229-239

LUDWIG Th. (1978), Optimale Expansionspfade der Unternehmung, (Gabler, Wiesbaden)

LUHMER A., (1982), Optimal control with switching dynamics, in G. FEICHTINGER & P. KALL (eds): Operations Research in Progress, (Reidel, Dordrecht), pp. 247-260

MEHLMANN A., (1985), Differentialspiele: die Analyse dynamischer Konfliktsituationen, (Anton Hain, Konigstein)

MILLER M.H., (1977), Debt and taxes, Journal of Finance 32, pp. 261-275

MILLER M.H. & M.S. SCHOLES, (1978), Dividends and taxes, Journal of Financial Economics 6, pp. 333-364

MODIGLIANI F., (1982), Debt, dividend policy, taxes, inflation and market valuation, Journal of Finance 37, pp. 255-273

MODIGLIANI F. & M.H. MILLER, (1958), The cost of capital, corporation finance and the theory of investment, American Economic Review 48, pp. 261-297

MODIGLIANI F. & M.H. MILLER, (1963), Corporate income taxes and the cost of capital: a correction, American Economic Review 53, pp. 433-443

MOERLAND P.W., (1978a), Optimal firm behaviour under different fiscal regimes, European Economic Review 11, pp. 37-58

MOERLAND P.W., (1978b), Firm Behaviour under Taxation, (Pasmans, 's-Gravenhage)

NECK R., (1984), Stochastic control theory and operations research, European Journal of Operational Research 17, pp. 283-301

PONTRYAGIN L.S., V.G. BOLTYANSKII, R.V. GAMKRELIDZE & E.F. MISCHENKO, (1962), The Mathematical Theory of Optimal Processes, (Wiley, New York)

RUSSAK B.I., (1970), On general problems with bounded state variables, Journal of Optimization Theory and Applications 6, pp. 424-451

SCHAEFFER S.M., (1982), Tax induced clientele effects in the market for british government securities, Journal of Financial Economics 10, pp. 121-159

SCHIJNDEL G.J.C.Th. van, (1985), Dynamic tax induced return clienteles, in G. FEICHTINGER (ed): Optimal Control Theory and Economic Analysis 2, (North Holland, Amsterdam), pp. 341-361

SCHIJNDEL G.J.C.Th. van, (1986a), Dynamic results of financial leverage clienteles, Journal of Operational Research 25, pp. 90-97

SCHIJNDEL G.J.C.Th. van, (1986b), Dynamic behaviour of a value maximizing firm under personal taxation, European Economic Review 30, pp. 1043-1062.

SCHIJNDEL G.J.C.Th. van, (1986c), Dynamic shareholder behaviour under personal taxation: a note, in: L. Streitferdt et al. (eds): Operations Research Proceedings 1985, (Springer, Berlin), pp. 488-495.

SCHIJNDEL G.J.C.Th. van & P.A. VERHEYEN, (1986), Leverage and the value of a firm under a progressive income tax: reconsideration, working paper Tilburg University, pp. 1-11.

SCHIJNDEL G.J.C.Th. van, (1987), Optimal dynamic portfolio selection and firm behaviour under personal taxation, to be published in Engineering Costs and Production Economics.

SCHWORM W.E., (1979), Tax policy, capital use and investment incentives, Journal of Public Economics 12, pp. 191-204

SEIERSTAD A. & K. SYDSAETER, (1977), Sufficiently conditions in optimal control theory, International Economic Review 18, pp. 367-391

SEIERSTAD A. & K. SYDSAETER, (1986), Optimal Control Theory with Economic Applications, Advanced textbooks in economics 24, (North Holland, Amsterdam), to be published

SENCHACK A.J. jr., (1975), The firm's optimal financial policies: solution, equilibrium and stability, Journal of Financial and Quantitative Analysis 10, pp. 543-555

SETHI S.P., (1978), Optimal equity and financing model of Krouse and Lee: corrections and extensions, Journal of Financial and Quantitative Analysis 13, pp. 487-505

SETHI S.P. & G.L. THOMPSON, (1981), Optimal Control Theory, (Martinus Nijhoff, Boston)

SHALIT S.S. & U. SANKAR, (1977), The measurement of the firm size, Review of Economics and Statistics 59, pp. 290-298

SMYTH D.J., DOYER & D.E. PESEAU, (1975), The measurement of the firm: theory and evidence for the United States and the United Kingdom, Review of Economics and Statistics 57, pp. 111-114

SODERSTROM H.T., (1976), Production and investment under costs of adjustment, a survey, Zeitschrift fur Nationalokonomie 36, pp. 369-388

STAPLETON R.C., (1972), Taxes, the cost of capital and the theory of investment, Economic Journal 82, pp. 1273-1292

STAPLETON R.C. & C.M. BURKE, (1977), European tax systems and the neutrality of corporate financing policy, Journal of Banking and Finance 1, pp. 55-70

STEPAN A. & P. SWOBODA, (1982), Kontrolltheorie und Kapitalstruktur, ZFB Enzyklopadie 52, pp. 681-703

STIGLITZ J.E., (1973), Taxation, corporate financial policy and the cost of capital, Journal of Public Economics 2, pp. 1-34

TAPIERO C.S., (1977), Managerial Planning: an Optimal and Stochastic Control Approach, 2 vol, (Gordon and Breach, New York)

TAPIERO C.S., (1978), Time, dynamics and the process of management modelling, in A. BENSOUSSAN et al. (eds): Applied Optimal Control TIMS Studies in the Mangement Sciences 9, (North Holland, Amsterdam), pp. 7-31

TUOVILA O., (1983), Optimal Financing Policy of the Firm, Acta Wasaensia 19, (Vaasa)

VERHEYEN P.A., (1976), Een dynamische versie van het model van Gordon (A dynamic version of the Gordon model), in: Geld en Onderneming, opstellen aangeboden aan prof. dr. C.F. Scheffer, (Stenfert Kroese, Leiden), pp. 329-340

VERHEYEN P.A., (1981), Belasting in de bedrijfseconomische theorie (Tax in business economics), Bedrijfskunde 53, pp. 57-69

VERMAELEN Th., (1981), Common stock repurchases and market signalling, Journal of Financial Economics 9, pp. 139-183

VIND K., (1967), Control systems with jumps in the state variables, Econometrica 35, pp. 273-277

WEINGARTER H.M., (1963), Mathematical Programming and the Analysis of Capital Budgeting Problems, (Prentice Hall, Englewood Cliffs NJ)

YLA-LIEDENPOHJA J., (1978), Taxes, dividends and capital gains in the adjustment cost model of the firm, Scandinavian Journal of Economics 80, pp. 399-410

Vol. 211: P. van den Heuvel, The Stability of a Macroeconomic System with Quantity Constraints. VII, 169 pages. 1983.

Vol. 212: R. Sato and T. Nôno, Invariance Principles and the Structure of Technology. V, 94 pages. 1983.

Vol. 213: Aspiration Levels in Bargaining and Economic Decision Making. Proceedings, 1982. Edited by R. Tietz. VIII, 406 pages. 1983.

Vol. 214: M. Faber, H. Niemes und G. Stephan, Entropie, Umweltschutz und Rohstoffverbrauch. IX, 181 Seiten. 1983.

Vol. 215: Semi-Infinite Programming and Applications. Proceedings, 1981. Edited by A.V. Fiacco and K.O. Kortanek. XI, 322 pages. 1983.

Vol. 216: H.H. Müller, Fiscal Policies in a General Equilibrium Model with Persistent Unemployment. VI, 92 pages. 1983.

Vol. 217: Ch. Grootaert, The Relation Between Final Demand and Income Distribution. XIV, 105 pages. 1983.

Vol. 218: P. van Loon, A Dynamic Theory of the Firm: Production, Finance and Investment. VII, 191 pages. 1983.

Vol. 219: E. van Damme, Refinements of the Nash Equilibrium Concept. VI, 151 pages. 1983.

Vol. 220: M. Aoki, Notes on Economic Time Series Analysis: System Theoretic Perspectives. IX, 249 pages. 1983.

Vol. 221: S. Nakamura, An Inter-Industry Translog Model of Prices and Technical Change for the West German Economy. XIV, 290 pages. 1984.

Vol. 222: P. Meier, Energy Systems Analysis for Developing Countries. VI, 344 pages. 1984.

Vol. 223: W. Trockel, Market Demand. VIII, 205 pages. 1984.

Vol. 224: M. Kiy, Ein disaggregiertes Prognosesystem für die Bundesrepublik Deutschland. XVIII, 276 Seiten. 1984.

Vol. 225: T.R. von Ungern-Sternberg, Zur Analyse von Märkten mit unvollständiger Nachfragerinformation. IX, 125 Seiten. 1984

Vol. 226: Selected Topics in Operations Research and Mathematical Economics. Proceedings, 1983. Edited by G. Hammer and D. Pallaschke. IX, 478 pages. 1984.

Vol. 227: Risk and Capital. Proceedings, 1983. Edited by G. Bamberg and K. Spremann. VII, 306 pages. 1984.

Vol. 228: Nonlinear Models of Fluctuating Growth. Proceedings, 1983. Edited by R.M. Goodwin, M. Krüger and A. Vercelli. XVII, 277 pages. 1984.

Vol. 229: Interactive Decision Analysis. Proceedings, 1983. Edited by M. Grauer and A.P. Wierzbicki. VIII, 269 pages. 1984.

Vol. 230: Macro-Economic Planning with Conflicting Goals. Proceedings, 1982. Edited by M. Despontin, P. Nijkamp and J. Spronk. VI, 297 pages. 1984.

Vol. 231: G.F. Newell, The M/M/∞ Service System with Ranked Servers in Heavy Traffic. XI, 126 pages. 1984.

Vol. 232: L. Bauwens, Bayesian Full Information Analysis of Simultaneous Equation Models Using Integration by Monte Carlo. VI, 114 pages. 1984.

Vol. 233: G. Wagenhals, The World Copper Market. XI, 190 pages. 1984.

Vol. 234: B.C. Eaves, A Course in Triangulations for Solving Equations with Deformations. III, 302 pages. 1984.

Vol. 235: Stochastic Models in Reliability Theory. Proceedings, 1984. Edited by S. Osaki and Y. Hatoyama. VII, 212 pages. 1984.

Vol. 236: G. Gandolfo, P.C. Padoan, A Disequilibrium Model of Real and Financial Accumulation in an Open Economy. VI, 172 pages. 1984.

Vol. 237: Misspecification Analysis. Proceedings, 1983. Edited by T.K. Dijkstra. V, 129 pages. 1984.

Vol. 238: W. Domschke, A. Drexl, Location and Layout Planning. IV, 134 pages. 1985.

Vol. 239: Microeconomic Models of Housing Markets. Edited by K. Stahl. VII, 197 pages. 1985.

Vol. 240: Contributions to Operations Research. Proceedings, 1984. Edited by K. Neumann and D. Pallaschke. V, 190 pages. 1985.

Vol. 241: U. Wittmann, Das Konzept rationaler Preiserwartungen. XI, 310 Seiten. 1985.

Vol. 242: Decision Making with Multiple Objectives. Proceedings, 1984. Edited by Y.Y. Haimes and V. Chankong. XI, 571 pages. 1985.

Vol. 243: Integer Programming and Related Areas. A Classified Bibliography 1981–1984. Edited by R. von Randow. XX, 386 pages. 1985.

Vol. 244: Advances in Equilibrium Theory. Proceedings, 1984. Edited by C.D. Aliprantis, O. Burkinshaw and N.J. Rothman. II, 235 pages. 1985.

Vol. 245: J.E.M. Wilhelm, Arbitrage Theory. VII, 114 pages. 1985.

Vol. 246: P.W. Otter, Dynamic Feature Space Modelling, Filtering and Self-Tuning Control of Stochastic Systems. XIV, 177 pages. 1985.

Vol. 247: Optimization and Discrete Choice in Urban Systems. Proceedings, 1983. Edited by B.G. Hutchinson, P. Nijkamp and M. Batty. VI, 371 pages. 1985.

Vol. 248: Plural Rationality and Interactive Decision Processes. Proceedings, 1984. Edited by M. Grauer, M. Thompson and A.P. Wierzbicki. VI, 354 pages. 1985.

Vol. 249: Spatial Price Equilibrium: Advances in Theory, Computation and Application. Proceedings, 1984. Edited by P. T. Harker. VII, 277 pages. 1985.

Vol. 250: M. Roubens, Ph. Vincke, Preference Modelling. VIII, 94 pages. 1985.

Vol. 251: Input-Output Modeling. Proceedings, 1984. Edited by A. Smyshlyaev. VI, 261 pages. 1985.

Vol. 252: A. Birolini, On the Use of Stochastic Processes in Modeling Reliability Problems. VI, 105 pages. 1985.

Vol. 253: C. Withagen, Economic Theory and International Trade in Natural Exhaustible Resources. VI, 172 pages. 1985.

Vol. 254: S. Müller, Arbitrage Pricing of Contingent Claims. VIII, 151 pages. 1985.

Vol. 255: Nondifferentiable Optimization: Motivations and Applications. Proceedings, 1984. Edited by V.F. Demyanov and D. Pallaschke. VI, 350 pages. 1985.

Vol. 256: Convexity and Duality in Optimization. Proceedings, 1984. Edited by J. Ponstein. V, 142 pages. 1985.

Vol. 257: Dynamics of Macrosystems. Proceedings, 1984. Edited by J.-P. Aubin, D. Saari and K. Sigmund. VI, 280 pages. 1985.

Vol. 258: H. Funke, Eine allgemeine Theorie der Polypol- und Oligopolpreisbildung. III, 237 pages. 1985.

Vol. 259: Infinite Programming. Proceedings, 1984. Edited by E.J. Anderson and A.B. Philpott. XIV, 244 pages. 1985.

Vol. 260: H.-J. Kruse, Degeneracy Graphs and the Neighbourhood Problem. VIII, 128 pages. 1986.

Vol. 261: Th.R. Gulledge, Jr., N.K. Womer, The Economics of Made-to-Order Production. VI, 134 pages. 1986.

Vol. 262: H.U. Buhl, A Neo-Classical Theory of Distribution and Wealth. V, 146 pages. 1986.

Vol. 263: M. Schäfer, Resource Extraction and Market Structure. XI, 154 pages. 1986.

Vol. 264: Models of Economic Dynamics. Proceedings, 1983. Edited by H.F. Sonnenschein. VII, 212 pages. 1986.

Vol. 265: Dynamic Games and Applications in Economics. Edited by T. Başar. IX, 288 pages. 1986.

Vol. 266: Multi-Stage Production Planning and Inventory Control. Edited by S. Axsäter, Ch. Schneeweiss and E. Silver. V, 264 pages. 1986.

Vol. 267: R. Bemelmans, The Capacity Aspect of Inventories. IX, 165 pages. 1986.

Vol. 268: V. Firchau, Information Evaluation in Capital Markets. VII, 103 pages. 1986.

Vol. 269: A. Borglin, H. Keiding, Optimality in Infinite Horizon Economies. VI, 180 pages. 1986.

Vol. 270: Technological Change, Employment and Spatial Dynamics. Proceedings 1985. Edited by P. Nijkamp. VII, 466 pages. 1986.

Vol. 271: C. Hildreth, The Cowles Commission in Chicago, 1939–1955. V, 176 pages. 1986.

Vol. 272: G. Clemenz, Credit Markets with Asymmetric Information. VIII, 212 pages. 1986.

Vol. 273: Large-Scale Modelling and Interactive Decision Analysis. Proceedings, 1985. Edited by G. Fandel, M. Grauer, A. Kurzhanski and A.P. Wierzbicki. VII, 363 pages. 1986.

Vol. 274: W.K. Klein Haneveld, Duality in Stochastic Linear and Dynamic Programming. VII, 295 pages. 1986.

Vol. 275: Competition, Instability, and Nonlinear Cycles. Proceedings, 1985. Edited by W. Semmler. XII, 340 pages. 1986.

Vol. 276: M.R. Baye, D.A. Black, Consumer Behavior, Cost of Living Measures, and the Income Tax. VII, 119 pages. 1986.

Vol. 277: Studies in Austrian Capital Theory, Investment and Time. Edited by M. Faber. VI, 317 pages. 1986.

Vol. 278: W.E. Diewert, The Measurement of the Economic Benefits of Infrastructure Services. V, 202 pages. 1986.

Vol. 279: H.-J. Büttler, G. Frei and B. Schips, Estimation of Disequilibrium Models. VI, 114 pages. 1986.

Vol. 280: H.T. Lau, Combinatorial Heuristic Algorithms with FORTRAN. VII, 126 pages. 1986.

Vol. 281: Ch.-L. Hwang, M.-J. Lin, Group Decision Making under Multiple Criteria. XI, 400 pages. 1987.

Vol. 282: K. Schittkowski, More Test Examples for Nonlinear Programming Codes. V, 261 pages. 1987.

Vol. 283: G. Gabisch, H.-W. Lorenz, Business Cycle Theory. VII, 229 pages. 1987.

Vol. 284: H. Lütkepohl, Forecasting Aggregated Vector ARMA Processes. X, 323 pages. 1987.

Vol. 285: Toward Interactive and Intelligent Decision Support Systems. Volume 1. Proceedings, 1986. Edited by Y. Sawaragi, K. Inoue and H. Nakayama. XII, 445 pages. 1987.

Vol. 286: Toward Interactive and Intelligent Decision Support Systems. Volume 2. Proceedings, 1986. Edited by Y. Sawaragi, K. Inoue and H. Nakayama. XII, 450 pages. 1987.

Vol. 287: Dynamical Systems. Proceedings, 1985. Edited by A.B. Kurzhanski and K. Sigmund. VI, 215 pages. 1987.

Vol. 288: G.D. Rudebusch, The Estimation of Macroeconomic Disequilibrium Models with Regime Classification Information. VII, 128 pages. 1987.

Vol. 289: B.R. Meijboom, Planning in Decentralized Firms. X, 168 pages. 1987.

Vol. 290: D.A. Carlson, A. Haurie, Infinite Horizon Optimal Control. XI, 254 pages. 1987.

Vol. 291: N. Takahashi, Design of Adaptive Organizations. VI, 140 pages. 1987.

Vol. 292: I. Tchijov, L. Tomaszewicz (Eds.), Input-Output Modeling. Proceedings, 1985. VI, 195 pages. 1987.

Vol. 293: D. Batten, J. Casti, B. Johansson (Eds.), Economic Evo tion and Structural Adjustment. Proceedings, 1985. VI, 382 pag 1987.

Vol. 294: J. Jahn, W. Krabs (Eds.), Recent Advances and Histori Development of Vector Optimization. VII, 405 pages. 1987.

Vol. 295: H. Meister, The Purification Problem for Constrain Games with Incomplete Information. X, 127 pages. 1987.

Vol. 296: A. Börsch-Supan, Econometric Analysis of Discre Choice. VIII, 211 pages. 1987.

Vol. 297: V. Fedorov, H. Läuter (Eds.), Model-Oriented Data Ana sis. Proceedings, 1987. VI, 239 pages. 1988.

Vol. 298: S.H. Chew, Q. Zheng, Integral Global Optimization. V 179 pages. 1988.

Vol. 299: K. Marti, Descent Directions and Efficient Solutions Discretely Distributed Stochastic Programs. XIV, 178 pages. 1988.

Vol. 300: U. Derigs, Programming in Networks and Graphs. XI, 3 pages. 1988.

Vol. 301: J. Kacprzyk, M. Roubens (Eds.), Non-Conventional Prefe ence Relations in Decision Making. VII, 155 pages. 1988.

Vol. 302: H.A. Eiselt, G. Pederzoli (Eds.), Advances in Optimizati and Control. Proceedings, 1986. VIII, 372 pages. 1988.

Vol. 303: F.X. Diebold, Empirical Modeling of Exchange Ra Dynamics. VII, 143 pages. 1988.

Vol. 304: A. Kurzhanski, K. Neumann, D. Pallaschke (Eds.), Optimiz tion, Parallel Processing and Applications. Proceedings, 1987. V 292 pages. 1988.

Vol. 305: G.-J.C.Th. van Schijndel, Dynamic Firm and Invest Behaviour under Progressive Personal Taxation. X, 215 page 1988.

GPSR Compliance

The European Union's (EU) General Product Safety Regulation (GPSR) is a set of rules that requires consumer products to be safe and our obligations to ensure this.

If you have any concerns about our products, you can contact us on ProductSafety@springernature.com

In case Publisher is established outside the EU, the EU authorized representative is:

Springer Nature Customer Service Center GmbH
Europaplatz 3
69115 Heidelberg, Germany

Batch number: 10844827

Printed by Printforce, the Netherlands